SAFEGUARDING CHILDREN
& YOUNG PEOPLE

Child Protection 0–18 Years

SAFEGUARDING CHILDREN & YOUNG PEOPLE

Child Protection 0–18 Years

Jennie Lindon

HODDER
EDUCATION
AN HACHETTE UK COMPANY

Dedication

To my parents, from whom I experienced respect and such very good care.
To my son and daughter, who taught me a great deal about being a parent.

Orders: please contact Bookpoint Ltd, 130 Milton Park, Abingdon, Oxon OX14 4SB. Telephone: (44) 01235 827720. Fax: (44) 01235 400454. Lines are open from 9.00–5.00, Monday to Saturday, with a 24-hour message answering service. You can also order through our website www.hoddereducation.co.uk.

British Library Cataloguing in Publication Data
A catalogue record for this title is available from the British Library.

ISBN: 978 0 340 94740 1

First Published 2008
Impression number   10 9 8 7 6 5
Year   2012 2011 2010

Hachette UK's policy is to use papers that are natural, renewable and recyclable products and made from wood grown in sustainable forests. The logging and manufacturing processes are expected to conform to the environmental regulations of the country of origin.

Cover photo © Stockbyte.
Typeset by Servis Filmsetting Ltd, Manchester.
Printed in Great Britain for Hodder Education, an Hachette UK Company, 338 Euston Road, London NW1 3BH by Martins the Printers, Berwick-upon-Tweed.

CONTENTS

Foreword   *vii*
Introduction   *ix*

Chapter 1: Safeguarding and child protection in the UK   1

   ★ Law and guidance for safeguarding   1

   ★ Changes in the child protection system   13

   ★ Process and steps of safeguarding   18

Chapter 2: Recognising abuse and neglect   39

   ★ Emotional abuse   39

   ★ Physical abuse   44

   ★ Neglect   49

   ★ Sexual abuse   55

Chapter 3: Child protection in action   69

   ★ Steps in dealing with concerns   69

   ★ Signs of possible abuse or neglect   83

   ★ Patterns of disclosure   98

Chapter 4: Equality practice and safeguarding   116

   ★ Key issues for gender and disability   116

   ★ Cultural background and faith   121

   ★ Cultural traditions that challenge protection   129

Chapter 5: Policy, procedures and good practice   143

   ★ Policies and procedures for safeguarding   143

   ★ Safety and security   152

   ★ Child protection and written records   175

Chapter 6: Taking care of children and young people   190

   ★ Physical care and nurture   190

   ★ Skills of personal safety   200

   ★ Troubled relationships between peers   213

Chapter 7: Supporting children and families   **228**

★ Working with parents to support children   228

★ Child protection and the courts   236

★ Families and children under stress   244

Further resources   *264*
Index   *267*

FOREWORD

This is a brilliant book and a godsend for anyone working in child care at any level. Jennie Lindon has put into easily understandable language the rapidly changing developments within the child care sector and in legislation. What I particularly like is the emphasis on partnership and working with both professionals and families – this has to be the best way forward for children and young people. I was pleased to see issues that are often ignored addressed, such as the climate of fear amongst teachers, social workers and other child care personnel about touching children, and the taboo subject of female sexual abuse of children.

The amount of research and work that goes into a book like this is enormous and Jennie Lindon has excelled herself by ensuring that the text is current and relevant to all those working in child care. Although I have been in this field for over 35 years, I learned such a lot reading through that I think it would benefit all of us to have a copy of this 3rd edition.

The other important aspect of this book is an overview of how far we have come in protecting children, with new laws and putting up safeguards to reduce the likelihood of sex offenders or violent people getting close to children. The caveat is that we now risk destroying the independence and self-confidence of children and young people by restricting their movements and becoming paranoid about dangers that will never happen. In a recent speech, I said that you were more likely to get hit by lightning in the UK than be abducted and murdered by a paedophile, yet the fear of child abduction remains high and out of proportion to the real risks. I was delighted to see that Jennie has raised this concern as well. In fact I cannot think of anything she has left out, which brings me back to why this book will be the standard for child care – it is quite simply the best book available anywhere on safeguarding children.

Michele Elliott, CEO
Kidscape

INTRODUCTION

I am highly aware in writing the third edition of this book how much I have learned over the years from conversations with children and young people, with the wide range of practitioners involved with children and their families and the experience of advisors and college tutors. I have undertaken a considerable amount of training on child protection and other areas of good practice. Shared experiences, just as much as 'Ah but. . . .' professional challenge, have been invaluable in helping me to understand about safeguarding in action, to reflect, to explain (hopefully more clearly) and to double-check. I wish to give particular thanks to the many residential social workers and foster carers who attended a series of child protection programmes I ran in Essex. I learned a great deal about court process by running joint workshops on the Children Act 1989 with local authority solicitors – with special thanks to Croydon and Lewisham.

Every organisation mentioned within the book was helpful to me through well-resourced websites and sometimes a real person on the telephone when I could not find, or understand, a vital piece of information.

An author has to make some decisions about terminology and these are my choices.

* **Parent**: anyone who takes the main family responsibility for children and acts in a parental role, whether or not that person is a birth parent. Please assume the word always includes **and other family carers**.
* **Practitioner**: anyone whose work brings them into face-to-face contact with children and young people on a regular basis. I have been specific about the profession whenever the information is relevant.
* **Setting**: any group situation, attended by children or young people, when I am talking in general. Again, I have been specific about which kind of setting, when that information is necessary.
* **Pupil** or **student**: it feels appropriate to me to call children in primary school 'pupils' and reserve the word 'students' for secondary and further education.

The scenarios were developed from real people and places but in every case I have changed many of the details. Readers can use these examples to explore aspects of practice – either on your own or in discussion with colleagues or fellow-students.

The information in *Safeguarding children and young people* is accurate to the best of my knowledge and up to the time of writing in early autumn 2007. It is the professional responsibility of all readers to be willing to check and to update themselves. This responsibility is especially sharp if you, or your colleagues, seek to reach a difficult decision that is dependent on interpretation of the law or a precise understanding of guidance or local guidelines. No section of this book claims to offer legal advice.

You will find a wide range of suggestions for further resources – both in the **If you want to find out more** sections throughout the book and in the **Further resources** at the end of the book. A considerable amount of useful information can now be found on the internet. Any references to websites were correct at the time I completed the book. However, just as books go out of print or move into revised editions, so, too, website organisation may change.

Otherwise, I take the usual responsibility for the content of my book, the ideas within it and any errors that I have failed to recognise. Please let Hodder Education know if you identify mistakes or misunderstandings and I will correct them as soon as possible.

All practitioners need to understand their own role within safeguarding: what they do, as well as those parts of the process that are the direct responsibility of another professional or service. You can only make sense of your involvement by understanding the larger picture: how the broad framework for child protection developed in the UK and key issues for the system to work effectively.

> **The main sections of this chapter cover:**
>
> ✳ **Law and guidance for safeguarding**
>
> ✳ **Changes in the child protection system**
>
> ✳ **Process and steps of safeguarding**

LAW AND GUIDANCE FOR SAFEGUARDING

The view is now well established that parents, or any other family members, cannot simply deal with children and young people as they please. Society, backed by legislation, leaves parents considerable flexibility in how they raise their sons and daughters, but reserves the right to intervene when their safety or continued well being is under threat. Services and settings are also accountable for their practice; professionals cannot argue that their knowledge or expertise places them beyond challenge. Of course, laws do not automatically change people's behaviour or attitudes. However, legislation makes a very public statement about what is acceptable or unacceptable within society.

Leading up to current practice

The current framework of child protection in the UK is a relatively recent development. But it would be wrong to assume that previous generations were uncaring about the ill-treatment of children. Some of the national children's charities were set up before the 20th century, by individuals who were deeply moved by the plight of abandoned children. Captain Thomas Coram fund-raised tirelessly to open his Foundlings Hospital in 1741 and the Coram Family organisation still operates in London today. Dr Thomas Barnardo set up his first orphanage for homeless boys in 1870 and Barnardo's continues to be an active national organisation. The National Society for the Prevention of Cruelty to Children (NSPCC) was established in 1884 by the Reverend Benjamin Waugh and likeminded people, who were shocked by the fact that a law against cruelty to animals had been passed, with no equivalent legislation about children. Energetic lobbying by the NSPCC led to the first English Prevention of Cruelty to

Children Act in 1889, which created the option of prosecution. The NSPCC set up a national network of centres and inspectors and for many decades they were more active in child protection than local authorities.

Children with repeated, hard-to-explain injuries remained a medical puzzle until 1961, when Henry Kempe, in a presentation to the American Academy of Paediatrics, described what he called 'the battered child syndrome'. This public discussion opened up a serious debate about the notion that adults, including parents, sometimes intentionally injured children. Tragically, it took the non-accidental death of a child to bring the reality of physical abuse effectively into the public arena: when, in 1973, 7-year-old Maria Colwell was killed by her step-father. Maria was known to be at risk by the local authority (Brighton, England). The public inquiry in 1974 criticised the lack of communication between the various agencies involved with the family. The child protection register, first known as an 'At Risk Register', was established in 1975 as a national requirement for local authorities to improve contact in such situations.

Over the second half of the 20th century a far greater awareness grew of the complexity of child abuse. Children and young people could be physically attacked but they were also put at serious risk by neglect of their basic needs, emotional maltreatment and sexual abuse within, or from outside, the family. Initially, the focus for abuse was on ill-treatment of children from their own family. But cases emerged, some dating back many years, where children had been abused by adults within the context of their professional role. Physically abusive and neglectful regimes had sometimes been justified as necessary discipline or tough training regimes. Any hopeful predictions about likely abusers were swept away as it became clear that there are no neat certainties. Abusers have been men and women, from any social class, ethnic group, cultural background and faith. The most likely abuser is an adult, but young people (under 18s) have abused peers or younger children.

If you want to find out more

✤ Barnardos – www.barnardos.org.uk/who_we_are/history.htm=

✤ Coram Family – www.coram.org.uk/heritage.htm

✤ NSPCC – www.nspcc.org.uk/default.html – click on 'What we do'

Laws and guidance

Within the UK, some laws passed by the Westminster Parliament apply to all of the four nations: England, Wales, Scotland and Northern Ireland. However, some legislation only applies to England and Wales and those two nations may differ in their application of the final details of practice.

Scotland passes laws, applicable only to that nation, through the Scottish Parliament, and Northern Ireland has the same power within the Northern Ireland Assembly.

The laws described in this section are primary legislation and the requirements built into the laws must be obeyed. However, legal language is not expressed in ways that make it easy for people without a legal background to understand what laws mean for daily life. Sometimes the relevant government department issues further information through books of guidance. These documents do not have the same force as primary legislation. But when they are described as 'statutory', it is required that local authorities, or relevant organisations, follow the details of guidance or a code – or can provide a very good reason for variation. For example, *Safeguarding children and safer recruitment in education* (2006) www.teachernet.gov.uk is statutory guidance for England. Guidance documents often describe good practice for wherever you work within the UK. However, you need to recall that statutory guidance may refer to law that does not necessarily apply to your part of the UK.

Some good practice guidance is 'recommended', meaning that the associated government department strongly advises that the suggestions and examples are followed. An example would be *Pastoral care in schools: child protection*, which is 'strongly recommended' by the Northern Ireland Department of Education www.deni.gov.uk/print/dc1999-10-5.pdf The process of developing guidance often now goes through a consultation phase. The draft guidance, or a report with practical recommendations, is available on the relevant website and anyone can make comments and suggestions.

WHAT DOES IT MEAN?

Primary legislation: laws that have been passed for a given country. The detail of law defines what is legally required or has been made illegal. The name of a law is given with the date when it was passed by Parliament or Assembly. Sometimes parts of a law do not become fully applicable until a given later date.

Statutory guidance: material issued by the relevant government department to explain in non-legal language what must be done or not done.

Good practice guidance: material to support professionals to put law and statutory guidance into daily practice. These publications may be 'recommended' by the relevant government department.

Consultation: the process by which draft guidance is made available, usually now on a government website, and anyone can make comments or suggestions.

Procedures, guidelines and advice

Statutory guidance, backed up through the process of inspection, sometimes requires that services have a clear code of practice or policy on an important issue. It is expected that local authorities will develop their own child protection guidelines, grounded firmly in the relevant law and statutory guidance, in order to support local practice. Some procedures apply across authorities, with the aim of creating consistent application of safeguarding practice. For example, the London Safeguarding Children Board has published the *London Child Protection Procedures* (third edition, 2007, see www.londonscb.gov.uk) The *All Wales Child Protection Procedures*, issued by the Social Services Improvement Agency (SSIA) applies legal requirements within the context of every Welsh authority (revised edition due in 2007 www.ssiacymru.org.uk).

These substantial documents not only explain the details of good practice, linked with national requirements, but also give information about relevant services and organisations for the area or country. Reliable websites, such as the LSCB and the SSIA, are also a valuable source of information and procedures for professionals facing a particular safeguarding issue. For instance, the LSCB addresses difficult issues about sexual activity under the legal age of consent – *London procedure for safeguarding sexually active children* www.londonscb.gov.uk/procedures/supplementary_procedures/ safeguarding_sexually_active_children/ The SSIA is one of several websites with procedures for dealing with illness induction and for physical abuse through female genital mutilation.

The law and child protection

The shape of child protection across the UK was determined during the late 1980s and 1990s. The first new legislation was the Children Act 1989, which applied to England and Wales. The Cleveland Inquiry contributed serious concerns about a thorough process of assessment, avoiding sudden and unjustified removal of children from their family. Chaired by Dame Elizabeth Butler-Sloss, this report investigated claims of widespread sexual abuse during 1987 within families in Cleveland (England). However, plans for revising family law were already well advanced before the final report. A number of avoidable child deaths, caused by the actions or inaction of children's own family, during the 1980s had raised serious concerns that the existing legislation was not working effectively. Legislation followed in the rest of the UK: the Children (Scotland) Act 1995 and the Children (Northern Ireland) Order 1996. Subsequent legislation has changed some details of how the child protection system works, but much of this legal framework still applies.

All these laws cover child welfare and family support in the broadest sense. The sections covering child protection are part of more wide-ranging legislation that also encompasses services for children in need. The Children (Scotland) Act 1995 stands out as the legislation that most took account of the United Nations Convention on the Rights of the Child 1989. Each Act or Order also covered the registration and inspection of early years services that fell outside the state educational system. Each law shared the key principles that should underpin all practice with children and young people:

- The welfare of the child must be paramount in any work with a family; this is known as the paramountcy principle.
- Work must be conducted in partnership. Professionals are expected to work together in a spirit of inter-agency co-operation and to work in a co-operative way with parents.
- Children are not the possessions of their parents. Parents have responsibilities for their children, not absolute rights.
- Children should preferably be raised within their own family, but their welfare requires limits to family privacy and decision making.
- Each law assumed that childhood, and the need to protect, extended up to an individual's 18th birthday, with the exception of Scotland, which placed the boundary at 17 years of age.

Each law also established two broad areas of concern:

- Children and young people are judged to be 'in need' when their development and health cannot be guaranteed without extra support for children and their families. All disabled children were defined as 'in need', although Scotland extended the definition to include all children in a family where any member, adult or child, was disabled.
- Serious concerns about a child's health and development raise the possibility that they are at risk of suffering 'significant harm'. A child's parents or other carers are failing to ensure that the child can thrive and be safe, compared with what could be expected for children of a similar age.

Promoting the well being of children 'in need' and safeguarding children who are at risk of 'significant harm' should be seen as two sides of the same coin. The judgment that children are suffering, or are at risk of significant harm, triggers compulsory intervention in family life through the child protection process. However, a range of actions can be taken to protect children who are 'in need', as well as 'at risk of significant harm', including family support services. The legislation also established the types of abuse recognised in law: physical abuse, emotional abuse, sexual abuse and neglect. In Scotland, a fifth category of non-organic failure to thrive was given separately from neglect.

New laws do not always repeal (or revoke) existing legislation – that is, remove a similar earlier law from the statute book. Legislation relevant to safeguarding, introduced since the Acts and Order described here, have not repealed the legislation of the late 1980s and mid-1990s. In fact, some details of safeguarding are still decided by the Children and Young Persons Act 1933. Other laws also affect safeguarding and family issues around that task; you will find examples throughout this book. In general, law affecting child protection is of two kinds.

- Civil law includes the public law that has determined the systems of child protection. It also includes private law that deals with family proceedings such as divorce and the ways in which separating adults can continue to be parents to their children in relation to issues such as contact.
- Criminal law relevant to child protection identifies what are offences against children and young people: crimes that inevitably bring police involvement.

UK law to safeguard children and young people includes a wide range of provisions to protect that do not require there to be a crime, nor for evidence to be presented that meets the standard of a criminal court case.

WHAT DOES IT MEAN?

Civil law: guides and determines disputes or problems between individuals that do not involve a criminal act.

Criminal law: determines which actions are criminal under a specific law and the likely consequences of being convicted in court for that criminal act.

Repeal or revoke: the legal step, built into some new laws, that specific sections now replace named sections in an existing law.

Developments since the 1990s

Law, guidance and the application to practice does not stay still. Since the 1990s, there have been significant reviews of how well the child protection system is working to safeguard children and young people effectively from harm.

Review and public inquiry

Government departments sometimes commission research reviews: overviews of safeguarding as a whole or reports on specific aspects of child protection. Public inquiries follow those cases when child protection has failed in some way. The different strands of overview sometimes merge in practice, for example the review by Nina Biehal and Jim Wade of *Children who go missing: research, policy and practice* (www.dfes.gov.uk/qualityprotects/pdfs/missing-children.pdf). An overview of this kind often makes practical recommendations, leading into practice guidance.

Around the UK, a local inquiry to review the case has to follow the death or very serious injury of a child, when child abuse was either confirmed or suspected. A report is made to the Child Protection Committee or Safeguarding Board (currently the Health and Social Services Board in Northern Ireland) for the area. Such a report does not necessarily become public, although sometimes the decision is made that publication is in the public interest. That step is sometimes taken when the death of a child was avoidable and professional practice had been inadequate to protect. For example, it is possible to read the report from the Dumfries and Galloway Health Board on the death of 3-year-old Kennedy McFarlane in 2000. The review of the case, as usually happened, was led by a professional from outside the area: Dr Helen Hammond, a paediatrician and vice chair of the Lothian Child Protection Committee. (Download from www.dumgal.gov.uk/Dumgal/Documents.aspx?id=11832)

The Department of Health (for England) is obligated to commission regular overviews of serious case reviews, following avoidable deaths or serious injuries to children. These overviews draw out the consistent themes from many case reviews, while keeping the details confidential. See, for example, the report by Ruth Sinclair and Roger Bullock (2002) *Learning from past experience: a review of serious case reviews* London: Department of Health

Significant public inquiries are organised when the events of a particular case raise serious questions about the adequacy of the existing system to protect. Such reports make recommendations, often leading to a change in guidance, and sometimes to new legislation. There have also been public inquiries following investigations into child abuse when professional opinion has been sharply divided; for instance, Lord Clyde's judicial inquiry following the claims about ritual sexual abuse in the Orkneys (1990). Public inquiries also usually follow the discovery of significant professional malpractice in provision for children or young people; for example, the abusive 'Pindown' system used in Staffordshire Children's Homes (1990).

The long-term abuse in residential children's homes in Clwyd, North Wales, exposed finally in the mid-1990s, led to the report *People like us*, by Sir William Utting in 1997. The government's response was to introduce the Quality Protects Programme for England – Quality First in Wales – to improve provision for looked-after children and young people. A review in 2004 by Marian Stuart and Catherine Baines identified that changes made since the Utting report had brought improvements in some aspects of practice. However, improvements were slow in some areas, such as children and young people in custody or in psychiatric hospitals. (For a summary of the report *Progress on safeguards for children living away from home: a review of action since the 'People like us report'* see www.jrf.org.uk/knowledge/findings/socialpolicy/n54.asp)

LOOK, LISTEN, NOTE, LEARN

Public inquiries are precisely that – a matter of public and accessible information. Reports are now provided on the internet. You can search by the name of the person leading an inquiry or the name of the child, whose experience (usually fatal) has led to setting up this investigation. The full report can be very long; it varies, but there is usually a summary. Once an inquiry is closed, the material often remains on the internet for information.

■ Access at least one public inquiry on the internet. This may be either a report mentioned in this book, or an inquiry of which you are aware from media attention.

■ What are the main points that emerge? What were apparent problems within the system of safeguarding? What were mistakes made by people or by their failure to act?

Focus on professional practice

A major consequence of reviews throughout the 1990s was to show that children's welfare may not only be endangered by their families, but also that professionals may have the potential to harm children through their actions or inaction. The concept of 'professional dangerousness' came into use to describe behaviour from members of relevant professions that failed to protect children effectively.

WHAT DOES IT MEAN?

Professional (or organisational) dangerousness: when inappropriate values, priorities or methods lead professionals to act in ways that fail to reduce the risk to children or young people.

Significant practice issues could increase the risk for children and young people, even though professionals were involved with their family.

- Unsafe professionals had inadequate supervision and sometimes impossible case loads.
- Whole teams were sometimes perplexed about how to balance anti-discriminatory practice with child protection.
- A proper focus on children had sometimes been lost in favour of addressing the problems of adults and accepting their perspective on family life.
- Some professionals held on to an unrealistic optimism about the family's ability to cope, even in the face of poor outcomes for the child.
- Some professionals had avoided contact with the family because of unacknowledged fears for their own personal safety. This situation, combined with poor support within the team, meant that nobody confronted how a child could possibly be safe in a household that professionals were afraid to visit.

A key theme in professional dangerousness for work with families is that the child has been lost as the priority in child protection. Even where parents are doing their best, given serious stress or very limited understanding of a child's needs, the final judgment has to be the well being of the child. No child can be left at risk of abuse or neglect on the grounds that, although their care is seriously inadequate, the parents could not be expected to manage any better.

During the 1990s it became clear that the full possibilities of family support services were not always used. Each Children Act and Order was set up to enable support for children 'in need' as well as action to protect children at risk of 'significant harm'. Reviews highlighted that the key point of the process was not exclusively whether to place a child's name on the register and this action did not in itself protect children without effective follow-up. Family support services could be crucial to ensure that a child who was currently 'in need' did not slide towards 'at risk' and a crisis situation. Reports emphasised the obligation to involve parents as much as possible, but that professionals must not overlook listening to children and young people, taking their views properly into account.

Procedures are not optional

Carefully drafted procedures, like any safeguarding policy, do not in themselves protect children and young people. Three significant reports from Wales highlighted how abusive treatment was allowed to continue because the adults responsible for safeguarding made other considerations a higher priority than the welfare of children and young people.

Sir Ronald Waterhouse reported in *Lost in Care* (2000), the North Wales Child Abuse Inquiry on allegations of abuse of looked-after children and young people in the Gwynedd and Clwyd areas dating back to 1974. The Waterhouse Inquiry documented allegations made by some children about abusive treatment whilst they stayed at Gwynfa: an NHS facility in Colwyn Bay for children and adolescents with mental health problems. Sir Alex Carlile led the inquiry into these allegations, reporting in 2003 with *The review of safeguards for children and young people treated and cared for by the NHS in Wales*. This report highlighted risks that arose from secrecy and a feeling among staff that it was unacceptable to express any concerns about practice within their team. The Gwynfa facility had clear guidance on child protection but failed to implement procedures, using excuses such as staff shortages.

The Waterhouse Inquiry and Carlile Report can be accessed on http:/new.wales.gov.uk/topics/childrenyoungpeople/careandprotection/childprotection.

The Clywch Report by Peter Clarke in 2004 documented allegations of sexual abuse, dating back to 1991, by a drama teacher in a secondary school. The school and local child protection committee had relevant procedures, but failed to follow them. The report was highly critical of the head's refusal to take seriously the concerns of a series of distressed students about the behaviour of their drama teacher. Students were disbelieved and then treated as the source of false allegations. The teacher, whom the head eventually permitted to resign as a solution to the problem, had successfully blurred the boundaries of appropriate touch between himself and young people. He had also bullied students into using inappropriate contact and actions for themselves, within the context of drama. With few exceptions, external examiners of the drama productions did not challenge the inappropriateness of the content, in some cases citing a reluctance to censor creative projects. The report, *Clywch – report of the examination of the Children's Commissioner for Wales into allegations of sexual abuse in a school setting* is available on www.childcom.org.uk – go in through *News*.

Focus on the child in 'child protection'

The sub-title of the Carlile Report was *Too serious a thing*. The full quotation from Charles Lamb (a 19th century writer) is given on the front page of the report: 'A child's nature is too serious a thing to admit of its being regarded as a mere appendage of another being.' The reports from Wales highlight the great risk to children and young people when protection of them becomes less important to adults than their own concerns and priorities. Adults can be culpable of neglectful inaction, even when they are not the active abusers.

Good practice in protection also has to respect the welfare and development of children as individuals in their own right. A criticism made in the public inquiry on the Cleveland sex abuse cases in the late 1980s was that the children themselves ran the risk of being lost in the flurry of diagnosis and professional counter-claim. A telling phrase from that report is still quoted: 'The child is a person not an object of concern.' However, problems continued through the 1990s, as shown in later reports on professional misconduct in dealing with claims of widespread sexual abuse within a community, for example in the Orkneys. There is a significant risk to children and young people when professionals are so convinced that abuse has occurred that they refuse to believe the children's protestations; indeed, the denial was sometimes taken as a sure sign that something had happened (the child was 'in denial'). Such public inquiries also highlighted that professionals must follow codes of conduct for how a child is interviewed and a high standard of documentation of that process.

Agencies must work together

An additional problem arose when a service simply did not view children and adolescents as part of their brief. There are now stronger messages for professionals within adult disability, mental health or addiction services: to look beyond their own adult client or patient. Such services should at least check whether an adult who faces a daily struggle to take care of themselves is also responsible, in theory, for a child or young person.

If all the different sources of knowledge are brought together, then the seriousness of the situation for a child or young person can be far more obvious.

- The most useful image is that of a jigsaw, for which different professionals or services each have only a few of the total number of pieces.
- Children are not well protected when roles and responsibilities between agencies are not clear.
- It is too easy for everyone to assume that somebody else 'knows about. . .' or 'is doing something about. . .'. Yet the real situation is that nobody has taken responsibility for this matter.
- Action to protect has been undermined when there was a different professional approach to confidentiality and information sharing, perhaps worsened by feelings about professional territory.
- Those practitioners in different professions, who are vital to the full safeguarding picture, need to address potential communication problems that may result from placing a different meaning on terms such as 'vulnerable', for example.

More than one inquiry has stressed the need to use observations and assessments made by people who see the child(ren) regularly. If all the different reports and knowledge of children are brought together, then the seriousness of the situation for the children can be far more obvious than when considering one perspective. Some reviews stressed the great importance of consulting individuals and group settings where children and young people were seen on a regular basis, sometimes daily. To return to the image of the jigsaw, practitioners in nursery, school and out-of-school facilities, or the childminding service can hold significant pieces.

Learning from what has gone wrong
The impact of high profile cases is that everyone becomes unsettled, not only those in that geographical or professional area. The experience of tragedy or the discovery of professional misconduct shakes general morale and confidence. A well-run public inquiry identifies key issues for good practice that need to be addressed. However, systems and policies are only as effective as the people who put them into practice day by day, week by week. Changes in the law or guidance do not in themselves transform practice to protect children. Key adults have to change, or be enabled to change, their professional behaviour, priorities and outlook.

The final reports of public inquiries and reports of local reviews, that have been made public, usually make recommendations. (This section describes the far-reaching consequences of the Laming and the Bichard reports. See pages 13 and 14.) It is important first to consider how reviews of safeguarding, following the death of a child, contribute to decisions to change.

Nick Alford and Roger Bullock were commissioned to undertake a research overview of child death and significant case reviews as part of the Child Protection Reform Programme (CPRP) in Scotland. Their 2005 report highlights several key points:

- Child deaths resulting from abuse or neglect are relatively rare. It can be problematic, if significant changes are made to the safeguarding system, specifically to avoid the repetition of an unusual event. The point is not, of course, to ignore inexcusable failures to apply existing guidance to protect.
- The majority of children who are in need of protection experience levels of abuse that, although unacceptable, are not life threatening. Their safety can be ensured, with effective child protection practice, while they continue to live with their family and promptly receive appropriate services.
- Patterns of cause and effect can appear more obvious with hindsight. Indeed, some children's injuries, trauma or death have been the result of serious failures of people and services. However, it is much harder

in most cases to predict the likelihood of a very serious or tragic outcome, while the situation is ongoing.

- The important focus for safeguarding is that a great deal is now known about factors that increase the level of risk to a child or young person. The aim of detailed assessment procedures is to assess that risk and not try to predict the future in detail. Effective safeguarding is a matter of 'most probably could', 'easily might' and rarely of 'definitely will'.

This review can be accessed in full, or in the summary of *Insight 19: Child death and significant case reviews: international approaches* through the home page of the CPRP on www.scottishexecutive.gov.uk/Topics/People/Young-People/children-families/17834/10238

TAKE ANOTHER PERSPECTIVE

You need to remind yourself that serious mistakes and tragedies are far more likely to become public knowledge than when children have been protected and are therefore safe. Headlines are not created from, 'Social workers intervene and life is much better for young Matthew'. Partly, such events are not deemed to be newsworthy, but also the details remain confidential to the family and involved professionals.

There have been serious failures of safeguarding that have led to deep distress, injury and even death for some children. This section has focused on overviews, which highlight good practice, as well as that which is less adequate, and public inquiries, which arise because safeguarding has not worked to protect children or young people. The clear message of more recent inquiries is that problems are not simply historical. Systems still fail some children and young people through the actions, inactions and inadequate knowledge of people.

CHANGES IN THE CHILD PROTECTION SYSTEM

Two public inquiries have exerted a significant impact on changes to child protection that continue to evolve at the time of writing in 2007.

The Laming Report

The lack of effective change for protection was brought home forcibly by the suffering and death of 8-year-old Victoria Climbié in 2002. The avoidable death of this young girl was especially shocking, because she was known to a wide range of North London services, professionals and community groups. The public inquiry led by Lord Laming identified twelve separate occasions when Victoria could have been safeguarded through direct action or information sharing between agencies.

The report makes such depressing reading, because many practice issues, clearly identified over the 1990s, were shown to have undermined effective child protection in the early years of the new century. The Laming report documents a list of serious problems: poor inter-agency working and information sharing, under-resourced social work departments and inadequate support for front line professionals and continued confusion over anti-discriminatory practice. For more detail see *The Victoria Climbié Inquiry*, 2003, www.victoria-climbie-inquiry.org.uk

The Bichard Report

Sir Michael Bichard reported in 2004 on the circumstances that led to the employment of Ian Huntley as a college (secondary school) caretaker. This position of trust enabled him, in 2002, to murder Holly Wells and Jessica Chapman, who attended the nearby primary school (in Soham, Lincolnshire, England). Huntley was known to police and social services in Humberside as a result of a series of sexual relationships with young adolescents who were under the age of consent. These incidents had been viewed separately, rather than brought together as a pattern to reveal an individual who posed a risk. The police database in Humberside was inadequate for effective safeguarding. Also, ignorance in the team about the working of data protection law meant that vital information was not passed on to the Lincolnshire police authorities. The final report has led to changes in the law around vetting and barring individuals for work in close proximity to children and young people (see page 153). The report can be accessed on www.bichardinquiry.org.uk

Changes in England and Wales

The recommendations of the Laming report have led to the overarching framework created by *Every Child Matters*. This approach established five key outcomes by which to judge the success of any policies for children and young people: being healthy, staying safe, enjoying and achieving, making a positive contribution and economic well being. Legal changes were made through the Children Act 2004 and Section 11 introduced a duty on agencies involved with children and young people both to safeguard them and promote their welfare.

The Children Act 2004 was followed by a revised version in 2006 of *Working together to safeguard children*. This updated guidance confirms much of the main structure of the system for England and Wales, but uses the term 'safeguarding children' alongside 'child protection'. (The phrase 'local authority children's social care' has also largely replaced the term 'social services'.) Safeguarding includes conventional child protection: actions to protect children and young people, once a risk or actual harm has been identified. However, the concept extends that approach to be more proactive: an obligation for all agencies and services to take effective measures to minimise risks and to anticipate what might threaten the welfare of children and young people.

In summer 2007, *Staying safe: a consultation document* was published and made available for comment until the end of October of the same year (available on http://www.dfes.gov.uk/consultations/conDetails.cfm?consultationId=1500)

This document, available in summary as well as the full version, shows the three main layers of what is regarded as safeguarding:

- Helping all children and young people to stay safe
- Protecting vulnerable children and young people
- Responding when children and young people have been harmed.

(Chapter 6 in this book deals with the first layer of safeguarding.) Good practice is not exclusively about children known to be vulnerable, nor about putting all the energy into reacting to a crisis in protection.

WHAT DOES IT MEAN?

Safeguarding: the process of creating a safe environment for the whole younger generation, as well as protecting those children and young people who are vulnerable or have already been harmed.

The main changes for England and Wales, brought about by the Children Act 2004, include that Area Child Protection Committees are replaced by local Safeguarding Children Boards. These are statutory, rather than just recommended, and are given a more formal responsibility to ensure local inter-agency working. The boards still bring together relevant agencies and services. The government now has powers to intervene if local social services are unsatisfactory – in a similar way that works already with schools. The Act creates the option of addressing the problems of unregulated private foster care – the situation in which Victoria Climbié lived. Local authorities now have a legal duty to promote the educational achievement of looked-after children and young people. The Act also introduced the appointment of a Children's Commissioner for England, although without the same remit and power of those commissioners already in post elsewhere in the UK.

The Children Act 2004 also created the legal possibility of a national electronic database of all children and young people. There are two planned, linked databases, which are in the final stages of development during 2007–8. The avowed aim of this new system is to ensure effective information sharing: so that professionals can identify and contact other practitioners working with the same child, young person or family. The overall purpose is to work together for the benefit of children and young people and to ensure that they are not 'lost' between services, professionals or different local authorities.

- ContactPoint (initially called the Information Sharing Index or IS Index) will hold basic information about every child and young person up to the age or 18 in England and Wales.
- The Integrated Children's System (ICS), also in process, will be a separate database with more sensitive information (including case files) on under-18s for whom an assessment has been, or is being, made on the Common Assessment Framework. This database would show the existence of a child protection plan for an individual child or young person: a step that is currently only taken when a name is added to the register. Access to the ICS would be more restricted than for the ContactPoint database. However, ContactPoint will include an indication that a child protection plan exists for a child or young person.

The plan is to phase out local child protection registers in 2008 or 2009 and replace that function through the Integrated Children's System. The system has been piloted in a small number of authorities in England and Wales. It is not possible to know how well the databases will eventually meet the aims. It is also important never to forget that any records are only ever as good as the quality of the information that is added by people. An electronic system is no more immune than paper records to human error. The records should be archived for six years after young people reach the age of 18, or 25 years (if they are looked-after or disabled), or when they leave England or Wales with no intention to return. The files should then be deleted and not slide into a population database.

The plan is that ContactPoint will show a child's name, gender, date of birth and an identifying number. The personal file will also provide contact details for parent(s) or other family carer, education provider and GP practice. It is intended that information will also be entered by practitioners who provide the child, young person or their family with a specialist or targeted service. ContactPoint will have basic information about settings and services involved with a child or young person. However, guidance has so far left undefined what is meant by 'involvement' or 'higher than average activity' for a particular profession. So different local authorities may vary on how they decide to include, or exclude, details of a service or involved practitioner. A problem arises because information about specific professionals could reveal sensitive information and private family matters on ContactPoint. It seems likely that a parent, older child or young person will be able to refuse permission for information about contact with services like sexual health, mental health or substance abuse. That information would be entered into the less accessible ICS.

A related issue remains for ContactPoint, or the ICS, of how parents will be enabled to check the information for accuracy and, if necessary, challenge the data in their child's file. The same issue of access applies to young people themselves. Right of access to information about oneself, or someone for whom you are responsible, is ensured by legislation on data protection. It is also not clear from briefing papers whether professionals in Scotland and Northern Ireland will be able to access the database, or make a formal request for information. One aim of this database is to overcome the risks when children are moved by their family from one area to another, as well as between services: family mobility can, of course, extend across the UK.

Changes in Scotland
The Child Protection Reform Programme (CPRP) is a significant audit and review of the system in Scotland. The programme has been led by a report commissioned by the Scottish Executive entitled *'It's everyone's job to make sure I'm alright' Literature review* (2002 www.scotland.gov.uk/ Publications/2003/05/17127/21840). This detailed overview combined information from research studies, public inquiries in Scotland and elsewhere in the UK and information about child protection in some countries outside the UK.

The CPRP has covered a range of safeguarding issues, including the implications of the Laming and Bichard reports, a review of how local Child Protection Committees operate in Scotland and the operation of child death and significant case reviews. Interim reports and reviews for the CPRP can be accessed on www.scottishexecutive.gov.uk/Topics/People/ Young-People/children-families/17834/10238. The programme is being completed throughout 2007, including the introduction of an Integrated Assessment Framework (IAF).

Changes in Northern Ireland
An audit in 2004 by the Department of Health, Social Services and Public Safety considered the child protection system in Northern Ireland against

the 108 recommendations in the Laming report. The Social Service Inspectorate for the province then reviewed all aspects of safeguarding in Northern Ireland. The final report acknowledged good practice and positive developments in the province but also made a series of firm recommendations. These changes are ongoing at the time of writing and include proposals for:

- A Safeguarding Board for Northern Ireland that will bring together the services involved in protection and work to improve practice across the province.
- The creation of five local safeguarding panels, to replace area child protection committees. The aim is to ensure that child protection remains a top priority and with clear lines of accountability. It is proposed that these panels, and the Board, will have legal status.
- Clear criteria for local Case Management Reviews (when a child has died or suffered life-threatening injuries) and steps to improve the quality of inter-agency working.
- The development of a Single Assessment Framework: *Understanding the needs of children in Northern Ireland*.
- A database bringing together the details of children on all the local child protection registers and better coordination on safeguarding with the Republic of Ireland (Eire).
- Action to ensure a consistent approach across the five Health and Social Services Trusts, and their associated Health and Social Services Boards.

You can access the SSI report, *Our children and young people – our shared responsibility – inspection of child protection services in Northern Ireland by* downloading from www.dhsspsni.gov.uk/oss-child-protection.htm

PROCESS AND STEPS OF SAFEGUARDING

The process of responding to concerns about children and young people is determined by law and related guidance. There are agreed steps in the sequence to protect vulnerable children or to act decisively for children who have been harmed. Once concerns have been raised about a child, these steps are not negotiable depending on local or personal preferences. The procedures are laid down by the national guidance and local authorities have to follow time limits on steps in the process; it is not allowed to drag on indefinitely. Practitioners need to understand the big picture of how protection works in the UK in order to place their own role in context (which is covered from page 69).

Who is involved?

A considerable range of professionals and services share the responsibility to protect children and young people. The situation is summed up well by the title of the review in Scotland, *'It's everyone's job to make sure I'm alright.'* Their roles are different but equally important. In brief the range includes:

- Social workers, who take the lead in assessment and investigation, but who will not be directly involved in much of the safeguarding practice that ensures the well being of children and young people who are not at risk.
- The police service, who will be involved in some steps for emergency protection and when there is the possibility that actions could be criminal.
- Related services like the courts, probation service and youth offending teams, the prison service and young offenders' institutions.
- Services for looked-after children and young people: residential homes, foster care and secure accommodation.
- Health services of all kinds: hospitals, clinics, health visitors and the wide range of specialist medical professionals.
- Education services for children and young people of school and college age, including related services such as careers advice.
- Early years services of all kinds: full day and sessional groups, drop-ins and crèches, and the childminding service.
- Out-of-school services for children and young people of school age.
- Local services such as housing that have contact with families.
- The wide range of play, sport and leisure services.
- Faith groups and communities that have contact with families and sometimes also offer religious instruction to children.
- Organisations such as the armed services, which have a responsibility for families through the nature of the job, but also accept under-18s into the service.

The community as a whole has a responsibility to look out for children and young people. It is possible for anyone to contact social services with a concern; it is not exclusively professionals who can make that phone call. Community groups and organisations have a definite responsibility, when they have regular contact with families, children and young people. Many informal services depend on an atmosphere of trust that anyone involved will not take advantage of younger or vulnerable members of that community.

Children's Hearings in Scotland

In this part of the UK a unique system deals with juvenile and family matters, including some aspects of child protection. Concerns about a child are dealt with by local social work departments through a similar process described in this section, including the use of case conferences. However, a referral to the Children's Reporter must be made whenever a local authority has information that suggests compulsory measures, including emergency legal action, may need to be taken as the result of abuse or neglect, or arising from a child or young person's own behaviour. Anyone, not only professionals, can contact the Children's Reporter with such concerns.

The Reporter will work in partnership with social workers to decide whether the case should be dealt with by the Children's Hearing, comprising volunteer lay people drawn from the local Children's Panel. The Children's Hearing can deal with emergency orders, but the Procurator Fiscal is the person who decides if a child protection case should go on to court within the criminal system.

Children and young people have not only a right to attend their own Children's Hearing, but also an obligation to do so, with few exceptions. A safeguarder can be appointed to support individual children and young people to enable them to express their views and to speak on their behalf.

If you want to find out more

✤ *The Children's Hearings System in Scotland 2003: Training Resource Manual* www.scotland.gov.uk/Publications/2003/12/18611/29855

Step 1: Initial concern and referral

The aim of this section is to give readers an understanding of the whole process. The simple flow chart in Figure 1.1. on page 21 has been designed to support that understanding. You may find that local child protection documents will have a more complex chart, or more than one chart. You will find a flow chart in Figure 3.1 on page 72, which is included as part of the section on the role of practitioners. That description occupies the part of the flow chart here that is summed up briefly by 'Practitioners would have made appropriate information gathering'. Unless you work with vulnerable families, children and young people, a high proportion of your concerns will remain at this lower level.

The child protection process is started when someone expresses concern about the welfare of a child, which can include disclosure by children or young people themselves. This concern may be expressed from one or more of the professionals and services listed on page 19. However, it is not always professionals who first voice worries about a child. Some child protection

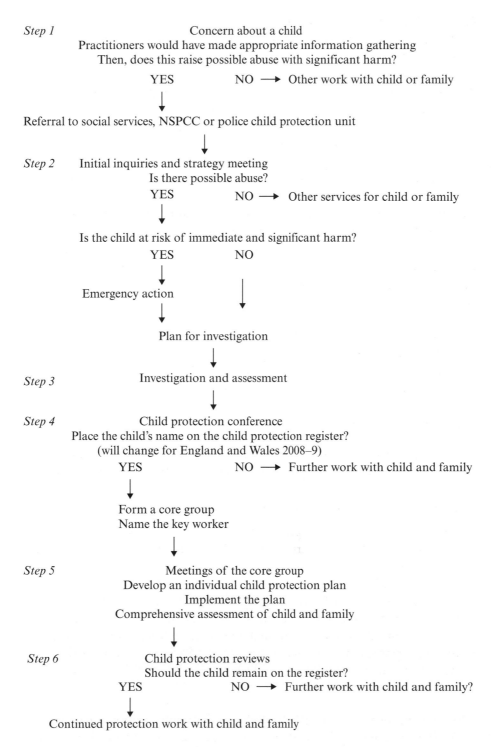

Step 1   Concern about a child
Practitioners would have made appropriate information gathering
Then, does this raise possible abuse with significant harm?
             YES   NO ⟶ Other work with child or family

Referral to social services, NSPCC or police child protection unit

Step 2   Initial inquiries and strategy meeting
Is there possible abuse?
             YES   NO ⟶ Other services for child or family

Is the child at risk of immediate and significant harm?
             YES   NO

Emergency action

Plan for investigation

Step 3   Investigation and assessment

Step 4   Child protection conference
Place the child's name on the child protection register?
(will change for England and Wales 2008–9)
             YES   NO ⟶ Further work with child and family

Form a core group
Name the key worker

Step 5   Meetings of the core group
Develop an individual child protection plan
Implement the plan
Comprehensive assessment of child and family

Step 6   Child protection reviews
Should the child remain on the register?
     YES   NO ⟶ Further work with child and family?

Continued protection work with child and family

Figure 1.1 Steps in the process of a child protection investigation

inquiries start as the result of fears for a child that have been communicated by members of the child's own immediate family, other relatives, friends or neighbours.

It is most likely that child protection concerns will be communicated to the local social services department or the local NSPCC. The NSPCC are more active in some local systems than others, but representatives of this national charity have 'authorised person' status because their inspectors protected children for decades throughout the 20th century, when local authorities were not active in that role. The police would not usually be the first point of contact, unless the situation seemed dangerous for everyone. However, the local police may well become involved and should have a designated officer and probably a unit for child protection.

Step 2: Initial inquiries and strategy

Any concern regarding the possible abuse of a child or young person has to be considered and an initial investigation made. The steps in the child protection process are intended to be steady as well as timely. The aim is that any concerns are checked carefully, but that no further measures are taken unless it is judged necessary. At the start of any investigation, a decision has to be made about whether the inquiries will be made by the social services on their own or whether the investigation will be a joint one, also involving the police and possibly an NSPCC social worker.

An initial assessment of the child or young person, and their family situation is undertaken. At this early stage, the main aim is to assess:

- The developmental, or other, needs of the child or young person.
- Whether parents are able to respond to those needs, so as to safeguard the child from significant harm and promote the child's health and development.
- The impact on the above of family history and anything that affects family functioning from the immediate social environment.

This information gathering will be led by a social worker, who in most cases will not know the child and family. So, reliable information has to be gained from services and practitioners who are more knowledgeable about the situation. The informed decision at this point has to be whether some kind of action is needed, either to safeguard the child from harm, or to promote their welfare.

Even when there is serious concern about an entire family situation, each child or young adolescent has to be approached as a distinct individual.

Consequently, child protection investigations can reach different conclusions about the needs or level of risk for different siblings.

Assessment frameworks

It is possible that some information may already have been gathered about the child, young person and family. Each part of the UK has, or is developing, a tool for the full assessment of children and young people.

- The Common Assessment Framework (CAF) for England and Wales.
- The Integrated Assessment Framework (IAF) for Scotland.
- The Single Assessment Framework (SAF) for Northern Ireland.

The framework is, in each case, provided to ensure that information is gathered consistently and to bring together assessments from different sources. Professionals should use the framework because a child or young person is in need of help, though at lower levels of concern than trigger a child protection inquiry. The assessment framework is a tool that provides general support to a child and family and is not exclusively about child protection. However, if there has previously been no reason to complete an assessment on a child and family, the relevant framework would now be used.

Strategy meeting

If there is any concern about likely or actual significant harm, then there has to be a strategy meeting to plan any future investigation and, at this point, there are three main possibilities:

- On the basis of the information available, it may be decided not to go further with the protection process for this child or young person. This decision does not mean that any concerns are ignored. Sometimes, though not always, the decision will be that low-key support will help and that parents, or other key family carers, are willing to accept that support. At this point the social worker should communicate with the professional who made the referral.
- It may be decided that the case requires investigation on the basis of child protection concerns. Initial plans will then be made for an investigation and assessment.
- The third possibility may be that the risk to the child or others in the same family is judged to be so great that steps must be taken immediately. The investigation and other steps in the process will also be undertaken, but the child is judged to be in danger of serious and immediate risk and action cannot be delayed.

Possible emergency actions

The principles guiding child protection stress that professionals must act in the best interests of the child, but not take more action than is necessary. If the child cannot be protected in the very near future, given all the facts of the nature of the risk (who, what, where, when, how), then the child is judged to be at risk of immediate and significant harm. A professional, who is most likely to be a social worker, then applies to the court for a relevant emergency court order, given the nature of the risk. It is judged too risky to wait for a meeting and the court order is a swift but temporary response to the situation.

Emergency legal steps might be taken at any point in the child protection process, because the situation suddenly changes. Such actions are not taken lightly and the key principles of legal process are that:

- The welfare of the child must be the prime concern.
- Professionals avoid and reduce delay that would leave children in a seriously unsafe situation.
- Making a court order (emergency or other kinds) is clearly in the best interests of the child. Orders are not to be used as a matter of routine.

In England and Wales:

- An Emergency Protection Order operates to allow the removal or detaining of a child for their own safety, for up to eight days. The order will be granted if the child is not safe at home, the parent(s) will not permit the voluntary removal of the child and there is nowhere for the child to be kept safe with the parents' consent.
- The effect of an Emergency Protection Order is to compel a parent, or other relevant person, to produce the child and allow the local authority to remove them to a place of safety. The order can also be used to prevent the removal of a child by parents, or other persons, from a place that is judged to be safe for the child.
- The court can additionally issue a warrant authorising a police officer to assist in the removal of children, or in preventing their removal by the family. Alternatively, the police have the powers to remove the child to suitable alternative accommodation or to prevent the child being removed from a specific place: such powers last a maximum of 72 hours.
- It is also possible to apply for an Exclusion Order, under which a child stays in their own home and a named person, who is alleged to be the source of risk, has to leave the home or not visit, if he or she lives elsewhere.

In Scotland, application for emergency orders is made to a sheriff.

■ In a similar way to the process in England and Wales, a Child Protection Order may require a relevant adult to produce a child, about whom there are serious concerns. Under the order a child can be removed to a place of safety, or it can prevent the removal of a child to a place where it is judged to be safe.

■ An Exclusion Order, like that used in England and Wales, deals with the alleged abuser, so that children can remain in their home, unless their removal is the only safe option.

In Northern Ireland:

■ An Emergency Protection Order enables a child to be made safe.

■ For longer-term protection of children at significant risk, one option is a Care Order, making a child the responsibility of the local Health and Social Services Trust.

■ A Supervision Order places the child under the supervision of the Board but without assigning parental responsibility.

Developing a plan for investigation

The initial strategy meeting must plan the investigation, if it has been decided to proceed with a child protection enquiry. The details have to be decided, on the basis of the information available so far, the strands that have to be followed and the other professionals involved with the family. It has to be clear who will be responsible for conducting the investigation and making contact with the child, family and other involved agencies. The strategy meeting basically assesses the evidence so far. It is possible that, at this point, the police representative might say that there is insufficient evidence to suggest a possible criminal prosecution in the future. Then the police will not be involved further in this process.

Understanding the role of the police

The work of the police in the child protection process is rather different from that of other professionals. They can only justify their continuing involvement with a child protection case on two related grounds:

■ That if the abuse is proven then the abuser(s) will have committed a crime. The alleged actions have to fall within one of the possible categories that define a crime under law.

■ There has to be sufficient evidence that a prosecution is likely to succeed. In England and Wales the police who have investigated a case then pass on the evidence to the Crown Prosecution Service (CPS) which makes the final decision about whether to go ahead with criminal proceedings. In Scotland this decision rests with the office of the Procurator Fiscal and in Northern Ireland with the Department of Public Prosecutions (DPP).

In Scotland, the police have a general duty to investigate on behalf of the Procurator Fiscal, when they have reason to believe that a criminal offence has been committed. Each Procurator Fiscal is the local representative of the Lord Advocate, and can interview witnesses.

If the police withdraw from the child protection process, it does not mean they believe the abuse of this child does not matter, nor that they think someone is mistaken or lying. It means that either there is no identifiable crime, however powerful the information collected, or that the evidence collected is not strong enough to stand up in court. On other occasions, it is judged not to be in the child's best interests to attempt a prosecution (see page 242). Of course, some cases do go to trial and, for various reasons, do not result in a prosecution. It is important that you understand the limits placed on the police force, since you may support parents and children who have unrealistic hopes that a recognised abuser will definitely be punished in law.

Generally speaking, the police are only involved in a child protection case when there is possible physical or sexual abuse or neglect, since the actions of the abuser may, but will not definitely, constitute a crime. Emotional abuse, even when well supported by a child protection investigation, cannot produce evidence that falls into a category of a crime. So it is very unlikely that police involvement will continue through the child protection process if emotional abuse is the only strand in the investigation. But it is important to realise, for yourself and in supporting parents and children, that very serious steps can be taken on behalf of a child at risk, regardless of whether there is an identifiable crime.

Step 3: Investigation and assessment

A full investigation has to be carried out after the strategy meeting and before the child protection conference. This investigation is carried out as part of the requirements under child protection legislation and is a necessary part of the later decision at the case conference (Step 4) whether or not to place the child's name on the child protection register (or in England and Wales from 2008–9 to develop a child protection plan). The safeguarding process cannot continue without this prior investigation. Guidance has established that the prime tasks of a child protection investigation are to:

- Establish the facts about the circumstances giving rise to the concern.
- Identify whether there are grounds to consider that the child is suffering, or is likely to suffer significant harm. If that is the case, then the investigation has to identify the sources and level of risks, and then decide on the necessary protective, and other, actions in relation to children.
- Secure by interview or medical examination the evidence from which a decision can be made regarding civil or criminal proceedings (the difference between these is explained on page 236).

At this point in the process, some children are judged to be 'in need' rather than 'at risk' of actual or likely significant harm. In such instances the process of investigation should identify the support services that would best improve the situation. Gathering information about the family would also include making an assessment of whether parents, or other significant family carers, would accept and work with a given service, or professionals who would visit the home on a regular basis.

The principles of an investigation are that it should:

- Always be child-centred and any procedures should be undertaken with the child's feelings and experiences in mind. Interviews or examinations should be explained and undertaken with consideration, avoiding further distress to an already hurt or confused child.
- Have due regard to the legal requirements. However concerned professionals may be about a child or young person, they must act within the law.
- Fully assess the child's circumstances before any action is taken. It has to be clear, and properly documented, detailing how any decisions have been reached.
- Undertake interviews with an open mind, having regard to different child care practices and cultural diversity, but with the welfare of the child as central. (See also chapter 4 about equality practice and safeguarding).

The investigation and assessment process should involve parents and carers, unless it can be clearly justified as prejudicial to the investigation. For instance, parents might be excluded if they continually disrupt meetings or intimidate the children. In that case the parents' views should still be sought and they should be given information. If parents refuse to co-operate in the investigation, a Child Assessment Order can be obtained in any of the four nations of the UK. This court order requires parents to allow an assessment to be made of a child at risk, when that co-operation is being withheld unreasonably. This order would not usually require the removal of a child from their home, unless obstruction from the family was such that professionals could not otherwise assess the child.

Guidance, for example in *Working together to safeguard children* (2006), makes it clear that the social worker leading this investigation should continue to be in contact with the professional who made the initial referral. Communication might be made not only for brief feedback on the progress of the case, but also for the appropriate involvement of that person and their setting or service.

Step 4: The child protection conference

Not all child protection concerns reach this stage. The whole point of initial inquiries and the investigation is that further steps are not taken unless there is genuine cause for concern. Some children are best helped by organising different kinds of family support services, when parents show that they are willing, perhaps keen, to address the problems that have given rise to concerns.

The child protection conference, sometimes known just as a case conference, brings together any professionals who have relevant information to share, and the family itself. The conference is attended by some, but not necessarily all, of the following people. Representatives from different professions are not invited unless they are involved with the family or have a direct contribution to make:

- A social worker will definitely be present.
- A practitioner who is directly involved with the child or young person; this may be a residential social worker or foster carer, key person from early years provision or a child's class teacher (or possibly the member of staff with designated child protection responsibility in the setting).
- In Scotland, the Children's Reporter.
- The police, represented by the liaison officer from a child protection unit or the investigating officer. In Scotland the police would usually represent the Procurator Fiscal.
- A medical professional, such as the family's GP or the school nurse.
- If relevant, someone from the Probation department.
- Perhaps a local NSPCC social worker.
- A representative of the local authority legal department.

Studies of the child protection process have suggested that detailed co-operation between different professionals is most likely at the beginning of the process and at the investigation stage. Social workers are the most likely professionals to carry on with the work and good practice has to ensure that all the relevant parties continue to contribute information and take action to safeguard.

Involvement of parents

Law and guidance across the UK firmly stress that parents should remain a part of the child protection process. Parents – or another key family carer – must be invited to the case conference, unless it can be shown that there is a very good reason why they should not be there. These family members might be excluded if there is reason to suppose that they are likely to become violent or very disruptive. At the case conference, parents can hear the views of everyone else and they can contribute their own views. However, they do not participate in the conference decision making and they may not be present for the full meeting.

Any professional involved in a case conference needs to understand what the experience can feel like from the parents' point of view. It is very stressful, as is all the investigation. Parents can feel seriously outnumbered when sat around the table and especially threatened if the police are present – as they will be if the suspected abuse could lead to criminal prosecution.

Family group conferences

Some local authorities have developed the use of family group conferences (FGCs) as a way to involve the immediate and extended family in steps to protect a child or young person. This meeting does not replace the child protection conference and any decisions have to be carefully considered, so that the child's well-being is assured.

It is possible that an independent co-ordinator will lead the FGC and work with the immediate and extended family. The aim is to reach a plan for the safe care of a child or adolescent, to which the family, social care services and children themselves all agree. The FGC can work well when there are other family members who are able to take care of a child or young person at risk. Sometimes there will be a clear agreement that a child or young person will become the specific responsibility of a relative. A formal arrangement of this kind is called kinship care. Such arrangements can avoid the situation in which a child or young person becomes looked-after by the local authority.

Involvement of children and young people

It is expected that an older child or young person should also be invited to attend their own case conference. They can bring a friend or other person to support them, who does not have to be a relative. If an older child or young person does not want to attend the conference, then the professional most involved with them needs to make their wishes and feelings clear to the conference, and to communicate the results of the meeting. The same pattern applies to family group conferences, since care plans will not work if a child or adolescent feels left out of the decision making or even opposed to the end result.

The child protection register

The conference decides on the basis of the evidence whether to place the child on the local child protection register. The register is maintained by the local social services on behalf of all the agencies involved in working with children who have been abused or who are judged as being at risk of abuse, and for whom there is a need for a child protection plan. It is also possible for the NSPCC to maintain the register on behalf of the local authority.

From 2008–9, in England and Wales, the creation of a child protection plan on the Integrated Children's System (ICS) will replace local registers. This step should operate in the same way as the current register, combined with an individual plan. Scotland and Northern Ireland are set to continue with the child protection register. (So this section is written with the register as part of the process.) Practitioners who work in England and Wales need to read the following paragraphs aware that putting a child's name on the register will, in the future, mean developing a child protection plan for a named child.

Serious concerns can be expressed at birth, or even prior to the birth of a baby. A case conference is called to make a decision about what should be done, given the capability of the pregnant woman and family situation. The conference can decide to place the unborn infant, or a newborn, on the register. The key point is that babies or children are judged to be at risk of significant harm through abuse or neglect. The children may not necessarily have been harmed already, but all the information gathered for the case conference leads to a decision that abuse is a real possibility. For some children, there may be very strong indications that they have already been harmed.

Children can only be placed on the register if the following criteria for registration are met:

- There must have been one or more identifiable incidents that can be described as having adversely affected the child. These incidents might be something that was done to a child, or failures to act on behalf of a child.

- The professional judgment is that further incidents involving this child are likely to occur.
- The abuse must be categorised under one, or more, of the following four types: neglect, physical injury, sexual abuse or emotional abuse. In Scotland, a fifth category of non-organic failure to thrive has to be considered.

If a child is not placed on the register, there may still be further work with the family, led by the relevant social worker or involving local family support services, including early years or school settings. The investigation will be written up in the family's file but no further steps will be taken within this child protection process.

If the child's name is placed on the register, other actions must follow:

- A core group is formed of the professionals most involved with the family. This group will not be very large and the aim is that it should not be unwieldy. (See under Step 5 for more details).
- A named person has to take responsibility for this case and ensure that the necessary planning and further assessment is undertaken. The person who leads may be called the key worker or the case co-ordinator. It is most likely that this individual will be a local authority or NSPCC social worker.
- A child protection plan must now be developed specifically for this child.

Usually, there is only one child protection case conference and the work is continued by the core group. Another case conference would only be called if there was evidence that procedures had not been properly followed. Another reason would be if it becomes clear that all the relevant information for the decision had not been shared at the time of the first conference.

Protection and use of the register
Statistics about the implementation of child protection are public information and data are gathered separately for England, Wales, Scotland and Northern Ireland. If you want to find out more, use the suggestions on page 37. Some key points follow, drawn from statistics for England over the period 2005–6 (the most recent available at the time of writing):

- There are a large number of children and young people on the child protection registers across the UK. But this figure has to be put in context for the total child population. For example, from 2005–6 the names of 31,500 under-18s were added to the local child protection registers across England. However, that figure represents 2 or 3 children per 1,000. That proportion has been consistent over the years that statistics have been gathered.

■ Of course, the numbers on the registers are not a final measure of child abuse or neglect. Not all children or young adolescents about whom there are concerns are necessarily judged to be best protected by joining the register. For example, over the same time period there were 569,300 referrals in total to social care services in England. Of those referrals, 300,200 went on to the stage of initial assessment.

■ The names on the registers do not remain constant. From 2005–6 the names of 31,000 children were taken off the register (de-registered). This pattern of turnover has been consistent throughout the years that statistics have been collected.

■ In many cases, the child protection plan has worked to protect the children. However, concerns about some families do not go away: 14 per cent of the names added to the register during 2005–6 were for children or adolescents who had previously been registered.

The numbers of children and young people are lower in the population of Wales, Scotland and Northern Ireland but the patterns are similar. The total number of children and young people on the child protection registers has been steadily declining during the 1990s and into the 21st century. The reduction does not necessarily suggest that fewer children are at risk. It is more likely that, in response to new guidelines in the mid- and late 1990s, professionals in the child protection system are more alert to bringing in family support services, which may avoid the need for use of the register and child protection plan.

The child protection plan
In good practice, professionals do not focus most of their energy on identification and investigation of children at risk. Children will be protected and helped through actions that follow. When faced with children at risk, the involved professionals have several options:

■ They can start a child protection inquiry under the requirements set out in the relevant Children Act or Order. A comprehensive assessment of the child or young person will often prove to be important in identifying how best to help. The earlier investigation is made only to establish whether the child is being abused or at risk of abuse and to determine immediate actions.

■ They can look at the possibilities within family support services. Each of the Children Acts and Orders in the UK is concerned with children in need as well as child protection. There are possibilities for support services covered in the legislation: Part III of the Children Act 1989, Part II of the Children (Scotland) Act 1995 and Part IV of the Children (Northern Ireland) Order 1996.

These options are not on an either/or basis. A child protection inquiry often leads to developing the use of family support services as the way to safeguard or promote the child's welfare. With younger children, the support services might include attendance with their parent(s) at a family centre, home support for parents or placement of the child in a daily early years setting.

Care proceedings

Early years, school and out-of-school practitioners are sometimes worried that a child protection investigation is very likely to mean that children are taken away from their families. Parents can be very anxious that their children will be taken into care. However, in the great majority of cases, children and young people stay in their own home, even when concerns about abuse or neglect have been substantiated. Guidance is clear that children should remain with their family, unless there is clear evidence they can only be effectively protected elsewhere.

Emergency court orders are temporary measures and do not automatically lead to care proceedings. However, if children or young adolescents are assessed as being at serious risk then more permanent steps will be taken. Social workers may apply for a Care Order, which starts the legal process of care proceedings: removal of a child or young person into the care of the local authority. If the order is successful, then children or adolescents have looked-after status: the local authority has assumed parental responsibility for them. Children may be placed in foster care or in a residential home but a minority of looked-after children remain with their own family, but under the close supervision of a social worker.

Families whose children are taken into care have long-standing difficulties, frequently from more than one factor. Problems that affect children's safety include serious mental health problems, substance abuse, persistent domestic violence, a chaotic family lifestyle that leaves children consistently at risk and an inability to cope with or control the child or young adolescent. Additionally, circumstances are such that it is very unlikely that parents, or other key family carers, will cooperate with support services. Sometimes a family may have received a great deal of support, yet the circumstances for the children are no better and there is no prospect of improvement to ensure a child's safety and well being.

LOOK, LISTEN, NOTE, LEARN

The need for everyone to understand how child protection really works was brought home in 2007, when a private family problem (in North Tyneside, England) became very public.

The predicament of Connor McCreaddie, 8 years of age and weighing 14 stone, was reported in newspapers with headlines of 'Fat boy may be put into care' (*Sunday Times*, 25th February) and 'Mother's anger as obese boy, 8, faces care order' (*Guardian*, 26th February). Muddled reporting implied that removing children from their family was a prominent choice for social workers. *The Times* (26th February) went further, with the headline, 'Go on diet or be taken into care, 14 stone boy is told': a message that being taken from your family is used as a threat to children.

There was limited explanation of the significant role of family support within safeguarding, even in the briefer follow-up reports. The child protection conference, in North Tyneside, had decided that the best route was to continue to support Connor's mother and grandmother while he remained at home.

QUESTIONS

- Follow up this story on the internet, by typing Connor's name into a search engine like Google. What do you think people, who are not professionally involved at all in safeguarding, may take away from these media stories?

- Connor's story became public property because his family decided to speak to their local newspaper, followed by GMTV and to be filmed for the ITV programme 'Tonight with Trevor McDonald' (broadcast on 26th February 2007). What do you think about this choice? What could be the impact on Connor himself?

Step 5: Meetings of the core group

The core group will consist of the key worker, who is most likely to be a social worker, and other professionals directly relevant to this family. The group also includes the parent(s) and the children, if they are judged to be old enough to be involved. As with the child protection conference, there would have to be a very compelling reason for not inviting the parent(s). The core group meets on a regular basis (often about fortnightly) and has to:

- Develop and then implement the child protection plan, which includes the need to identify objective criteria about protection for this child or young person.

- Organise a comprehensive assessment of the child and family. The case conference has decided that on the basis of the initial investigation there is cause to put the child's name on the register and develop this plan.

- Ensure that the details of the plan are discussed with the parents, and with the child or young person as well, and that they are all given a written copy.

- Set up a matrix: a pattern of formal monitoring of the child's welfare and well-being. The matrix lays out who will see the child on which day of the week.

Assessment of the child or young person

Part of the child protection plan may be to make a comprehensive assessment of the child through the assessment framework used in this part of the UK. This action includes gathering information from all the agencies who know the child and family and can include a developmental and/or medical assessment of the child. Any assessment must also include the views and wishes of the children and young people themselves.

Good practice is that any assessment directly involving the child, whether a developmental assessment, an interview or a medical examination must be undertaken with respectful concern for the child, both in their physical care and their feelings. No assessment, at this stage or at the earlier investigation stage, should further add to a child's distress or feelings of being used or abused. Any collecting of evidence should always be balanced against avoiding further trauma to the child. Some public inquiries have made the specific point that children should not be subject to repetitive and long interviews, nor to repeated medical examinations.

Medical examinations would not always form part of the assessment of children at risk. This step would be undertaken for specific reasons, such as to:

- detect traumatic or infectious conditions;

- evaluate the nature of the abuse;

- provide evidence, including forensic proof;

- provide a developmental assessment that could provide a benchmark on children's future health and development;

- reassure children who fear that the abuse has seriously damaged them physically and help in the process of recovery for an abused child.

A medical examination, including the use of technology like X-rays, does not always produce clear-cut results, for instance about how an injury was caused or whether it is accidental or non-accidental, beyond reasonable doubt.

A comprehensive assessment is presented to the first child protection review meeting or less often to a reconvened case conference. The core group is responsible for taking action on the basis of the assessment, always bearing in mind the child's wishes, feelings and perceptions.

Step 6: The child protection review

Children do not just remain on the child protection register forever, as you can see from the statistics on page 32. The first review for a child is usually set for three months after the child protection conference, and then every six months. The point of the review is to assess whether the child's name should remain on the register, or whether a child protection plan is still necessary. This review includes the involvement of all those with relevant information including the parents and an older child or young person themselves.

A child's name is taken off the register, or there is judged to be no further need of a child protection plan, when the original factors that led to registration no longer apply. Specific examples are:

- The child or young person is still at home but the risk is reduced through work with the family.
- The child is away from home and the source of harm.
- The alleged abuser – adult or young person – has gone from the home.
- Assessment and analysis shows that child protection is no longer necessary.

In other cases the name is removed if:

- The child has died of natural causes. (If the death were suspicious then there would have to be an investigation.)
- The child and family have left the area and the area to which they have moved has assumed responsibility for the case.
- The individual who was previously at risk is no longer deemed to be a child: reached 18 years in England, Wales or Northern Ireland or 17 years in Scotland. Or they have got married and are therefore viewed as adult.
- A disabled young person might still need protection and support but will now come under legislation to protect vulnerable adults.

If the review decides that the child's name will be taken off the register, work can continue with the child and family, involving whichever professionals and services are appropriate. The child and family may still need help but the child or young person is judged to be no longer at risk.

If you want to find out more

About statistics and child protection

- ✤ The NSPCC website is a good source for summary statistics, from across the UK or relevant to different aspects of abuse and neglect. Search from this home page: www.nspcc.org.uk/Inform/informhub_ wda49931.html and go to *Resources for professionals.*

- ✤ For concise data about children and young people on child protection registers see www.nspcc.org.uk/Inform/ resourcesforprofessionals/Statistics/ChildProtectionRegisterStatistics/ childprotectionregisterstatistics_wda48723.html

- ✤ If you want to research more about your own part of the UK, the NSPCC pages give their sources and you will gain valuable information if you follow those links. National statistics are organised in slightly different ways and the pattern can change between years. Some provide useful summaries, for instance see the following link for England. www.dfes.gov.uk/rsgateway/DB/SFR/s000692/SFR45-2006V1.pdf

- ✤ If you go into some of the government sites, the search or index facility is sometimes useful, but not always. Some reports are very long; check the page length before you press the print button!

About the child protection system

- ✤ A specific internet search (like child protection system + Scotland) will take you to useful sites. You may also find information from:

- ✤ The Fact sheets from the NSPCC, such as *An introduction to child protection legislation in the UK* and *An introduction to the child protection system* www.nspcc.org.uk/Inform/informhub_ wda49931.html and go to *Resources for professionals.*

- ✤ *Children Act Enterprises* which produces pocket size guides, mainly applicable for England and Wales. 103 Mayfield Road, South Croydon, Surrey CR2 0BH Tel: 020 8651 0554 www.caeuk.org

Practitioners working in England and Wales can access the website for *Every Child Matters*, a source for many papers and guidance documents about the safeguarding process www.everychildmatters.gov.uk/socialcare/ safeguarding. You will find useful information, such as the revised, 2006, edition of *Working together to safeguard children: A guide to inter-agency working to safeguard and promote the welfare of children.* Chapter 5 is most relevant for practitioners. The shorter booklet, *What to do if you're worried a child is being abused,* can also be downloaded from the same home page. The new electronic databases are explained in briefing papers on www.everychildmatters.gov.uk/socialcare/ics/

Practitioners working in Wales can also explore through www.childreninwales.org.uk and www.allwalesunit.gov.uk

Practitioners working in Scotland will find materials on www.scotland.gov.uk and on www.scottishexecutive.gov.uk

Practitioners working in Northern Ireland will find materials on www.deni.gov.uk

This chapter explains and describes the main types of abuse and neglect, as they are covered within the child protection systems for the UK. It is important that practitioners understand the different kinds of abuse and that they are all equally important and unacceptable.

> **The main sections of this chapter cover:**
>
> ✳ **Emotional abuse**
>
> ✳ **Physical abuse**
>
> ✳ **Neglect and failure to thrive**
>
> ✳ **Sexual abuse**

In broad terms, child abuse covers:

- Doing something to a child or young person that should not be done: anything that will injure them physically, distress them deeply emotionally or seriously disrupt their development or well being.
- Failing to do something for a child or young person that should be done, for the sake of their well being, safety or continued healthy development.

Within this broad framework there are different types of action, or inaction, which could be considered abusive and neglectful because of the consequences for children. This chapter discusses those issues from the perspective of what is considered to be ill-treatment of children or young people. In chapter 3 you will find a discussion of what practitioners may notice that arouses concerns.

EMOTIONAL ABUSE

Any kind of direct ill-treatment or neglect affects children's sense of security and trust. Such experiences shake their belief in themselves as worthwhile individuals who deserve care. Therefore, it is reasonable to say that emotional abuse plays a part in all types of abuse or neglect. However, for some children, a pattern of emotional abuse is the main or only form of abuse in their lives.

Emotional abuse is a persistent pattern of deliberate uncaring or emotionally cruel treatment of a child. A judgment of emotional abuse has to take account of patterns and a continuing experience for a child or children in a

WHAT DOES IT MEAN?

Emotional abuse: a persistent pattern of cruelty by words or rejecting body language, such that children or young people feel disliked or unloved by carers, from whom they have the right to expect such affirmation.

family, or in a setting, in which a child or young person is regularly targeted. It can sometimes be hard to identify, especially when the burden seems normal to a child, but it is crucial not to underestimate the impact.

Persistent or severe emotional ill-treatment or rejection of a child has a negative effect on their all-round development and their behaviour. Children need to experience affection, security and encouragement. If these experiences are denied, children can doubt their ability to make relationships or their capacity to learn and deal with life. Children may be physically unharmed, but so badly affected by emotional abuse that they are in poor health or react by harming themselves. Children and young adolescents can be seriously depressed by this experience, so that psychological scars last well into adulthood.

Ways children and young people may be emotionally abused

Emotional abuse might take any of the following forms:

- Children are verbally abused, told they are 'stupid', 'useless', 'ugly' or 'should never have been born'.

- Some children and young people are burdened with the accusation from a parent that their birth 'ruined my life and stopped me being. . .'. The claims of lost opportunities that follow are often unrealistic and, in any case, children cannot be held responsible for their own conception.

- Sons or daughters are subjected to continuous criticism or faced with unrealistically high adult expectations, which no child or young person could ever meet. Perhaps their interests and achievements are ridiculed or compared unfavourably with someone else, for example a favoured sibling.

- Any apparent affection felt by the parent is made dependent on the child's behaviour or achievements. Children may never feel sure of their parents' love, nor easily predict what will make them withdraw signs of affection.

- Children may be overprotected, to an unrealistic extent, so they cannot gain any sense of confidence or appropriate self-reliance. The continuous message is that they are incompetent to deal with ordinary daily life. Parental over-protection can be hard to judge, especially where a child or young person's disability or health condition means that a higher level of care is necessary.

■ Communication with the child may be distorted so that adults use their maturity inappropriately to make a child or young person feel guilty for family situations that are not, and cannot be, the child's responsibility.

■ One child in a family is sometimes pushed into the role of 'serious behaviour problem' as a way of explaining away entrenched family strife. The argument is that everything would be fine, if it were not for this child or young person. The targeted child may be given little option but to behave in disruptive ways. Family support of any kind has then to separate the child's reaction from the unhealthy family dynamics.

■ Children may also be emotionally damaged by experiences of domestic violence (see also page 248) or general family conflict. Children may feel torn between two disputing parents and the adults may deliberately use the children to vent their own feelings.

■ Some children and young people face such a barrage of verbal threats and personal attack, even without physical abuse, that they describe their experience as a kind of emotional terrorising.

Some children and young people experience an emotional rejection, akin to abuse, when their non-abusing parent retreats from them following a disclosure. Some children who speak up about serious physical or sexual abuse by one parent, or a step-parent, are further devastated when the other parent continues to doubt their word and chooses the abuser over their son or daughter. Such an event may lead a child or young adolescent no choice but to go into care, unless other family members can provide an alternative home.

MAKE THE CONNECTION WITH . . . BULLYING

Children and young people can be emotionally cruel to each other: from minor taunting, that still causes distress, through to vicious campaigns, sometimes now supported by technology such as mobile phones, email and other cyberbullying through websites (see also page 218).

An effective bullying policy and practice in school, out-of-school settings and residential care needs to recognise that verbal cruelty can be as devastating to a child's well being as physical attack. However, rather like physical aggression, you should be concerned about children and young people who have a pressing need to be emotionally cruel to other people. You should wonder to what extent they are recycling verbal abuse and emotional threats that shape daily experience in their own family.

Families can go through difficult times and the majority of parents try their utmost not to take out their feelings of stress on their children. Some parents respond well to help from relatives, friends or trusted practitioners who are involved with the children and the family. Parents acknowledge the difficult situation that has developed and are prepared to work towards changing it. Other parents, and some carers, are resistant to acknowledging what is happening or changing the situation. They persist in believing that the child deserves the emotional abuse, and that the fault and responsibility all lie with the child.

SCENARIO: PIKE LANE PRE-SCHOOL

Students on placement at Pike Lane have reported back to their tutor their distress on discovering how the children are treated. 3 and 4-year-olds are subject to a very structured session, in which they have no choice about activities. The children are expected to sit still for a long time. Children who fidget or who try to move across to the 'wrong' activity are told off at length and threatened with losing their short time out in the garden.

The students report that children who have toileting accidents are told they are 'dirty'. The end of session group time is run mainly as a way to highlight which children have failed to behave well during that day. The ground rules for the setting are all phrased as 'don't' or 'you must not. . .'. Adults regularly contravene the rules, such as not shouting. One student has written up an incident in which a child tentatively said to an adult, shouting across the room at him, 'But we're not supposed to shout. You said it's rude'. The practitioner strode across the room and, pointing a finger towards the child's face, yelled, 'That means you, not me!'

The students tried to raise their concerns with the pre-school leader and were told firmly that all the parents wanted this kind of approach to education and discipline. So the pre-school was meeting the demands of partnership.

Questions

■ **What would concern you about this situation?**

■ **What issues would you want to raise if you were directly involved?**

You will find a commentary on page 66.

Possible, underlying reasons

No adult, however caring, manages to be patient and considerate with children all the time. Parents are not perfect and sometimes they get cross, or their own concerns temporarily overwhelm them. Normally considerate practitioners may look back and feel that they did not give children the attention they needed. Adults may recognise they jumped to an unfair conclusion about a child or young person's behaviour.

Mainly kind and reflective adults treat children with respect. Parents or practitioners will admit their mistakes and make the effort to put right their oversights. They will listen to another adult, fellow-parent or colleague who points out that a child is being treated too severely, or that their expectations of the child are unrealistic. They will listen to the child or young person: the words they manage to express, or the messages of their sad and disheartened body language. In contrast, an adult who is culpable of emotional abuse carries on with this treatment, regardless of the obvious distress of the child or young person. Some abusive adults look as if they actually enjoy the pain they cause.

TAKE ANOTHER PERSPECTIVE

This section about possible reasons appears for each of the different types of abuse and the following points apply every time:

- There is no single pattern of cause-and-effect for abuse. So any hope of changing circumstances to benefit children and young people has to be attuned to what probably created fertile ground for this abuse or neglect.
- Possible reasons or likely explanations are not, ever, excuses for ill-treatment of children and young people. Professionals try to make some sense of unacceptable adult behaviour to gain a perspective on the possible dynamics.
- Some adults are breathtakingly cruel and will not be stopped without extraordinary measures, including imprisonment and other, severe restrictions on their civil liberties.
- However, many adults whose behaviour brings them into the child protection system will be amenable to change, levered from an understanding of why and how. Practitioners may be in a position to offer support to a child or young person, who needs to believe the situation is not their fault.

There may be different factors that cause adults to abuse children emotionally:

- Some adults may be reliving their own childhood experiences of cruel words and relentless criticism. It does not occur to them, without outside support, that there are better ways to treat children. Parents may really believe that they are unaffected by the treatment they received, and so they cannot possibly be harming their child(ren).

- Adults' own troubles may be projected onto children or young people. In a life plagued by worries and doubts about their own competence, adults may boost their own self-esteem by verbally abusing more vulnerable individuals.

- Such twisted thinking and unacceptable behaviour is not restricted to the family. Self-centred adults working as practitioners may follow the same track: unloading their stress onto children in their nursery or school class. Such bad practice is excused by claims that their actions are justified by a child's behaviour, or that it does not matter, because the children take no notice anyway.

- Some emotional abuse in any environment seems to arise from an adult's dislike of a child. The abuse is excused on the grounds that the child is persistently naughty, awkward or insolent.

- In group settings, such as a school or leisure activity that takes place in a sports club, some adults argue that highlighting or shaming a child also keeps the rest of the group in line. Such a tactic of motivation through fear is seriously inappropriate in any setting or service. Even at a low level this behaviour sets an unacceptable example of bullying by adults.

- Emotional cruelty from adults is connected with an abuse of their authority. The adult feels powerful by ridiculing a child or always finding something to criticise, however hard a young person strives to please.

- Some adults believe that children will not learn without being hit, or the threat of such punishment. In a similar way, other adults believe children only learn by being criticised and punished for their mistakes and that encouraging words will make them proud (in a negative way) and spoiled.

PHYSICAL ABUSE

Physical abuse is defined as actual or likely physical injury to a child or young person. Children may be physically abused through direct attack or by an adult's deliberate failure to protect them from injury or suffering; the two forms of abuse sometimes merge together. Physical abuse, with accompanying neglect, is a very dangerous form of maltreatment of children and young people. Serious injuries and damage to health can result; babies and children can die. It is important to bear this fact in mind, since some media coverage implies that sexual abuse is the dominant risk for children.

WHAT DOES IT MEAN?

Physical abuse: non-accidental injury to children or young people, caused by direct attack or actions highly likely to put them at significant risk of physical harm.

Ways children and young people may be physically abused

Children and young people who are physically abused may be ill-treated in different ways. It is important to realise that attack and severe physical cruelty is inflicted even on babies. In fact, babies and very young children may be at increased risk from physical abuse, as a direct result of their reduced ability to fight back or escape.

- Children have been hit with hands, fists and implements. They have been shoved, thrown against walls and furniture or shaken hard, so that injury is almost inevitable.
- It is potentially dangerous to shake any child with violence, but babies are especially at risk from shaking. An older child or young person may manage to brace their head and shoulders, at least against limited shaking. However, babies do not have the muscle strength to protect themselves and their heads are relatively heavy. Babies easily sustain neck injury and brain damage.
- Children have been bitten, burned or deliberately scalded, squeezed with violence or half-suffocated. Physical abuse has included deliberate poisoning of children with household substances, the inappropriate use of alcohol, drugs or prescription medicines.
- Abuse has also included physically rough handling and dragging of children. Ill-treatment, often in the name of discipline, has frightened children, for instance, who have been shut in confined, dark spaces.

It is the responsibility of adults to help protect children and this obligation extends to members of the family in which one adult poses a danger to the younger members. The Domestic Violence Crime and Victims Act 2004 (applicable across the UK) has made it possible to prosecute a parent or other adult family member who knew about the risk of violence and did not act so as to protect children. When a child has been killed, the parent or other family carer can be judged guilty of causing or allowing that foreseeable death. They failed to act directly to protect a child or left a child or vulnerable adolescent with a person known to be violent. This provision also covers the situation when it is impossible to prove which of two or more adults, definitely present at the time of a fatal attack, actually killed a child.

MAKE THE CONNECTION WITH . . . A RESPONSIBILITY TO CARE

Physically abusive actions are not always directly inflicted through attack by an adult. In 2007 four women appeared in court in Plymouth (England) as the result of their behaviour towards a 2- and 3-year-old. The mother of these young children, together with three of their adult female relatives, had bullied the boy and girl into fighting each other and had recorded the event on video.

Information became public through the trial, that the children's father, who was not resident with the family, had borrowed the camera, seen the footage and himself contacted the police. Public statements by the women showed that they justified their actions as 'toughening up' the children and claimed to be doing no worse than many other people they knew. The women were convicted of causing the children to be ill treated in a way that was likely to lead to unnecessary suffering or injury. The brother and sister were removed from the home for their own safety and custody was then given to their father's family.

The behaviour of these women was judged to be abusive, because their actions could, in no way, be justified as supporting children's personal safety skills. It is abusive to ill-treat children as a means of entertainment. The women could be heard laughing in the background to the video recording and the children could be seen distressed and trying to escape.

Possible reasons underlying physical abuse

Children are physically abused by adults, or by young people, for a number of reasons. Support work with families and individuals has to take account of circumstances. But reasons are not, of course, justifications for abuse.

- Family stresses are sometimes taken out on the children. Financial and other worries may make parents less patient, or they may focus their anger on the person close at hand, the child.
- Young parents or carers who are unsupported may become overwhelmed with the responsibility for babies or young children. Their frustration or panic may combine with a genuine ignorance of how their actions can injure children. Leaflets in health clinics often stress the serious danger of shaking.
- Physical discipline may get seriously out of hand as a parent's frustration or temper leads to fiercer attempts to control a child's perceived misbehaviour.
- Some adults, for a variety of reasons in their own background, relish inflicting cruelty on others, and children are easy targets. Powerless adults may enjoy wielding control over the young and vulnerable.

SCENARIO: SAJIDA

Sajida is 7 years old and attends your after-school club, which is linked with her primary school. Sajida has Down's syndrome and her development is closer to that of a 4-year-old. She has a helper, Alan, who stays with her during school time but does not attend the club. Your impression is that Sajida's mother still has difficulty in reconciling herself to having a disabled child and speaks with much more enthusiasm about her son, who is nearly 5 years old. You have never met the children's father.

Sajida seems to have a lot of accidents, both at school and at home. Within the last year, she has had a badly twisted ankle, a fractured arm and numerous bruises. Each time there has been a plausible explanation and Sajida's mother and Alan agree that the child is very clumsy. You have seen Sajida bump into tables and sometimes other children, but she has never sustained more than a mild bruise at the after-school club.

Today, Sajida arrived at the club with Alan, who said that the child had slipped in the school toilets and hit her head on the taps. Sajida has a large swelling and bruise over one eye and a reddened area on one arm, which, Alan says, is the result of his trying to catch the child to prevent her fall. Later that afternoon, you are sympathising with Sajida, saying, 'You have a lot of bangs, don't you? How did you slip?'. Sajida looks puzzled and you say, 'Alan says you slipped over in the toilet.' Sajida shakes her head and says, 'No, didn't slip. Alan banged me.'

Questions

■ **What would concern you about this situation?**

■ **What should probably be your next step?**

You will find a commentary on page 66.

They may exercise this power by other forms of abuse, in addition to physical. The consistent strand is that adults regard children, or vulnerable young people, as acceptable targets for adult frustrations or a twisted sense of entertainment.

- Within families, one child may be abused, when another is left unharmed. The distorted thinking in the family may be that this child is the bad one or the unwanted child.
- An abused baby may be harder to comfort or feed, or cry a considerable amount. Parents under stress, or with little support, may find it very hard to put the baby safe in the cot and walk away to calm themselves.
- An abused child may sometimes show challenging behaviour, but it can be hard to determine to what extent the child's behaviour led to

the abuse (as a justification in the adults' eyes) or resulted from physical abuse.

■ Physical abuse can follow actions that parents or other family carers strongly feel are for the child's own good. Girls are abused through the injuries that result from the cultural practice of female genital mutilation (see page 133).

Illness Induction Syndrome

Deliberate creation of illness in a child or young person by their carer is recognised as a form of physical abuse. The pattern was first identified in the late 1970s by Roy Meadow and others. Adult carers, in most cases the mother, reported a series of imaginary symptoms for the child, actually made the child ill (for instance poisoning to cause fits) or interfered with medical investigations to make the claims appear true. This disturbed adult behaviour is called fabricated illness syndrome or illness induction.

WHAT DOES IT MEAN?

Illness induction or fabricated illness: physical harm when a parent or other carer feigns, or deliberately causes, symptoms of ill health in a child or young person for whom they are responsible.

Roy Meadow, and another medical professional David Southall, were severely criticised during 2003–4 for the frequency with which they had diagnosed the syndrome in families who had experienced more than one unexplained infant death. As an expert witness in criminal and family court cases, Roy Meadow's certainty of opinion was crucial in jail sentences for some mothers and removal of other children from their family. Several convictions for child murder were eventually overturned on appeal. Sally Clark never recovered from the traumatic experience and died in 2007, four years after her release from prison. These miscarriages of justice raised a vital practice issue about safeguarding that had been highlighted nearly 20 years earlier in the Butler-Sloss inquiry into the Cleveland sex abuse cases (see page 4). The clear recommendation of that report was that serious steps, such as removing children from their families, let alone conviction for child murder under uncertain circumstances, should not rest solely on medical opinion.

The problem in these cases was that of enthusiastic over-diagnosis, unsupported by any other clear evidence. A serious problem also arises with swift diagnosis of illness induction, because it becomes a circular argument, which is very difficult for parents to disprove. The syndrome is not common and is different from parents who are highly anxious. It is important that nobody swiftly assumes illness induction, when a parent is persistently concerned about the health of a child. There is plenty of anecdotal evidence that concerned parents have been proved to be right, although medical professionals could not initially reach a diagnosis.

However, there is support that illness induction syndrome does exist and poses a threat to children. The most pressing action is to take steps to protect the child or young person. There also needs to be appropriate psychiatric help for the adult, often a parent but sometimes an adult in a position of trust and authority, such as a medical professional. Parents and other carers who claim that healthy children are ill, or who deliberately harm children to create a medical emergency, seem to feed off the drama of the situation. They seek the reflected attention onto themselves of having a dramatically ill child. Some seem to like the kudos of being seen as an important and self-sacrificing carer for the child. The end result for children is unnecessary illness and medical intervention and confusion over their own health and well being. Some children have died as a result.

Concerns should be raised when:

- Children or young people have unexplained and recurrent illnesses.
- There is a mismatch between the medical history and what the carer claims is the current problem or health history of the child or young person.
- Extensive medical investigation has failed to explain the symptoms.
- There is an unexplained presence of drugs, chemicals, blood or other substances in the urine, stools or stomach fluids of the child.
- The symptoms do not occur if the child and carer are separated.

NEGLECT

Abuse through neglect is a continuing pattern in the treatment of a child or dependent young person. Persistent and severe neglect includes different kinds of failure to care properly for a child, or for young people who still need effective care from their family or other responsible adults.

The reviews of child protection practice over the 1990s identified that neglect could be difficult to assess, especially when a family was not known to social care services. In that situation, services such as nursery or school were doubly important, since those practitioners could be the first ones to realise that a child's basic needs were not being met by family carers. Serious case reviews stressed the significant risks to children, and vulnerable young people, when their dire state failed to be recognised, even when a social worker had been assigned to the family. Revised guidance strengthened the importance of attention to the risks of neglect and highlighted that professionals must insist on seeing a child and not depend on continued reassurances from a parent or other carer.

Children suffering neglect of their basic physical needs have died, or been in a desperate state when they were found. However, neglect at less extreme levels can slow down all areas of development, including physical growth. This condition, which is caused by neglect and not an indentifiable genetic or medical cause, has been called faltering growth and, more recently, failure to thrive. In Scotland, the child protection system includes non-organic failure to thrive as a fifth category, separate from neglect.

WHAT DOES IT MEAN?

Neglect: failure of a carer, responsible for a child or young person, to ensure their safety, health and general well being.

Non-organic failure to thrive: when neglect of a child's basic needs leads to persistent health and development problems, not explained by other causes.

Ways children and young people may be neglected

Neglectful treatment could arise in the following ways, all of which arise when adults responsible for the care of children and young people fail to meet their basic physical needs for health and survival.

- Children may be given inadequate food, so that they are malnourished or actually starving. Neglected children have been found going through dustbins for food, sometimes from homes where their parents had enough to eat. Very young children are at even greater risk, since they are less likely to be able to scavenge in this way.

- Very young children, and some older children with disabilities, need considerable support with feeding. Neglectful adult carers may unrealistically expect children to feed themselves. They may rush to feed a baby or child in such a careless way that the food will almost inevitably come back up again.

- Until the 21st century, neglect of children's nutritional needs was focused on insufficient food and malnutrition. However, it is now recognised that parents, and other key carers, are responsible for any aspect of diet-related health. It can become a child protection issue if children are allowed to eat excessive amounts of food, possibly also a seriously unbalanced diet, so that they become clinically obese (see also page 92).

- Children are not given warm enough clothes for the time of year, so are cold and ill throughout the winter months. Children may be left in unheated bedrooms with insufficient bedclothes for the temperature.

- Children, especially very young ones who are unable to climb out of their cot and find more layers, have died of hypothermia and related neglect. Some babies have died, lying in their own urine, while their parents were warm and healthy in an adjacent room.

- Sometimes, parents or other carers have grossly neglected a child's basic physical needs so that they are dirty, remain for ages in unchanged nappies or have infections that would have improved with basic medical attention.

- Older children still need parents to pay attention to their physical needs – not only when disability or ill-health makes it difficult for children to take care of themselves. However, neglect of older children can arise because parents fail to set safe boundaries, have no idea of their children's whereabouts or are unable to control the behaviour of a son or daughter.

It is important not to underestimate the risks of severe neglect to babies, young children and older children or young people, whose disabilities mean that they cannot take responsibility for their own basic care needs. Inquiries into child abuse have raised awareness that families who are neglectful of their children have sometimes drifted for a long time, perhaps years, even with social work support, because nobody had made a comprehensive assessment that the family had gone beyond the bounds of 'acceptable parenting'. The input of practitioners who see the child regularly can be crucial in this kind of situation. You notice what is happening with children, observe and record their health and general well being.

A concern that parents are doing what appears to be their best under difficult circumstances has to be balanced by an objective view of what is happening to the children. Some local child protection guidelines have explicitly recognised that support work focused on adults, for instance because of drug or alcohol addiction, must never be allowed to mask the importance of assessing children's well being when these adults are parents.

Home alone and young carers
Young children, or older children with disabilities, are not able to take care of themselves without adult support. So parents, or other carers, who leave them alone will be judged neglectful, because of the high risk that children could come to harm. Across the UK there is no legislation that determines

an age at which a child can be left alone at home. However, adults can be prosecuted for wilful neglect, under the Children and Young Persons Act 1933 (and equivalent laws across the UK) because they have left a child unsupervised in a way that is likely to cause unnecessary suffering or injury to health. However, practitioners need to recall that child protection concerns can be raised, and serious action taken, regardless of whether a criminal prosecution is feasible.

Concerns about family decisions of this nature would consider the age and capability of a child or young person, how long they were left and whether this occurred during the day or night-time. Older children could well be judged safe to be left during the daylight hours or adolescents able to manage without an evening sitter. Part of growing up is that children are steadily taught the practical life skills that enable them to take care of themselves. However, concerns multiply if children, even adolescents, are left for long periods of time. Examples would include those cases that have hit the headlines since the 1990s when a parent has left children alone, or with adolescent siblings, while the adult takes a holiday.

Across the UK it is not possible for under-16s legally to take responsibility for children. Parents make their own decision to pay a 14- or 15-year-old for evening or daytime sitting and some young people of this age are competent and trustworthy. However, parents remain legally responsible for the welfare of their own child. They can therefore be judged neglectful for entrusting a baby or young child to a young adolescent, who proved to be unreliable or who reacted with panic to a crisis. Young sitters can themselves also be held accountable for abusive or neglectful actions that they can be expected to have understood.

Neglect by practitioners

Individuals or teams can be neglectful of children or young people: through direct poor practice, reluctance to challenge colleagues, or acceptance of what they are told is centre policy.

- Children's physical needs must be met to a good standard. Cost cutting in poor provision can undermine a healthy diet for children. Disregard for the importance of feeding routines and mealtimes can mean that children are not enabled to eat well. Refusal to deal with wet or soiled underwear may mean that children's clothing remains unchanged (see page 196).
- Neglectful practitioners, who work alone or unsupervised, may target one or more children through the same twisted logic used by abusive parents: the child is badly behaved and does not deserve care. The withdrawal of basics like food may be justified as a punishment.

SCENARIO: DANNY

You understand that Danny is the youngest child of five in the Sanders family. Danny attends the nursery class where you work and his three brothers are in the primary school. Danny is frequently dressed in clothes that are torn, dirty and smelly. His shoes and socks appear to be too small for him and affect how he walks. You have spoken with teachers in the classes of the other Sanders boys, who say that these children are usually in clean clothes and quite expensive trainers. When you mentioned Danny's shoes to his mother, Mrs Sanders told you firmly that she does not have money to burn and Danny should be grateful that he has any clothes that his brothers have not already ruined.

You continue to be concerned about Danny. Something he says to you makes you suspicious that he is shut in an enclosed space. But, when asked, Mrs Sanders says that Danny was shut in the cellar by one of his brothers as a joke and then the boy forgot. A singed area of hair and what looks like a burn on Danny's scalp is explained as, 'I got the hair dryer a bit close to him last night. Kid wouldn't sit still!'

One afternoon you overhear Mrs Sanders talking to another mother, who is expecting her second child and says she is hoping for a girl this time. Mrs Sanders says that Danny should have been a girl. 'I wanted a daughter. Do you think I wanted all these boys! But Danny fixed that for me. It ruined my insides having him and he was such a sickly little runt. They had to change all his blood when he was born, so it's not like he's really mine, anyway.'

Questions

- **What would concern you about this situation?**

- **What pieces of the 'jigsaw' do you and your colleagues have already?**

- **What do you not know and perhaps need to explore?**

You will find a commentary on page 66.

- Children may be left in unsafe conditions by practitioners who are more interested in talking with colleagues, or who have been allowed to develop unacceptable habits, such as taking calls on their mobile phone during working hours.

Possible underlying reasons

Different factors can combine in leading to neglect and the accompanying risk to children and vulnerable young people (please recall the points on page 43). By definition, neglect occurs in families that are functioning poorly, but there are different reasons for the difficulties. Some adults appear to be fully aware of what they are doing and the consequent risks to the child. In this situation neglect is often combined with emotional abuse, perhaps physical as well, because the adult does not care and may even be pleased by the child's dire plight. In other families, neglect has arisen mainly through ignorance or the pressure of cirumstances.

Neglect from lack of knowledge

Some parents may not know what to do because their own childhood has given no useful experience of how adults care for children. They may themselves have been abused or neglected as children and have no positive model to help them. Parents with severe learning disabilities may not understand what a baby or young child needs and the consequences of poor care. Adolescent parents, especially those without family support, may have little idea of what baby and child care involves. They may feel overwhelmed by the responsibilities and the change brought about in their life. Young mothers may also be stunned that a baby who they hoped would satisfy their own emotional needs is a very needy individual.

Parents of any age can be ignorant of the consequences of their actions, for instance over diet. There have been tragic events, in which babies have died of malnutrition. In one case that hit the headlines, very young parents fed their baby with an instant breakfast cereal, assuming it was the same as the more expensive packet baby food. In another instance, older parents had insisted on feeding their baby on a strict diet of fruit, which again failed to provide enough nourishment.

These are all possibilities but, of course, there is no absolute link between these circumstances and child neglect or abuse. Some adults who have experienced disrupted childhoods can be good parents to their own children. They have looked for positive models outside their own experience or been guided by a supportive partner whose childhood was much happier. Parents with learning disabilities or very young parents can often cope with appropriate support.

Neglect from pressures

Some families would not be neglectful under more favourable circumstances. Adverse events have overwhelmed the ability of one or both parents to cope and the well being of the children suffers.

▪ Parents may be experiencing extreme financial hardship, debts and all the worries associated with this. It is important to realise that some families with serious money worries care well for their children and some parents, with no financial problems, deliberately neglect one or more of their children.

- Physical or mental illness in the family may have incapacitated the main carer of the children. Psychological disturbance in the main carer may also lead this adult deliberately to neglect one child in a family, who is seen as a problem, unwanted or the 'wrong' sex.

- Alternatively the parent's energy may be diverted to caring for a very sick or elderly family member. The children are being overlooked, effectively forgotten or expected unrealistically to take care of themselves.

- Parents who have continuing problems of alcoholism, substance abuse and other addictions, such as gambling, are likely to lose sight of the needs of their children. Time, attention and family money may be diverted away from the children's needs and towards the addiction.

In some families deeply held religious or philosophical views may lead to what is judged to be neglect from outside the family. Parents may refuse conventional medicines, even when their preferred alternative methods have failed to help a very sick child. Parents may also refuse life-giving interventions such as blood transfusions. These situations are very difficult since an outside authority has to judge the limits to any parent's right to decide. When the consequences for a child are likely to be fatal, parental preference will usually be over-ruled legally.

SEXUAL ABUSE

Sexual abuse is defined as the actual or likely sexual exploitation of a child or adolescent, who is dependent or developmentally immature (because of age in years or the impact of learning disabilities). The point about sexual abuse is that the younger, more dependent or vulnerable individual is not in the position to give consent to acts that would be acceptable between genuinely consenting adults. Additionally, some sexual abuse involves acts of force that would constitute a crime even if adults were the only people involved.

The majority of identified sexual abusers are male. But there has been increasing awareness that sexual abuse by women happens and has been underestimated. Part of the problem seems to be that many people, even within safeguarding professions, resist believing that women would act in this way. Additionally, a strand of feminist tunnel vision has continued to assert that men are violent, sexually as well as in other ways, and not women.

Most sexual abusers are known to the children whom they abuse, either because they are a relative, a family friend, or a trusted person who has access to children through their work or voluntary activities. Abduction and sexual assault by total strangers is very rare by comparison. It is because such incidents are so infrequent that they receive significant media coverage.

WHAT DOES IT MEAN?

Sexual abuse: the exploitation of a child or young person, who has not reached an age or maturity to be able to give informed consent to involvement in any kind of sexual activity.

Adults who sexually abuse children are desperate to satisfy their own sexual desires and impulses. The situation with young sexual abusers – children or adolescents – follows a different pattern (see page 219). Abusers often claim that the younger, or less mature, individual was a willing partner. However, abusers twist the idea of informed consent. Genuine consent means an agreement within an equal relationship and abusing relationships are unequal. Abusers are in a greater position of power because they are older, larger or stronger and may have a position of authority over the child. Anyone who abuses a child usually builds a web of coercion to try to prevent discovery and reduce the likelihood that a child or young adolescent will be believed. But sexual abusers are especially keen to force apparent cooperation and to impose secrecy: they know they are breaking an important social taboo.

A child's compliance and silence about the sexual abuse may be coerced through various means by the adult, and sometimes an adolescent who abuses peers.

- Abusers may directly threaten to hurt the child or young person or someone they care about (a person or a loved pet).
- Abusers may claim that nobody will believe the child if they tell or that other people will blame and despise the child if the sexual activity is revealed.
- This threat can be especially effective if the abusing adult holds a position of authority over the child (through family or profession) or is a respected member of the local community.
- Some abusers attempt to bribe children with presents or treats and then induce a sense of guilt because the child accepted the gifts or outings.
- Some abusers work to convince children that what they are doing is normal or acceptable, as an activity within the family or between people who supposedly care for each other.

Ways children and young people may be sexually abused

The key point is that sexual abuse operates to exploit the vulnerability of children or young people, by coercing or forcing them into activity that is outside the boundaries for appropriate contact and interaction with minors.

- Sexual abuse of children sometimes involves full sexual intercourse, or abusers work their way towards this goal. Children and dependent young people have been coerced into tolerating oral or anal sex.

- But abusive use of children in a sexual way also includes intimate fondling and masturbation, either using a child in this way, or requiring that they perform such acts on the abuser.

- It is also regarded as abusive for adults to engage in sexual activity in front of children. Sex between consenting individuals is a private, adult activity and trying to involve children as watchers is regarded as an abusive form of sexual exhibitionism.

- It is also regarded as abusive to coerce children into looking at pornographic photographs or films or to make them take part in such filming.

Available statistics indicate that more girls than boys have experienced some form of sexual abuse. However, both sexes are definitely at risk and it seems very probable that boys, especially from late childhood and into early adolescence, may under-report sexually abusive experiences. Some children are sexually abused only once, or for a very short period of time, but for some children and young people the experience carries on for years.

Abuse of trust

Concerns can still arise when young people are older than the age of consent for sexual activity: 16 years across the UK for heterosexual or homosexual relationships and 17 years in Northern Ireland. It is judged to be an abuse of trust for someone in a professional position with a young person to become sexually involved. Undoubtedly, some long-lasting relationships have evolved between student and teacher. However, the law and supporting guidance is now very clear that an intimate relationship must not start while one person is in a position of trust and responsibility vis-à-vis the other individual. The laws about abuse of a position of trust apply to women just as much as men and are the Sexual Offences Act (2003) for England, Wales and Northern Ireland and the Sex Offences Amendment Act (2000) for Scotland. Such a situation may seem harsh when there is a minimal age gap, but, apart from the law, it has always been sound professional practice that the boundary is not blurred between personal involvement and professional commitment.

SCENARIOS

For each scenario consider the following questions. Ideally discuss the scenario with colleagues or fellow-students.

■ **What would concern you about this situation?**
■ **What should probably be your first step now?**

You will find a commentary on each scenario on pages 67–8.

Sam

During the morning break, in the playground of the school where you work, you watched a vigorous physical game between the 8-year-olds that gradually began to concern you. The game involved a lot of shrieking and chasing in which the boys and girls were equally active. But one small group of boys, which appeared to be led by Sam, seemed to push the game beyond the limits that some of the girls wanted. A couple of girls were pushed against the fence and kissed, although they were shouting, 'Stop it!' You cannot be sure, but it looked also as if Sam was trying to put his hand up one girl's skirt. Sam is a boy who has concerned you because of the sexually explicit jokes that he makes sometimes.

Kayleigh

You are a nanny to a family in which there are two younger children, for whom you are responsible. Their half-sister, 14-year-old Kayleigh, is often in your household at weekends, but lives with her mother a few streets away. You have got on well with Kayleigh and she has chatted to you in a confidential way, but not over any subject that caused concern.

Recently, you have seen Kayleigh out on the street at times when she should be in her secondary school. You have asked friendly questions like, 'No school today then, Kayleigh?' You have received non-committal answers or unlikely explanations about being 'out doing a project'. You have now seen her several times with the 14-year-old daughter of a family in your street. This young adolescent is known to truant and you have regularly seen her in town at weekends with a group of young men in their early 20s.

You do not want to appear to tell tales on Kayleigh, and she has never been your responsibility. But you are now concerned that she may slip into serious trouble and wonder if at least one of her parents should be told.

Sexual exploitation

Young people of both sexes can become sexually exploited. Children and young people can be at risk when they run away from home but they can be exploited and never leave their own neighhbourhood.

- Some children and young adolescents have been effectively prostituted by their own families, who have welcomed relatives or a network of friends to abuse their daughters and sometimes sons as well.
- Adolescents who are not at risk from their own families have sometimes become involved in an exploitative and sexually abusive relationship with one or more adults who live locally.
- Young and naïve adolescents initially feel flattered by the attentions of a group of older men, including the first sexual contacts. Even if the young women come to accept that the men regard them with total disdain, it becomes difficult to break away from individuals who will not easily let go of a source of cheap sexual activity.
- Young women are groomed for exploitation by an older man, maybe no more than in his 20s, who initially behaves like a boyfriend. The young woman becomes infatuated, and is possibly also encouraged into drug use. She is then persuaded to have sex with someone else, allegedly to solve the man's financial problem. Coercion and intimidation follows.
- Predatory adults target adolescents who are likely to be vulnerable, for instance those who are looked-after and live in residential homes.

Some young people who run away, from their family or a residential home, have been pulled into prostitution. Other young people in the support network they find may already be living by this means, so the option seems more viable. If young people on the streets have no other means of support, there may seem to be no alternative to selling themselves. Use of drugs or alcohol to alleviate a miserable existence soon creates a vicious cycle of dependency, even when a pimp is not also involved. However, projects undertaken by Barnardo's have identified that some young people enmeshed in this kind of exploitation are not literally on the streets. A proportion of young females and males, coerced into having sex for the profit of someone else, live in a flat or other accommodation which other abusers visit. Some of these young people insist on seeing the pimp who controls their life as a friend or genuine partner.

Adolescents who trade sex for money could in theory be prosecuted for common prostitution. However, the police involvement now is much more likely to follow the need to protect vulnerable young people, whose behaviour is the result of sexual exploitation and other forms of abuse. The specialist Sara Swann was active for many years in persuading police forces, and other professionals, to stop treating such young people as criminals.

Trafficking and exploitation

Some children and young people, brought illicitly to the UK (also adult women) with the intention to exploit them for sexual means, are trapped without means of escape in accommodation that operates as a brothel. However, some young people who are trafficked, with or without the involvement of the family left behind in their country of origin, have ended up as household servants. Families who seek young people in this way are pleased to exploit and in some cases physically ill-treat them. Some children or young people arrive accompanied by an adult who claims to be a friend of the family, if not a relative. Unaccompanied young asylum seekers, especially females, can be especially vulnerable, despite the fact that they automatically have looked-after status. Immigration authorities sometimes challenge the adolescent's age or there is a delay before they are provided with a safe place to live. A considerable proportion of these young people appear to go missing once they reach the UK.

WHAT DOES IT MEAN?

Sexual exploitation: abuse of children and young people by adults not only for sexual satisfaction but for personal gain.

Trafficking: movement of people, usually across national borders, for the purpose of exploitation, whether sexual or forced labour.

If you want to find out more

✤ ECPAT UK – End Child Poverty, Child Pornography and the Trafficking of Children for Sexual Purposes – a coalition of UK children's rights organisations and part of an international network www.ecpat.org.uk

✤ Swann, Sara and Balding, Valerie (2002) *Safeguarding children involved in prostitution – guidance review* London: Department of Health

Possible underlying reasons

Sexual abuse is possibly the hardest of the types of ill-treatment for practitioners, or anyone else, to consider in terms of possible underlying explanations. (Look back at page 43 at the points made for considering 'why' as well as 'what' and recall the important point that reasons are not ever excuses.) Adults, or young people, who sexually abuse others, remain accountable for their actions, even when they have themselves suffered abusive treatment in the past, or it is still ongoing. They are not responsible for what was done to them; they have to accept the impact of what they have done to others.

Paedophiles

Adult sexual abusers are now frequently called paedophiles. The roots of this term come from two Greek words: 'paedo' meaning boy or child and 'phile' meaning a strong or excessive liking. Sexual attraction to children and very young people is a compulsive pattern of behaviour. Paedophiles do not stop unless they have been pressed to acknowledge the genuine damage done to their victims. Focused therapy through group work can be effective in persuading men (it is usually males) to accept that they must inhibit their compulsion. By all accounts, the sexual feelings remain.

A paedophile is, by definition, an adult who is specifically sexually attracted to children and very young people, below the age of sexual consent. Paedophiles lose sexual interest in children as they grow out of childhood into adulthood. Children are their preferred objects for sexual activity and fantasy. Paedophiles may be heterosexual or homosexual. A disruptive myth still persists that gay men can be regarded as potential paedophiles. This assumption is false and can lead to discriminatory behaviour towards gay men. However, the outlook is also likely to put children at increased risk, if adults are reluctant to believe that 'happily married' men could ever be sexual abusers.

Paedophiles spend a great deal of time gaining a position of trust with children, in a paid job or through voluntary activity. Some target particular children and spend time getting to know the child and gaining the trust of their family, before attempting to create a relationship with the child. This process is called 'grooming' and some paedophiles target several children or young adolescents at any one time. Paedophiles feel sexually excited by steadily increasing their contact with a child and their plans fuel their sexual fantasies. Some paedophiles become known to older children and young adolescents as the person who runs 'open house', where anyone (young) is welcome with no questions asked. Under these circumstances paedophiles may have contact with many children and some are not abused.

The process of grooming works if paedophiles are reasonably socially skilled. Some people are very adept at making contact and, in a twisted way, could be described as 'good with children'. They are very alert to children or young people who are emotionally needy and without effective support from family or safe friends, either temporarily, or over the long term. However, some paedophiles are socially unskilled and their attempts to make contact are so clumsy that even isolated children avoid them. Such abusers tend to make the headlines because they have abducted or attempted to abduct a child. The other type of paedophile, who hits the headlines, is a sub-group who are predatory in a violent way. Such people are very dangerous indeed but appear, from available evidence, to be the less common pattern for paedophiles.

WHAT DOES IT MEAN?

Sexual abuser: an adult or young person who uses children or vulnerable peers to satisfy their own sexual needs.

Paedophile: an adult who is specifically attracted sexually only to children or young adolescents.

Grooming: the process by which any kind of sexual abuser creates a relationship with a child or young person, making possible a pattern of sexual abuse.

Child pornography: the visual or written record of the sexual abuse of a child, or fantasies about this abusive behaviour.

Images of abuse: the visual record of sexual abuse. This term tends to be used now alongside, or instead of, 'child pornography'.

Other sexual abusers

Some adult sexual abusers are also in a sexual relationship with another adult, or have been in the past. These abusers seem to target children and young adolescents because they are available or easier to intimidate. What seems to happen is that such abusers, mainly men, turn to children or under-age young people when they feel under stress or rejected in their adult relationship. They find children – their own, stepchildren or children of friends – less threatening and justify their abuse on the grounds that they are not harming the child, or that the child sought and welcomed their form of affection.

In isolated families, or whole communities, that close themselves away from outside contact, an abusive pattern has sometimes developed. A tradition is established that men have a right of sexual access to girls or very young women. Again, in examples that have come to public attention, the sexual abuse has been perpetrated by males. Most often, the women have been intimidated through pressure that this behaviour is acceptable, even required by the imposed cultural or faith tradition.

Some sexual abusers have themselves been abused as children. As a child or young person, they developed a distorted understanding of how to form affectionate relationships. As an adult, they may be exercising a sense of power over children, because they feel incompetent in relations with adults. However, children who have been sexually abused do not all go on to abuse as an adult.

Adults, usually men, who are part of sexual exploitation through prostitution, either formal or informal, may argue that they did not know the adolescent's age. But often the attitude seems to be that these young women are of no value, therefore effectively disposable, or have brought their problems on themselves by being promiscuous.

Organised groups

The majority of sexual abusers, whatever their exact nature, appear to act on their own. However, there have been cases of groups of adults engaging in systematic sexual abuse of children. Such cases within families have involved either several generations of the same family or a linked group of local families. The organised abuse of groups of family and friends have involved men, women, boys and girls, although there are still proportionately more men involved than women. Scandals have broken about organised sexual or physical abuse in a few group settings, where children or young people were coerced into secrecy. They have also been told, with tragic justification in some cases, that nobody will believe them if they tell, because they are bad children with a track record of misbehaviour and absconding.

Use of the internet

Pornography involving children can be part of sexually abusive behaviour. Organised groups of abusers not only pass children between adults in real time contact, but also have increasingly used webcam technology to provide interactive access to other abusers who may live at a considerable distance. Visual and written pornography involving children is not new. But communication via the internet has offered an easy expansion of the opportunity to access and exchange images of abuse. In their email communications in website chatrooms, sometimes linked with such websites, paedophiles support each other in the stance that their behaviour is acceptable and just another sexual orientation.

International police operations have uncovered significant internet websites. The ring called the 'Wonderland Club' was exposed in 2001 and during 2002 a huge subscriber website was discovered that operated out of Texas in the United States. In 2007 another international operation, led by the Child Exploitation and Online Protection Centre, dismantled an online ring that extended to more than 35 countries. This paedophile network was by that time largely controlled by one man, living in Suffolk (England).

Such cases have shown the extent to which paedophiles exchange abusive images within well-hidden websites. Some participants in such websites claim not to be sexual abusers, because they only download the images. But, of course, children have to be abused in order to create the pornography. It is a profound shock for children and young people, who have been sexually abused, to discover their traumatic experiences have become public through the internet. This knowledge brings new levels of distress and a sense of powerlessness to children and young people who have already been damaged.

The harm of sexual abuse

Unless the sexual practices are very intrusive or violent, children are less likely to suffer direct physical injury than to be psychologically damaged by the experience. Sexual abuse matters because of the short- and long-term impact that the abuse has on children and young people:

- It is the responsibility of adults, especially those in a close relationship of trust, to help children and young people to establish boundaries for appropriate physical contact and respect for others. Sexual abusers cross and disrupt the very boundaries that adults should help to create.

- Sexual abusers confuse and distort children's growing understanding of relationships, because they replace proper affection with sexual contact. The emotional upheaval is worsened by an atmosphere of coercion and secrecy. The experience disrupts children's legitimate wish for attention and care, because these needs are met with an inappropriate sexual reaction.

- Children's natural wish for physical contact and affection is manipulated through sexual abuse and children can feel responsible. Yet it was entirely the adult's responsibility to offer appropriate intimacy to a child or young person, not such an abuse of trust. Adolescents can be further confused and distressed, if they felt a level of sexual excitement, for instance a young male may have had an erection, despite not wanting the abusive attention.

- Children can experience, and be left with, painful feelings of guilt that somehow they brought the experience on themselves. They continue to believe they are to blame because they accepted gifts or treats from the abuser.

When children's disclosures of sexual abuse lead to the break-up of their family, they may feel that this crisis is their fault. Some members of the family may be keen to blame the child or adolescent.

- Children may not be believed or considered to be at least partly responsible when the abuser is a respected member of the community and 'not the kind of person who would do this'. Children can be disbelieved about any kind of abuse or neglect. But claims of sexual abuse, perpetrated by an adult with high status in the community, seem especially likely to be rejected.

- Depending on the reactions that children experience when the abuse is disclosed, they may feel dirty, as if they are unpleasant and unworthy. The abuser may also have threatened children that they will be disliked and rejected if they break the secret.

- Children should be able to trust adults to protect them and not to violate them. The experience of sexual abuse can leave children feeling powerless and betrayed. The abuser can have shaken their trust in adults in general.

- Children's emotional and sexual development can be disrupted. They may have later doubts about their sexuality and how healthy relationships should operate. Adults who experienced sexual abuse may fear, with some justification, that their later adult partners would be disturbed or reject them if they knew what had happened.

- Children who are sexually abused by adults of the same sex may experience confusion about their sexual identity and what would have been their chosen orientation, without the imposition of abuse.

If you want to find out more

The NSPCC website offers many short briefing papers that will enable you to explore each broad area covered in this chapter. Useful sources on the site can be accessed through this page: www.nspcc.org.uk/Inform/informhub_wda49931.html

The following sources are recommended for information about aspects of abuse that are less acknowledged or distressing to consider. For example:

- Barter, Christine (2003) *Abuse of children in residential care* (reach through *Research, Child protection research briefings*)

- Bunting, Lisa (2005) *Females who sexually offend against children: responses of the child protection and criminal justice system* (reach through *Research, NSPCC Research findings*)

- Creighton, Susan (2003) *Child pornography: images of the abuse of children* (reach through *Research, Child protection research briefings*)

- Elliott, Michele (ed.) (1993) *Female sexual abuse of children* London: Longman

Commentary on the scenarios

In each example, the commentary offers possibilities and suggestions.

Pike Lane Pre-school (page 42)

The students need to be reassured that their concerns are valid; they have observed bad practice and they were right to challenge what they observed.

Their tutor needs to contact the pre-school leader and meet to discuss the concerns. If the students' account is correct, there are serious concerns about practice in this setting. The team has bad practice in terms of young learners, the adult approach to behaviour and setting a good example to the children. Even if some parents are in favour of such an oppressive regime, this agreement does not excuse the team and the leader. The pre-school is not a suitable work placement for students, as they are being given a negative model for early learning and partnership with families.

If the tutor meets with the same reaction as the students, then the matter will need to be taken further, both verbally and in writing. The most likely first step would be to contact the local advisory team for early years provision. It is possible to make a complaint, with descriptive support, to the regulatory body that inspects the group. However, it would be appropriate first to contact the local department responsible for this setting.

Sajida (page 47)

The after-school club team needs to talk now with Sajida's parents and the school, either through Sajida's key person at the club or the CPO of the club.

It is important, of course, not to leap to conclusions. Perhaps Alan did 'bang' Sajida, but it was in the course of trying to catch her. However, the child seems to have more accidents at school and home than in the club. This difference between settings raises concerns that Sajida is either poorly supervised elsewhere, or is being directly hurt by somebody. Sajida has the ability to express herself in spoken words, but she may need help through signs and images to communicate the details of her accidents.

It is important that nobody comes to a premature conclusion that Alan or Sajida's family have hurt her. But equally, it is time to challenge the simple explanation that Sajida's clumsiness explains a series of accidents.

Danny (page 53)

The information about Danny raises the real possibility that he is neglected and possibly physically abused, by his mother or older siblings. Teachers in the primary school are not concerned about his older siblings. But, in some families, one child is singled out for neglect or abuse. The way that Mrs Sanders talks about her son sounds very rejecting.

The nursery class team and the head need to keep descriptive records of Danny's condition each day and be clear with Mrs Sanders that their concerns are serious and could well be taken further. The nursery team need to bring together what they already have observed and discuss with the designated teacher for child protection (in the school) what kind of regular contact they will plan, in order to make a more concerted effort to address the problems for Danny.

It will also be important to bring together, if this has not already happened in a thorough way, the knowledge of the Sanders family that is spread across the school staff team. For instance, is Danny's father at home or in contact with the family; may he be of any help? There appear to be five boys in the family but only four in the nursery and school. Have there been any concerns in the past about this other son and where is he placed in the birth order of siblings? Once all the information is made available to the school staff team, and if Danny's well being does not improve, it is probable the CPO will judge it is time to make a referral.

Sam (page 58)

The adults need to intervene in a game that has unacceptable elements of pressure and possibly touch. A first step would be to tell children that 'Stop it!' means precisely that and a game is no longer playful if anyone is hurt or distressed. It is also appropriate to explore the issue with the girls in question. You could ask, 'I was concerned about what was going on by the fence. What exactly happened?' The girls may need to be reassured that they were not responsible for the chasing game going too far. Depending on what emerges, there may be a need for a whole group discussion about appropriate touch, listening to 'No' and play without pressure.

If Sam was putting his hand up a girl's skirt, that behaviour is unacceptable between children. It will be necessary for an appropriate person, possibly his class teacher, to have a serious conversation with him about what is and is not alright in play. If Sam was aware of being observed, and nothing is said, he is likely to assume that either his actions are acceptable, or that adults do not have the confidence to challenge him.

Depending on the seriousness of what has emerged, there may also need to be a conversation with his parents. There should have been an earlier conversation, when the practitioner raised with Sam's parents what has been said to him about the sexually explicit jokes and why they are offensive. If nothing was said about that matter, then it is overdue that the team addresses the situation.

Kayleigh (page 58)

It is right to be worried about Kayleigh and to consider what may happen if nothing is said. Adults can be genuinely concerned about the well being of young people for whom they do not have direct responsibility.

A possibility is to have a quiet word with Kayleigh at some time during the next weekend. Explain what you have seen and your concerns and give her the choice to talk with her father this weekend. Make it clear that you are worried enough, given her new friendship, and that otherwise you will have to speak with him. It would not be appropriate effectively to keep secrets with Kayleigh about truanting. There are also real concerns that could arise, if she joins the other adolescent in spending time with older males. If the young men are, as it appears, in their early 20s, then it is a significant age gap between them and 14-year-olds.

Part of the whole process of child protection will be the involvement of your own setting, service or home-based practice as a childminder or foster carer. This chapter focuses on ways in which child protection concerns can arise and offers guidance on good practice in how to respond. The pattern will be different, depending on your type of provision and your role if you work in a group setting. However, everyone contributes to the safeguarding of children and young people.

> **The main sections of this chapter cover:**
>
> ✶ **Steps in dealing with concerns**
>
> ✶ **Signs of possible abuse or neglect**
>
> ✶ **Patterns of disclosure**

STEPS IN DEALING WITH CONCERNS

Social workers lead an investigation when there are child protection concerns. Other professionals will not take on this role, no matter how experienced they are in their job. However, the child protection system cannot work well without the full involvement of practitioners who work on a regular basis with children, young people and their families. You could therefore be directly involved in different ways:

- Concerns might be raised first within your setting, or by you as an individual childminder or foster carer. (This section of the book focuses on this possibility.)

- On the other hand, you might be contacted by a social worker or other professional, because concerns have been raised elsewhere.

- You, or a member of your team, should contribute to the steps of child protection described in chapter 1. Your knowledge will be an important part of the assessment, investigation and full discussion at a case conference.

- One element of a child protection plan should be what will be best undertaken during your time with a child or young person. Your contribution will arise from your professional skills, as well as the important basics such as ensuring a child or young person does arrive at the setting each day.

Certainly, if a child or young person is on the local child protection register (or has a child protection plan), then a social worker should inform and involve you and your setting. Without this professional communication, a significant piece will be missing from the protection jigsaw.

Making sense of concerns

Nobody should dismiss the possibility of child abuse with the claim that 'I don't work with that kind of family' or that 'no practitioner would ever behave like that'. On the other hand, individuals, or a team, must not become so focused on the likelihood of abuse that they assume all problems or accidents are caused by deliberate ill-treatment.

Every practitioner needs a sound basis of knowledge about development across the age range. Some problems are ordinary for an age group: 'toddler tantrums' still merit attention but are not usually a sign that should worry adults. Teams in specialist services still need to consider what they hear and see. Residential and foster carers have to bear in mind that adolescents who have experienced abuse also pose ordinary problems. Sometimes they behave like any other cranky 14-year-old who does not want to get up for school. Yet, it is equally important not to explain out-of-the-ordinary behaviour as 'just a phase'.

Practitioners may be worried about being wrong in their concerns. It is responsible to allow for doubts, but it would be against the children's interests if those doubts led practitioners to do nothing. The child protection system described in chapter 1 shows that there are steps between expressing a concern and serious action to protect a child, including intervention in the family. Nor is it safe to assume that, 'surely someone else will speak up'. Perhaps nobody else has noticed, or perhaps this childminder or key person is the only one to whom this child or young person has confided their experience.

This uncertainty should not be seen as a problem for practitioners because:

- It is not your responsibility to determine exactly what kind of ill-treatment is threatening a child's health, or a young person's emotional well being.
- It is your responsibility to be knowledgeable about patterns of development within the normal range and familiar with children and young people as individuals. You are then in a strong position to be alert to what is out-of-the-ordinary for this age or for this child or young person.

TAKE ANOTHER PERSPECTIVE

Child protection materials sometimes describe worrying signs in brief, but good practice is not led by simple checklists. Careful observation and discussion will raise a number of 'if's and 'but's, because practitioners are usually looking for patterns rather than single incidents. Bland statements about 'obvious' symptoms of abuse can also be disruptive of genuinely good practice, because worrying signs are not a matter of simple cause and effect.

Bed wetting is often on an abuse checklist and some children who wet the bed are reacting to the distress of being abused. But not all children who wet the bed have definitely experienced abuse and the child's age is obviously a key issue in making sense of this. Children who have been reliably dry at night sometimes start to have wet sheets because they are very worried and the stress leads them to regress in this skill. The bed wetting is a sign of children's distress and the need for emotional support. However, the cause may be that they are feeling upset at their parents' separation, being bullied at school or experiencing panic because of the impending maths test.

A possible plan of action within your own practice is given in Figure 3.1. If your setting or service does not have such a flow chart, you could use this plan as a working chart from which to develop your own. Minor concerns will often be resolved within your setting and through conversation with parents. Look back at the flow chart in chapter 1 (page 21). This section deals with practitioners evaluating their concerns within the very first step on that chart.

The role of the child protection officer

It is now expected that any group setting or service attended by children and young people will have a specific member of staff who is the named practitioner with special responsibility for child protection. This area of practice is judged to be sufficiently important to require someone who takes an overview and is the known contact point for everyone. This person is usually called the designated child protection officer (CPO).

- The CPO should be a more experienced member of the team but does not have to be the head of the setting. CPOs are central in effective safeguarding for a setting but they are no more responsible for starting a child protection investigation than their colleagues on the team.
- Their task is to ensure that policy and procedures for child protection are up to date and that practice follows policy. This obligation is

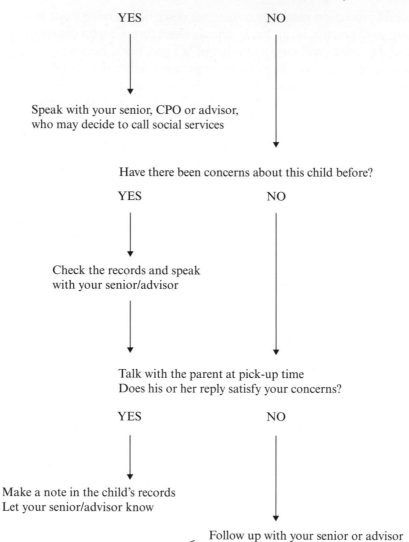

You are concerned about a child or young person
Are you seriously concerned about this child's immediate safety or health?

YES   NO

Speak with your senior, CPO or advisor,
who may decide to call social services

Have there been concerns about this child before?

YES   NO

Check the records and speak
with your senior/advisor

Talk with the parent at pick-up time
Does his or her reply satisfy your concerns?

YES   NO

Make a note in the child's records
Let your senior/advisor know

Follow up with your senior or advisor
Is there serious cause for concern?

YES   NO

You/your senior should contact social services

Make a note in the child's records
Plan – do you need to make observations?

*Figure 3.1 Weighing up concerns: a practitioner within a setting or
your home as a childminder*

shared with the team; the CPO should not be made responsible for all aspects of safeguarding.

- Conversation with the CPO does not replace careful discussion between colleagues, when practitioners work together with the same group of children. However, it should be easy for any practitioner to consult with the CPO.

- The CPO should be told promptly when a child or young person has made a disclosure that suggests the possibility of abuse or neglect (see page 98). The only reason not to talk with the CPO would be if the disclosure implicated that practitioner in some way. Then any concerns should be taken to the head of centre or other person in a management role.

The CPO will be responsible, in partnership with the head of a setting, for the continued professional development of all staff with regard to safeguarding.

- CPOs should keep the team up to date with developments in safeguarding practice and resolve any mixed messages.

- They may not themselves run any workshops, but should facilitate information sharing from team members who have recently attended child protection courses.

The CPO offers well-informed support that respects other practitioners' ongoing relationship with children or parents, but does not take over the task. Every team member needs to have sufficient understanding of child protection so that they are able to talk and listen to a child or young person who has chosen to confide in them. Any setting has to ensure that all staff can be trusted to understand their role, including what is meant by confidentiality.

Talking with fellow-professionals

Good practice within every setting or service is that it should be possible to raise concerns at any level. Practitioners need to be able to say their worry is at a low level and not have the CPO or an advisor insist on making a referral 'just in case'. Equally, practitioners need to feel confident that their knowledge of child development, and of this individual in particular, is respected when they express serious concerns. Practitioners need to be able to think over what they have observed, but it is often useful to talk in confidence with a fellow-professional.

- In a group setting, you would talk with your room colleague or the CPO. The only reason for not talking with these colleagues would be if you had serious concerns relating to their behaviour.

SCENARIO: CIARAN

Consider the following scenario and the two options at the choice point.

- **What do you judge are the likely consequences of each option?**
- **Overall which option do you think would be best for the child?**

You will find a commentary on page 109.

You are a specialist teaching assistant (STA) and also undertake lunch time duties in the playground. Ciaran is now 8 years old and, in the time you have known him, has been a quiet child but recently he has chatted much more to you.

One lunchtime last week he started to discuss one of the regular 'soaps' on television that has a current storyline of serious rows in the fictional family. Soon, you got the impression that Ciaran was talking about his own family. He has continued to chat with you on most days and you have been very careful not to lead the conversation in any way. Over the last week you have become sure that Ciaran's mother and father have serious rows, that Ciaran and his younger sister have been hurt at least once, that they are distressed and frightened, yet under pressure to say nothing to outsiders.

Yesterday you made notes of what had emerged so far and discussed the matter with the CPO in your school. This teacher agreed that you should continue to listen to Ciaran and says she will inform the head about the situation. Today, the CPO passes on the head's instruction that any further conversations with Ciaran about his home situation must be undertaken only with her.

Choice point: you have two main options here and both have consequences.

1. **You feel that the head's instruction has to be followed: as an STA you are not in a position to argue. During the next lunch time, as Ciaran starts to talk about his family, you say that he needs to have that conversation with Ms Reilly.**
2. **You question, with the CPO, whether the head's instruction is appropriate for Ciaran. You want to support and protect Ciaran effectively and ask the CPO to talk now about other possibilities.**

- Some duty social workers will listen on the telephone and give advice about a non-specific concern. However, local teams vary and some insist on details for a referral before they will continue a conversation with a fellow-professional.

- Every local area will have departments responsible for the different types of settings. If you do not know the details, find out by going on your local authority's website. You may find a good contact for advice within the specific team covering your service.

- There will be someone with local responsibility for the childminding service and there should be a support worker linked with any childminding network. Foster carers should have their own link worker.

- The national organisations for childminding are willing to listen and give professional support (during office hours). The NCMA (England and Wales) offer a safeguarding children's service on 0845 880 0044. The SCMA (Scotland) can be called on 01786 449063. The NICMA (Northern Ireland) can be called on 028 9181 1015. Or call the number of your local branch.

- Nannies are the most isolated practitioners if child protection concerns arise. The childminding organisations encompass home-based child care in general and will listen to nannies who call in need of a sounding board.

- The NSPCC has a 24 hour 7 day a week helpline, open to anyone – call the Child Protection Helpline on 0808 800 5000.

Talking and thinking

Practitioners will think through some issues without the need for support, but sometimes a sounding board is necessary. The following points will help as you listen to a fellow-professional and, phrased differently, are also relevant when you mentally talk yourself through your observations and possible concerns.

- Listen to what the other person is telling you, without prejudging the issue one way or another.

- Ask open-ended questions that do not direct or assume. You might ask, 'What else did he say to you?' or 'What sense do you make of this?'

- Intuitions are important, but vague yet persistent concerns need to be grounded in what a practitioner has actually observed. You might comment, 'So, you feel Justin humiliates his son. Can you give me an example of something that's happened recently?'

- Another approach can be to invite: 'You say your worries about Karen came to a head this morning. Can you talk me through what happened?' Sometimes it helps to be encouraged to re-run 'this morning', like a visual and sound recording in your memory. It is important that the person listening only encourages and does not lead the memory with direct questions.

- Encourage the other practitioner to make notes on their observations, if this work has not yet been completed.

Talking with parents

Your usual next step would be to talk with the parent of a child or young person. Practitioners are often uneasy about the prospect but this conversation is not always awkward. Sometimes a direct question brings a straightforward and credible explanation. Alternatively, parents may be pleased you have spoken, because they share your concerns. The appropriate follow-up action may go no further than your own setting, because no child protection concern arises. Perhaps the key issues are about the child's development or an understandable reaction to distress in the family, such as bereavement.

Without doubt, this kind of conversation will be easier if you have taken the trouble to build a friendly working relationship with parents. Such a relationship gives parents a different context in which to make sense of your question about Sandra's bruises on her thigh or Mike's puzzling remark about 'seeing a strange man's willy'. Regular conversation will have created a two-way relationship: you have shown you believe parents have a right to be informed and offered explanations. A good working relationship with parents may also mean that Mike's mother tells you, without your having to ask, that yesterday she and her son had an unpleasant encounter with a flasher in the park, or Sandra's father tells you that his daughter fell out of the tree-house at the weekend.

Anything that you say to parents needs to be in your own words and so come across as a genuine communication. There is no format that is always right or that will avoid any unpleasantness. However, there are better, as well as unwise, ways of expressing your concern or question. Your aim is for clear and honest communication: avoid unnecessary apology as well as any tone of confrontation.

Decide what you want to tell or ask a parent (or other relevant carer).

- What exactly is puzzling you about what the child said or did?
- What and where are the bruises, cuts or other marks?
- What patterns of behaviour from the child or young person have concerned you? What is happening or not happening?

Which of your feelings are relevant and could be voiced? Some examples are:

- 'I'm uneasy about the games Jared tries to play with two other children.'
- 'I'm confused about what Tara said. What sense does it make to you?'
- 'I'm concerned that Nathan is so very quiet when your au pair picks him up. He's a different child from the one he is on the days that you or your husband come.'

It is unlikely to be appropriate to add apologies like 'I'm sorry but . . .' or riders like 'Please don't think I'm interfering but . . .' The communication will be more straightforward if you express the facts and any relevant feelings simply. See also the example on page 185.

You could take time during the day to consider, with a colleague or the CPO in a group setting, what you will say to a particular parent at the end of session or the day. You could practise the words you intend to use, either in your head or out loud with your colleague. Keep your message simple, for instance, 'Wai has several big bruises on her upper arms. Do you know how they came about?'. Or 'Davie said an odd thing to me today. He said, "The ghosties will get me if I tell about Uncle Ned". He seemed very upset. What sense do you make of it?'

In some neighbourhoods, older children may be allowed to walk home with friends or accompanied by older siblings. Adolescents will often, although not always, travel home by public transport. So there will be situations when you have to contact parents and ask for a meeting with them.

You should never avoid talking with parents because:

- You are too busy. It is crucial that you make the time and, if necessary in a group setting, a senior practitioner must rearrange their time to enable you to have an uninterrupted conversation with the parent.
- You are concerned that the parent will get angry or start swearing. Having someone shout at you or disagree in a loud voice is not a pleasant experience, but you need to face this possibility for the child's sake.
- You cannot believe that anything dubious could possibly happen in this family, so you are going to ignore the whole incident. There are no certainties for patterns of abuse or neglect, so you must take further appropriate action.
- You are worried about the consequences if your concerns are groundless: that you will spoil a friendly relationship with the parent that has been hard to establish. Social work practice has been criticised when undue priority has been given to maintaining good relations with the parent. All the UK child protection legislation stresses that the welfare of the child must be the most important consideration and should therefore take priority over adult feelings.

Undoubtedly, some teams have gained the impression that even minor concerns should be referred immediately to social care services. Sometimes this message has been given through child protection courses, with the rationale that talking with parents raises the possibility that abusers will cover up the evidence. However, the law and official guidance is clear: it is good practice is to talk with parents, unless there are very sound reasons not to have this conversation. Bear in mind that practitioners would be seriously taken aback, if parents' first reaction to their own concerns were to contact social care services, rather than first have a conversation with their child's key person or childminder.

Reasons not to talk with parents

A sound reason for not talking with parents, and going straight to a referral, is if the current situation, or past events with this family, genuinely support a belief that the child or young person is at immediate and significant risk. High levels of concern might arise from the nature of what a child or young person has disclosed, such as a serious level of physical threat.

Local guidelines sometimes specify that practitioners should go straight to referral if they have a sound basis for concerns about sexually abusive treatment, that a child or young person is involved in organised abuse by several people or there is good reason to fear that a carer is deliberately making the child ill (illness induction − see page 48).

Alternatively, you could have good reason for thinking that the parent will have an extreme and violent reaction to what you say. In such a case the safety of you, your colleagues and the children is paramount. Your judgment, on the basis of sound information, which you can explain clearly to other professionals, is that the child's immediate safety requires that you contact social care services to set other procedures in motion.

The police have an important role in child protection (see page 25), but it would be unusual for you to telephone the local police force about your concerns. The exception would be if a parent, or other carer, became aggressive, or threatened to become violent, so that you were concerned for your safety or that of any children or young people. You would then call the police, as you would for any incident where safety was an immediate concern.

MAKE THE CONNECTION WITH . . . SAFETY AT HOME

It is a serious matter if practitioners are already so worried about their own safety that they hesitate to raise concerns with a parent or other family carer. This fact increases the level of concern significantly. It also raises the crucial question of whether a child or young person can be judged safe from harm, if they are living with adults (or older siblings) who frighten practitioners working in nursery, school, club or as a childminder.

The results of talking with parents

You may talk with parents and they give a plausible explanation of what had concerned you. Good practice would still be to make a note of the conversation in the child's record. This is easier if you and the parents have a continuing relationship of openness and share written records appropriately.

Alternatively, you may talk with parents and your concerns are not put to rest. Perhaps what they say only adds to your concerns, or the parents are relieved you have opened the subject and make a disclosure about themselves or someone else involved with the family. Even if parents press you to keep the matter within the setting or your own practice as a childminder, you cannot agree to this request. Tell parents what you will be doing next and when you will speak with them again.

Making a referral

Your concerns may not be resolved or this incident may be part of a sequence that is not improving at all. In that case, your decision, or that of the CPO in a group setting, may be to make a referral to social care services.

You should already know the telephone number and, if appropriate, the name of the person to contact. This person would most likely be the duty social worker, or possibly the local NSPCC, if they are prominent in child protection in your area. Out of normal working hours, there should still be emergency social work cover at the end of the telephone. It is very likely that the relevant information will be on the website of your local authority or Health and Social Services Board in Northern Ireland. The site may also have other useful links and information. For example, look at the website of one authority in London: www.wandsworth.gov.uk/Home/Safeguarding/default.htm

You need to have all the information to hand so you can give details in a straightforward way. Your setting or service should have a pro forma: a prepared layout in which you can fill in the details of a referral. Use this form to ensure that you have all the information in front of you, while you make the telephone referral. You should then send the completed form, with a covering letter in confirmation of the referral. If your setting does not have a pro forma, then the CPO should contact the relevant department for your service to obtain the recommended local form.

SCENARIOS

For each scenario, please consider the following questions:

■ **Does this situation concern you? If so, in what way? Be specific by thinking about the concerns that you might have if you were the practitioner.**
■ **Should you talk with the parent in this situation? What will you say?**
■ **Practise some real phrases, or explore the situation in a role play with a colleague or fellow-student.**
■ **What further information might you, or the CPO, want to explore with care?**

Monica

You are an experienced childminder and have cared for Monica since she was a young toddler. Monica is now nearly 6 years old and you are about to take responsibility for her younger brother, a baby nearly 5 months of age. The parents are strict vegetarians and you have been happy to ensure that Monica's food in your home meets the family's requests. Monica has been healthy and full of energy until the last couple of months. Her family now explain that they have shifted to a new kind of vegan diet and want you to do the same for Monica, as well as following their food guidelines sheet as you help to wean the baby.

You are concerned when you see the family's food list, because the diet is very restricted even for vegan and seems to depend on excessive levels of vitamin pills. You are very uneasy that Monica, let alone the baby, will have nutritional deficiencies in some ways, yet could overdose on some vitamins and minerals. You had planned to talk with the parents about Monica's health, because she has become very listless, normal scrapes take a long time to heal and she has had a sequence of colds. A conversation this evening has not gone well. Monica's mother became very irritated and demanded that you respect the family diet or else she would find another childminder. You do not feel that partnership with parents can mean that you follow requests that could endanger the health of Monica or her baby brother.

Sergio

4-year-old Sergio has been persistent in trying to grope the female practitioners in your children's centre. When you started at the centre two weeks ago, you were warned never to turn your back on the boy, but this was explained as 'macho Italian stuff – it's the family'. Within a week you have noticed how practitioners stand with their back to the fence out in the garden and you noticed that your room colleague avoids sitting close to Sergio. Today, he tried to push his hand up your T-shirt and persevered despite your firm, 'No, Sergio, that is a private area of my body'. You had to hold his wrist and move his hand away. Sergio then grinned at you.

Rory

Rory is 2 years old and seems to have a lot of accidents at home. His mother, who runs her business from the house, has offered a reasonable explanation for each incident so far. You know Rory as a bold child whose curiosity and self-confidence can lead him into risky situations, even in the day nursery. This morning Rory has a very large bruise on his forehead and you ask his mother what happened. She replies, 'I think he pulled out the kitchen steps to get to the biscuits. He must have fallen off. It was a while before I realised.' You ask, 'Oh, weren't you in the kitchen with him then?' She looks a bit embarrassed and then says firmly, 'I had an assignment to finish. I can't turn down work and you won't have them later than 6.30. And his father won't watch him.'

Yvette

Yvette is 7 years old and attends your after-school club. Her mother dresses Yvette in what you feel are inappropriate clothes for a girl of her age. She wears mainly crop tops, tight short skirts and her shoes often have little heels. Yvette wears nail polish and has three ear rings in each ear. You have become increasingly uneasy on hearing Yvette's comments about someone called Martin. Yvette has said things like, 'I'm his little princess' and 'Martin is going to get me a CD player if I'm good.' Yvette seems to become even more flirtatious with your male colleague than previously. He has just said to you that Yvette wanted to sit on his lap this afternoon. He made an excuse to get her off, because she seemed to be wriggling back very firmly against his crotch.

Marsha

The local child protection team is making initial inquiries about Marsha's family because of concerns that their mother is hitting Marsha and the young baby in the family. Marsha is usually very quiet in the playgroup but today you hear her shouting in the home corner. When you go closer, you can see her violently shaking the baby doll and calling out 'Be quiet! Be quiet! I'll give you such a one!' Another child in the home corner is looking at Marsha with disapproval and says, 'You know you shouldn't shake the baby. You'll make him cry.'

You can return to these scenarios when you have read other sections of this chapter. You will find a commentary on each scenario on pages 109–12.

The social worker will want to know:

- Your details, including your name and contact details for your setting or service, and your involvement with the child and family.
- Personal details of the child or young person and family, including names and home address and who is in the immediate family. They may also want to know at this point about relevant details such as whether the child is disabled and the family language(s).

- The nature of your concern, expressed in a concise way, and any sequence of events.

- Whether this referral is about an incident that requires immediate or emergency attention. You might be seriously concerned about the well being of this child, or other siblings, given what has just happened.

- Whether you have spoken with the parent(s) about your concerns and what that conversation added to your views.

- Also whether you have informed parents that you are about to make this referral. You would usually tell parents, unless again the circumstances were such that you judged this action would increase the level of risk.

- Details of other services or professionals who (you know) are already involved with the child or family, such as their GP or the child's school, if you are a childminder or from the child's after school club.

Involvement in the steps of child protection

You should confirm your referral in writing within 48 hours and the social worker should confirm in writing to you that the referral has been made. It is important that you, or the CPO, keep alert to these steps and are ready to follow up, if you hear nothing back from the social worker within a matter of days. As the source of the referral you should be kept up to date with the process. Be ready to follow up, by telephone and letter, if the social worker fails to contact you beyond the initial confirmation.

The social worker should be in contact for your contribution to gathering information at the different stages of assessment and investigation, as described in chapter 1. You should be invited to a case conference and it would be an internal decision for a setting about whether the key person or the CPO will attend. It is wise to prepare thoroughly for any meetings, either informal ones with the social worker or a case conference.

- Act in advance by ensuring that you, or the representative of your setting, has a slot on the agenda. Talk with the chair of the meeting or lead social worker if you have not been contacted to attend.

- Organise in advance the information you have to contribute and the facts underpinning any opinions that are expressed. You have to be confident in presenting the perspective and observations of your setting or service.

- In formal meetings, including case conferences, you are likely to submit a written report in advance. Be ready to contribute the main points from that report, sharing your knowledge of the child, young person and family.

- Arrive promptly for the meeting, dressed in a smart style, and allow enough time so that you are present for the full conference.
- Continue to pay full attention throughout the meeting, not only during your slot. Another professional may raise issues about which you can appropriately add your understanding. Do not break into their contribution; make yourself a note and indicate to the chair that you would like to add a comment.
- Use straightforward language and be ready to explain any terms that are specific to your area of work, including shorthand by initials. Be ready to request an explanation in your turn. It is important to establish common goals and raise any professional differences in approach or terminology that could influence the effectiveness of any plan to protect a child.

In order to help a child, young person or family, practitioners need to know key points about an individual child protection plan: what you will contribute and the ways that your involvement will complement other sources of support.

SIGNS OF POSSIBLE ABUSE OR NEGLECT

This section covers separately the different types of abuse and neglect, with examples of observations that would concern you. You need to continue to bear in mind that a similar worrying pattern might link with experiences like bullying. A child or young person might really want your help, but the problem is not a child protection issue. Also bear in mind that some children's ill-treatment includes more than one type of abuse.

The possibility of emotional abuse

Any of the following patterns of behaviour in children should concern you. They may indicate emotional abuse by an adult, but are not, of course, proof that this kind of experience is the source of the problem.

- When your observations show that a young child is developmentally delayed, especially if your efforts to help a child have not led to much progress. There are many different reasons for developmental delay, but persistent emotional abuse can stunt children's motivation to learn.
- When children indicate, through words and body language, that they think they are worthless, stupid or unattractive.
- When children persistently blame themselves, or seem to expect you to blame them or punish them. Be aware of children who are very distressed by their mistakes. Some children are by temperament, as well as experience, hard on themselves, or set themselves tough standards. So, you cannot afford to jump to easy conclusions.

- When children harm themselves with persistent hair pulling, picking at their skin, or head banging, or have compulsive rituals such as very regular and lengthy hand-washing.
- When children find it difficult to make friends and the reason seems to be that they do not see themselves as worthy of being liked.
- When children mistrust adults and appear to expect them to be unpredictable and unpleasant.
- Alternatively, you should be alert to children, or young people, who are prone to cling in an undiscriminating way to any adult who is kind to them.

The above possibilities need to be placed in context and some of these developments arise because a child is being relentlessly harassed by one or more siblings. However, all practitioners in contact with children should know that it is not within the normal range of behaviour for children to harm themselves, nor for young people to have compulsive habits that cause them injury. It is not usual for children to say they wish they were dead or similar desperate statements. Adolescents are more given to dramatic door-slamming and shouting, 'I wish I was dead. Then you'd be sorry!' But even with adolescents it is necessary that responsible adults, in the family or elsewhere, realise that it is not within a range that is considered normal for young people to keep giving this message, especially when it is not accompanied by whining that, 'Everyone is so unfair.'

Deliberate self-harm during childhood and adolescence is provoked by serious distress, although not always by abusive treatment – emotional or otherwise. There is no typical profile of someone who self-harms: a wide range of older children, adolescents, and adults too, deal with their emotional turmoil by cutting or otherwise hurting themselves. Individuals who injure themselves are often female adolescents but their male peers also sometimes turn to self-harm. There is some indication that young men turn to very risky patterns of behaviour, such that they are almost certain to be injured. It is possible that deliberate self-hurting by younger children is misinterpreted by adults as accidental injury.

If you want to find out more

- ✣ www.selfharm.org.uk – a website with a range of useful resources and reports suitable for practitioners and some directed at young people themselves.

- ✣ Mental Health Foundation and Camelot Foundation (2006) *The truth about self harm: for young people and their friends and families* www.mentalhealth.org.uk

SCENARIO: SALLY

You are the manager of a large nursery and a parent asks to speak with you in private. Sally, her child, is 3 years old and spends her time in a group run by Richard (who is the child's key person) and Jessica. The parent says, 'I know it's awkward to ask you, but I'm worried that Richard is leaving. We've always been a bit concerned about Jessica. She's very sharp with the children. Our daughter says some amazing things when she's playing with dolls, and it's not the kind of stuff that we say to her. Richard seemed to keep a balance, but now he's going. Could you get our daughter moved into another group? I really don't want Jessica to become Sally's new key person.'

Questions

■ **What would concern you about this situation?**

■ **What else would you need to explore?**

■ **What should probably be your next steps?**

You will find a commentary on page 112.

The possibility of physical abuse

The most likely warning signs of the physical abuse of children are injuries, perplexing illnesses, or a continuing pattern of accidents to a child for which the responsible adult(s) give no believable explanation. It is important to recall that young children collect a large number of bumps and bruises in the normal course of their play. Physically lively children, with a limited understanding or concern about risks, can have a childhood full of minor, but understandable injuries. So, a consideration of possible physical abuse has to include both the visible injury to the child and the explanation of how this injury was caused.

Accidental or non-accidental?

It will not be your job to make an assessment of whether a child or young person's injuries are definitely accidental or non-accidental. However, your attention should be caught by aspects such as the age and mobility of a child. For instance, a baby or a profoundly disabled older child will not manage the kind of lively play and getting into 'mischief' that can be usual for an active 3- or 4-year-old. One good reason for keeping proper records (see page 180) is that documentation will show whether a child or young adolescent has many accidents, each of which have a credible explanation, but which build to a serious catalogue of events.

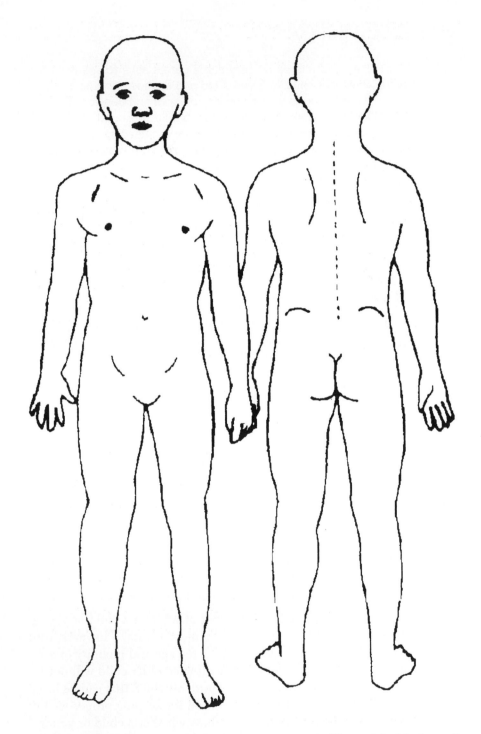

Figure 3.2 A body outline

There are no certainties about visible injuries, but in general:

- Accidents that occur during normal play or boisterous activities tend to lead to a small number of bruises to the bony parts of children's bodies, such as elbows and knees, which stick out and are likely to be hit in a fall.

- Children usually trip forwards so are likely to hit themselves on the forehead, face or other parts of the front of the body. They may also injure their hands, once children have learned to put them out to break their fall.

- However, children have been directly hit in the face by abusive adults or pushed with such force that they fell forwards. So, injuries to sites that are often the focus of genuine accidents cannot be overlooked.

- Injuries on the bottom and back of the legs are regarded as more suspicious sites, because that is where children are often hit, by an adult hand or with implements. However, if children accidentally lose their footing or lose control of roller blades or a skateboard, they can land very heavily on their bottom.

- Bruising to the less accessible parts of the body, such as upper arms or thighs, is more likely to result from deliberate pinching, biting or hitting. But you do not know by whom; it could be bullying from another child.

- The genital or anal area is a less likely site for accidental injury. However, children or young people have lost their footing on climbing apparatus, or when riding a bike, and landed heavily on their crotch area. This experience is painful for both girls and boys.

- Very young children, especially babies, do not usually bruise inside their mouths. It is, in fact, very hard to imagine how they could gain that kind of injury in what should be the normal pattern of a baby's day.

- Symmetrical bruising is unlikely to be accidental, since children tend to hurt themselves naturally in one place. It is difficult, although not impossible, to gain two black eyes at the same time by accident. Patterns can arouse suspicions, for instance, three to four small bruises on each side of a child's face could be finger marks. Outline rather than solid bruises may be the mark of a belt or hand. (See page 191 about benign skin markings that may look like bruising.)

- Young children sometimes bite each other. But an oval or crescent shape more than 3 centimetres will have been made by an adult or older child with permanent teeth.

- Burns or scalds with clear outlines are regarded as more suspicious by medical practitioners; so, too, are burns of uniform depth over a larger area or splash marks above the main burn area. Children who can step into their own bath do not sit down voluntarily in very hot water. So they cannot accidentally scald their bottom without also harming their feet.

TAKE ANOTHER PERSPECTIVE

Some sites for an injury will raise more concerns than others. But it is unwise to assume that some locations are sure indicators of non-accidental injury. In a group of colleagues or fellow-students, copy the front and back body outline that is given on page 86.

■ Now mark up the sites of injuries that you definitely know to have been accidental because you were there and observed events. Your knowledge may arise because you, or a sibling or friend, injured yourself in that way during your own childhood. Or you may be marking up genuine accidents for a child that you observed, but could not prevent, as an adult.

■ Maintain confidentiality about the details of any accident involving a child other than yourself.

Now look together at the patterns that have emerged. This exercise works best if your group, or combination of a number of smaller groups, brings contributions from at least a dozen or more people. If you have several groups then mark up one large outline on flip chart paper.

■ Where on the outline do you have most crosses?

■ What parts of the body outline have few, if any, crosses?

It is very likely that many sites of accidental injury will be the more predictable places. However, you will have reliable anecdotes that illustrate how a child or young person managed to sustain accidental injury in sites that usually raise concern about non-accidental injury.

Explanations of an injury
It makes sense to ask a child or young person about a visible mark or an apparent discomfort from part of their body. Your question does not have to be intrusive. It may include comments like, 'That's an impressive bruise, Jonathon. How did you manage that?' or 'Yasmin, you look as if your leg hurts. What's up?' The response in words or actions may reassure you or add to your concerns.

■ Many children are rather proud of their minor injuries from falls or understandable domestic accidents. They are only too keen to show you and tell their tale. Indeed, one story often leads to rolling up of trousers and sleeves as other children contribute their own dramatic narrative.

■ It is a different situation if children are evasive (rather than appearing genuinely perplexed about the origin of, say, a long scrape mark), look very uneasy or refuse absolutely to discuss the injury.

■ Initial unlikely explanations still cannot be seen as proof of abuse. Some children give a strange reason for their injury. But further conversation reveals they produced this story because they were doing something they should not. Under these circumstances, the children, even young adolescents, are most worried about getting into trouble themselves. They cannot foresee that their unlikely version of events could bring suspicion on their parent or other carer.

There are features in a conversation with a parent that could put your mind at ease, or alternatively add to your existing concern. The same considerations hold if you are a senior practitioner in conversation with a member of staff, who was responsible for the group when an accident happened. Injury as the result of a genuine accident is likely to have some or most of the following features:

■ The parent (or other carer) acted swiftly to help the child, with appropriate first aid or seeking further medical help. Some people are prone to panic, but what happened after the panic subsided? If a team member seems incompetent in a crisis, then this problem must be addressed.

■ After a full conversation, the explanation of the child's injury makes sense: given the nature of the injury, the child's age, what you know of the child (some children are reckless) and their overall development.

■ But again do not just be persuaded by your knowledge that these individual children are lively and fearless. Given their age, does it sound as if they were being properly supervised?

■ The description of the incident given by all the individuals involved, including children who are old enough to talk about what happened, is very similar. You hear a consistent story about what happened.

You would suspect non-accidental injury if the pattern varied significantly from the above, including if the explanation kept changing. But be aware that people are now aware of child abuse, so parents may seem uneasy even though nothing has happened that is wrong. Perhaps they are genuinely worried that matters may get out of hand and they will be accused of maltreatment.

A worrying pattern still cannot be taken as proof of abuse or neglect without further exploration. Careful consideration may reveal health problems. For example, some children have problems of physical co-ordination or may be found to have failing eyesight. A few children have brittle bone disease, which means that very minor accidents can create fractures and breaks. Recall that the child protection system across the UK is also set up to respond to these situations: the child and family are in need of appropriate support and help.

The behaviour of a child or young person

Children may tell you that someone is hurting them. But sometimes they are as concerned to hide their ill-treatment as the adults who inflict it. So, you should be alert to a child who is very reluctant to undress for games or for a routine medical check and to uncover their limbs in the hotter weather, unless there is an alternative explanation for their unease. Some families feel strongly about modest dress, for reasons of faith or cultural traditions. Children may continue to wear long sleeves and cover their legs when their peers are wearing shorts and a t-shirt. Other children are very self-conscious about their bodies because other children have been rude about their size, shape or skin problems like eczema.

There may be behavioural signs that all is not well with a child or young person, and the underlying reason may be experience of physical abuse. Children who are persistently aggressive towards other children will need clear adult guidance on how to change this pattern of behaviour; such information is most likely to be found within the policy on bullying. However, supportive adults need to notice children and young people who have developed strong habits of cruelty and physical attack. You have to

MAKE THE CONNECTION WITH . . . NORMAL RANGE BEHAVIOUR

Young children need to learn how to be careful with animals and understand that pets can be hurt. It is appropriate to be concerned about older children who are cruel to animals and unresponsive to clear boundaries set by practitioners.

Children may have been physically abused and are working out their anger and pain on a more vulnerable creature than themselves. It may also be that children imitate the cruelty that they have observed from other family members. Joint work between the RSPCA and NSPCC has identified that cruelty to animals within a family highlights the possibility of other risks. The RSPCA have a protocol for reporting concerns about children following a family home visit in connection with allegations of animal cruelty. Some social care services have strong links with the local RSPCA and share concerns in return.

question how they have learned this pattern of behaviour and whether there is a possibility that they are imitating what has been done to them.

If you want to find out more

✤ The Links Group is a joint venture between the RSPCA and the NSPCC www.thelinksgroup.org.uk

✤ NSPCC (2005) *Understanding the links: child abuse, animal abuse and domestic violence* www.nspcc.org.uk/Inform/informhub_wda49931.html (go through *Research*, *NSPCC Research findings*)

The possibility of neglect and failure to thrive

Children who are neglected will show a pattern of the results of their poor care.

- They may be thin and health records show that they fail to put on weight. A malnourished child can be tired and lethargic. Severe malnourishment in babies and very young children can cause damage, including to their brain, which can never be completely reversed, even with very high quality later care.

- If you feed children in your setting, you may find that a child arrives desperate for food and eats a large amount when it is available. Their state of hunger may be noticeably greater after the weekend.

- It is not usual for children to hide food because they are afraid that they, or their siblings, will be hungry later. It is relatively usual for children to hide food that they do not want to eat and when they feel nagged by the adults.

- Children may be seriously overweight and this condition may have affected their ease of movement, ability to join in physically active games and may be causing observable emotional distress.

- Children may be regularly dressed inappropriately for the weather, for instance, thin summer clothes and sandals on a cold winter day. They may show signs of being cold on a regular basis: chapped hands, chilblains or unnaturally reddened skin (noticeable against a light skin colour).

- Children and their clothes may not be kept clean – and it takes time for a child to develop an unpleasant body odour. Soiled clothes, such as underwear, may be put back on a child rather than removed for washing.

- Parents may be unreliable in bringing the child to the setting on a regular basis or in picking the child up at the end of the day or session. The parents themselves may be in an unsafe state to care for children: drunk or showing the effects of drugs.

▓ Children may have untreated medical conditions or infections that are left to worsen rather than improved with basic home care or medical treatment. Parents, or other key carers, are responsible for taking up ordinary health care services, such as dental checks and ensuring that young children's teeth do not decay in their mouths.

Sometimes all the children within a family are neglected, but it can happen that one child is singled out and is visibly treated worse than other siblings.

SCENARIO: FAZILA

You are playing tea parties with 4-year-old Fazila, who appears to enjoy making tea and laying out the table. Fazila lines up the dolls in readiness for joining you both for tea. But she puts one doll at some distance from the others. You ask if this doll is coming to the tea party and Fazila replies, 'She's a smelly-poo. Nobody likes her.'

You have been working with Fazila's mother to try to improve the child's care, but her clothes are still changed infrequently and some days Fazila has an unwashed smell about her.

Questions

■ **What would concern you about this situation?**

■ **What should probably be your next step?**

You will find a commentary on page 113.

Concerns about weight

Children who are neglected sometimes fall into the group described as showing faltering growth or a failure to thrive. Records of a child's physical and general development can be crucial in making sense of whether a child is being neglected. Careful monitoring may need to establish a child's pattern of ill-health and their weight gain, or lack of growth. When care for a child is shared, either inside or outside the family, neglected children may be in considerably better health and energy after spending time away from a particular family carer.

The experience and records of all the professionals involved with the child and the family have to be taken into consideration. Some babies and children have digestion or allergy problems that affect their ability to keep food down or to digest it properly. Other children have eating problems and parents' understandable concern over mealtimes has inadvertently worsened difficulties. Such families may appreciate advice from a practitioner, but they are not neglecting their children.

MAKE THE CONNECTION WITH . . . RELIABLE DATA

In 2006 the World Health Organisation issued new growth charts, based on a study of a substantial number of babies who had been breast-fed. It had been belatedly revealed that growth charts, used in the UK since the 1970s, were based on norms calculated from weighing babies who had been bottle-fed. The pattern of healthy weight gain is different when babies are breast-fed through the early months. So, a normal pattern for a baby thriving on breastfeeding often looked doubtful when set against these charts. Over several decades, many mothers who breast fed were made anxious that their baby was failing to grow in a healthy pattern. (Yes, readers can detect a personal story there!)

If you want to find out more

✤ Royal College of Paediatrics and Child Health www.rcpch.ac.uk/ Health-services/Nutrition-and-Growth

Being significantly overweight brings serious health problems, starting in childhood, and can also create emotional distress for children and young people. Obesity would not in itself trigger a child protection investigation and assessment. A public statement in June 2007 by the Royal College of Paediatrics and Child Health (www.rcpch.ac.uk/Media/news) expressed concern about the high numbers of overweight, and clinically obese, children in the UK. This professional group, however, made it clear that obesity should be tackled as a health issue, unless other circumstances combined to pose a child protection risk. So, practitioners would be right to monitor the situation and first of all to work in partnership with parents (and their health visitor or GP) to bring the weight of a child or young person back within healthy parameters. It is not usual practice to put children on a diet, as such. The best way forward is to establish healthy habits for eating, with sufficient physical exercise, and then let the natural upwards growth pattern even out the excessive weight.

Care by siblings

Within some social and cultural groups it is very usual that children help with domestic tasks and with the care of younger siblings. So, it would be important to avoid criticism of a family pattern only because it does not fit your own cultural experience. However, practitioners still need to be alert to situations in which inappropriate or heavy responsibilities are placed on a child and the well-being of young siblings, if an older brother or sister takes on much of their care. There would also be cause for concern if responsibilities meant that older siblings missed school or were unable to complete homework on a regular basis. (See also young carers on page 257.)

The possibility of sexual abuse

It is important to recall that, within normal development, children can be very physical in their contact with one another and often like to be close to adults whom they trust and like. Children often show curiosity about their own and others' bodies and are sometimes relatively uninhibited in their behaviour. Any concerns must be placed within an understanding of the normal range of children's development and their likely grasp of socially accepted behaviour.

Behaviour of the child or young person

Any of the following observations should catch your attention.

- Highly sexual behaviour from young children, rather than affectionate physical contact, should concern you. It is not within normal development for children to persist in trying to make physically intimate contact with other children or with adults, especially once another child or adult has said 'No'.
- Children who are being sexually abused may express their worries and experiences in their pretend play or with dolls and small figures. They may produce sexually explicit paintings or write stories, showing unusual knowledge for their age.
- You must consider how far this child's play is out of the ordinary – allow for the fact that younger children are interested in bottoms and 'willies'. Young children are often interested in these body parts in relation to going to the toilet, which is a direct part of their daily experience. The detailed sexual function of those same body parts should not be part of their knowledge.
- Young children often fiddle with their private parts, but you should be concerned if a child masturbates a considerable amount. Even if careful checking does not arouse child protection concerns, a child who self-comforts a great deal needs significant emotional support.
- Some children with learning disabilities behave like much younger children, and they may be less aware of the boundaries between public and private behaviour. Practitioners, and parents, need to focus on supporting children and young people as they learn, but should not easily dismiss worrying behaviour patterns as an inevitable consequence of a disability. You need to explore the loop of 'would we be worried if this child were not disabled?'
- What children say may concern you if it shows a sexual knowledge or curiosity unlikely for their age. Again, it is important to have a broad

framework in which to make sense of any concern. Some parents are honest in answering children's questions about the new baby. So a 4- or 5-year-old may be relatively well-informed about 'where babies come from'.

Children and young people may use language or show behaviour that raises concerns in different ways, which could also indicate other kinds of abuse or neglect. Possibilities might be that children regress in their development, start to have nightmares or many daytime fears. Reactions to sexually abusive treatment are varied: some children turn their distress inwards, perhaps with self-harm. But others express their turmoil through aggressive behaviour or abusing others in their turn (see page 219 about young sexual abusers). Children do not like everyone equally and sometimes they are uncomfortable with someone for reasons that have nothing to do with abuse. However, it is important to follow up if a child really does not want to be taken home by a family member or friend, or seems deeply uneasy about a practitioner or a frequent visitor to your setting.

Practitioners who work in schools and out-of-school services will know that the playground language of some children can be robust. Even when some families are careful about their own language and conversations in front of their children, those same boys and girls may hear some of the sex-related and sometimes offensive lyrics of some forms of music. Practitioners need to track the origin of dubious phrases that children say or sing. The words may need attention in terms of 'we don't sing that song here, because . . .', but there may be no further concerns about a child's direct experiences.

Practitioners who work with much older children and young adolescents need to keep a perspective on usual levels of flirtatious behaviour and physical contact. You would be right to feel concern about behaviour from the older age range that made you think they could be sexually active (and still under age) or that one young person was putting undue pressure on the other (see page 223).

Physical conditions
These physical symptoms should concern you and they need prompt attention. Most of them do not imply clear evidence of abuse, although all could be linked with this kind of ill-treatment of children or young people.

- Pain, itching or redness in the genital or anal area needs medical attention, but the condition could be the result of thrush or threadworms. Both these conditions cause very uncomfortable

SCENARIO: OLWYN

You are the specialist support assistant for Olwyn, who has learning and communication disabilities. Olwyn is 10 years old and her developmental level is estimated to be more like a 6- or 7-year-old. Olwyn has managed with support in mainstream school, but her pattern of behaviour has now raised concerns.

Olwyn appeared to have learned some of the boundaries between private and public behaviour, but has recently started to masturbate when she is in the classroom. You have raised this issue with her father, who is the main family contact for the school. He said that the behaviour had also become an issue at home. You were glad Olwyn's father seemed able to talk about this sensitive problem, but are now uncomfortable that he wants to recap the situation each time you meet.

Today you found Olwyn without her underwear in the boys' toilets and a couple of sheepish-looking boys just leaving. You have previously spoken with Olwyn's class teacher, who took the view that the child was showing immature behaviour as part of her disability. In that conversation, the teacher dismissed your unease about Olwyn's father, saying you are just embarrassed.

You feel today's events raise a new and different pattern and that it should be taken seriously, but you are disinclined to speak with the class teacher again. Additionally, you have become uneasy about how Olwyn behaves towards the new driver on her transport to school for some days of the week. You find it hard to identify what is awry, but are concerned to hear that he also runs a specialist sports club that Olwyn attends. You do not want to over-react, but equally you do not feel her behaviour should be explained away as part of the disability.

Questions

■ **What are the main issues that concern you about this situation?**

■ **What should probably be your next steps?**

You will find a commentary on page 113.

itching and can lead to broken skin if the child has scratched vigorously. Persistent constipation can cause redness and anal fissures, or bleeding from the strain.

■ Bruising or bleeding in the genital or anal area again needs a medical check as does any child's clear discomfort in walking or sitting down. But you have to keep an open mind, as does the doctor who examines the child, because children do sometimes slip or fall and land heavily on their crotch area.

- A vaginal discharge or apparent infection in a girl should be checked. Again, be aware that children sometimes stick small objects into their bodily orifices and an otherwise harmless object creates an infection if left.

- A doctor would assume sexual abuse if a medical examination showed evidence of a sexually transmitted disease in a child. STDs are caught from very close, intimate contact with an infected person, not from toilet seats.

- STDs in young adolescents, as well as pregnancy in under-age young women, all raise the strong possibility of sexual abuse. An alternative is that young people have developed very risky patterns of behaviour, and that prospect would also be cause for serious concern.

Sexual exploitation

Older children and young people who have experienced years of disruption and lack of care from adults can develop an outlook bordering on self-harm. They deliberately seek out dangerous situations and persist in making contact with other people whose aim is to abuse them. Children and young people of both sexes, who have already been damaged by their experiences, may continue to go to the home of a known sexual abuser. They persist in this contact even when the abuser has groomed the young person to the point of accepting sexual exploitation by other people.

Practitioners such as residential and foster carers, who work in specialist daily settings, can find themselves trying to protect children and young people from the dangerous consequences of their own behaviour. There are several key strands in how you work with these children and young people:

- As hard as it may be, persist in your attempts to boost their sense of self-esteem, letting them know that they are people who are worth protecting and that key adults in their life care and worry about them.

- Look for all possible ways to replace the social contact, personal identity or excitement that is being fed through risky behaviour.

- Use the authority that you have to create boundaries for acceptable behaviour and address the problems that seem to fuel children or young people's tendency to put themselves at risk.

For any of these exploitative patterns, early intervention is crucial and good practice has to recognise the significant difficulties that young people face in trying to make a change in their life. Children and young people who have been sexually exploited often have rock bottom self-worth, are frightened of violence from their abusers and may also have problems of drug dependency. A range of practitioners need to be aware of warning signs, not only those who work in services for children and young people who are known to be vulnerable.

■ Some risk indicators are similar to those for sexual or physical abuse.

■ Other signs include when a child or young person has unlikely amounts of cash or expensive clothes and consumer goods. The explanation is not necessarily that sex has been traded for these items; but there is unlikely to be a safe reason.

■ Practitioners need to be alert to unexplained patterns of contact between young people and older adults, especially when there is reason to be suspicious of the motives of an individual or group. Contact may also start over the internet; yet another reminder of the connections between different strands of safeguarding.

■ There should be concern when a young person joins the social network of a peer who is already involved with exploitative adults.

If you want to find out more

✤ Scott, Sara and Skidmore, Paula (2006) *Reducing the risk: Barnardo's support for sexually exploited young people: a two year evaluation* summary and full report on www.barnardos.org.uk/resources (then search by '*Reducing the risk*'). Other materials about the same area of practice are available on the Barnardo's website.

PATTERNS OF DISCLOSURE

Sometimes children and young people themselves communicate that they are worried: about what they fear may soon happen, what they are currently experiencing or what happened in the past that they now feel able to talk about in confidence. This kind of communication from a child or young person is called a disclosure and is not always made through words.

WHAT DOES IT MEAN?

Disclosure: verbal or non-verbal communication by a child or young person about ill-treatment: potential, current or in the past.

Ways of 'telling'

The communication that practitioners recognise as a disclosure can vary, and sometimes it is only later, on reflection, that you realise a remark should not have been left without your comment. So, do not be reluctant to revisit a conversation with a child or young person. You might use an open-ended phrase like: 'I'm been thinking over what you said yesterday. . .' or 'Can we go back to what you told me this morning . . . what did you mean by . . . ?'

Talking with you directly

Children may seize the chance to confide their fear or distress in response to your friendly question, perhaps about how they got a visible new bruise or cut, or that they have been looking 'sad' for much of this week. A child or young person may take the opportunity for a long conversation in which many details emerge. However, disclosures are not always 'big' events.

It can be possible to miss or overlook the significance, when a child or young person makes a brief, almost throwaway remark. Children or young people may approach a disclosure through an apparently unrelated comment, by asking you a question or for your opinion. Children, much like adults, sometimes may begin speaking with expressions such as, 'What would you think if somebody . . . ' or 'I have a friend who . . . '. But of course, the disclosure may actually be on behalf of a friend.

Some older children and young people may make 'testing' disclosures. These are comments that are not strictly accurate and their aim is to test your reaction, if they say something that could shock you. It is important to take each disclosure on its own merits. However, older children or young people need to understand that mixing truth and fiction makes it much harder for you to help them.

'Telling' through actions

Children may look fearful or very reluctant to follow a routine. Young children are unlikely to behave in this way deliberately; their distress is simply manifesting itself through their actions. Older children or young people may let their feelings show in a rather more conscious way, hoping that a trusted adult will pick up on the non-verbal message. Children, like adults, sometimes deal with extreme distress by burying the experience in their mind. The emotional pain may emerge in less obvious ways such as panic attacks or nightmares.

Children or young people who have been damaged by abusive experiences may have reactions that are out of all proportion to what seem to be ordinary events. Something in a normal routine (such as a story at

SCENARIO: CAMERON

Cameron is 6 years old and was born when his mother, Becky, was nearly 17 years old. Becky has tried to continue her own life and, although there have been no concrete worries about Cameron, neither his nursery nor his primary school feel that they have been able to get Becky to focus on being a parent to her son. This summer she went on holiday to Greece with a new boyfriend and left Cameron for three weeks with some friends of hers. Cameron was very distressed while Becky was gone and has been loath to let her out of his sight ever since. Becky finds this very irritating and continues to say that she explained everything to her son and that it was not a suitable holiday for a child and asks 'So what was I supposed to do?'

Cameron does not seem to like his mother's new boyfriend but Becky says that her son is only jealous and does not like sharing her. The teachers have noticed that Cameron is quieter than he used to be. Recently he said to the one male teacher in the school, 'I hold my willy, don't I? Nobody else should hold my willy?' Cameron was unwilling to say any more but he was later overheard saying to one of the other boys, 'Does your Daddy hold your willy?' Sometimes the new boyfriend comes with Becky to pick up Cameron from school and Cameron refuses to take his hand. This afternoon it is just the boyfriend, without Becky, and Cameron has flatly refused to leave.

Questions

- **What would concern you about this general situation for Cameron?**

- **How should you deal with the immediate problem today?**

You will find a commentary on page 114.

bedtime), an aspect of conversation or a television drama might have triggered memories, sometimes strong enough to be described as flashbacks. Younger children, and sometimes those who are older, may show the impact of abusive experiences through play, including the themes they weave into their imaginative play. Practitioners may realise that the theme of a game or long sequence of pretend play is not entirely imaginary.

Older children and young people sometimes use their drawings to communicate what is happening to them. Other channels have included story-telling, or acting out with puppets, in addition to story writing in all its forms and poetry. Children who cannot yet write, or adolescents who lack confidence in literacy skills, may dictate their story to a trusted adult. Some older children and adolescents first 'tell' through their diary, which they then offer to an adult to read, sometimes much later than when they wrote the entry. Children have sometimes written letters to the person who ill-treated them as a way to communicate their disclosure to another adult, not with the intention of posting the letter.

You may overhear one child speaking to another and the content of the conversation concerns you. Older children and young people sometimes deliberately talk about their worries, knowing that an adult will overhear. They want, at some conscious level, to invite adult comment. Sometimes older children tell a peer in the expectation that this older child or young person will pass on what was said to a trusted adult. Sometimes the way of telling can make it harder for a practitioner to respond. Older children and young people do not always find a quiet time and place to speak about their distress or fears. Some only tell after they have wound themselves up in some way, so that the disclosure is made in a highly emotional manner.

What stops children telling?

Children and young people sometimes do not tell about abuse or neglect, or they delay for some time before making a disclosure.

Fear of the consequences

Children and young people are especially at risk when cared for or educated within closed systems, such as boarding schools, residential children's homes, secure accommodation, young offender institutions and as young recruits to the armed services. Children and young people may have very limited opportunities to tell about abuse or neglect. They also have the realistic fear that telling will make matters worse, because they have to live with, or be controlled by, their abusers. A similar level of despair grows when children and young people are relentlessly bullied by peers in the same, closed setting.

Adults or young people who abuse sometimes make direct physical threats that ensure children's silence. The abuser may threaten to hurt the child if they tell or make realistic threats towards someone else for whom the child cares. Abusers also make emotional threats, which can be just as effective as physical ones. They may say that if the child tells, then the family will be broken up, or the abuser will lose his or her job. Sexual abusers may claim that nobody will believe the child or that others will think the child is 'bad' or 'disgusting'. The aim of these emotional threats is usually to make the child feel inappropriately responsible for the negative consequences of telling; effectively the abuser is saying 'It will all be your fault!'

Thinking the abuse is 'normal'

Children who have long experiences of abuse or neglect may simply assume that their experience is ordinary. They believe that it happens in all families or that that it happens to 'bad' children like themselves who deserve ill-treatment.

A number of abuse cases have emerged in sport and leisure services. Coaches or adults in other positions of power have not always behaved with care and consideration for children and young people. Parents and other adults have sometimes been loath to question someone who is generous with their time and skills. Children and adolescents have sometimes been unsure whether they are right to speak out, wondering if the verbal or physical abuse is a legitimate part of the training process in their sport.

Complex feelings
Children and young people may be blocked by their sense of shame about what has happened and the prospect of anyone else knowing, even adults whom they currently trust. Older children and young people are sometimes acutely concerned that their peers will find out about what has happened to them and that taunts will then add to their current distress.

Some children postpone telling because they keep hoping the situation will get better, especially if they are fond of the abuser. An adult who is a relative or family friend may further abuse the trust of a child or young person by continually promising to stop. Within a family, one child has sometimes said nothing, for example about sexual abuse, in the hope that suffering in silence will protect younger siblings. Some adolescents, even adults, have finally spoken when they discover the heartbreaking truth that their sacrifice did not work: the parent or other relative also abused other children in the family.

Some older children and young people may have difficulty in disclosing their own abuse, because that experience has now become entangled with their own maltreatment of a peer. They fear their disclosure will be taken as an attempt to excuse their own behaviour.

Responding to disclosure
When children or young people tell about ill-treatment, whether abuse by adults or bullying from their peers, they generally want:

- the abuse (or bullying) to end as soon as possible, ideally right away
- to feel safe from now on and to be able to access help as and when they wish.

They do not want:

- telling to make matters worse: because they are not believed or protected after telling

- to have their life, or that of their family, turned upside down and then to feel guilty about having told
- to find that circumstances spiral way out of their control, with additional adults, some of whom they do not know, presuming to know what is best.

It takes courage to speak out, even when children or young people feel confident about the person they tell. Older children, and especially adolescents, have some level of understanding that serious matters probably have to go beyond the individual in whom they confide. So there is always uncertainty about whether telling will, overall, make them safer or create more trouble in an already distressing situation.

Listening matters

There is no set pattern of response to be followed by all practitioners, as it would undermine an authentic reaction from a trusted adult. The most important skill you can offer is to listen to what the child is telling you. Good listening is a core strand in any work with children and young people, so practitioners should draw on existing skills when a child starts to confide.

- Hear the words children are using and the way they share this confidence. Watch children so that you can also 'hear' what they tell you through their facial expressions and whole body language.
- Be guided by the children or young people; the conversation finishes when they wish. If you are responsive, they are very likely to talk in confidence another day. On the other hand, if you press them now, they will almost certainly become evasive, silent and possibly distressed.
- Children may choose a time when they can speak with you without being overheard, but sometimes you need to create a confidential space. If other children come to get your attention, you can courteously ask them to wait by saying, 'I'll be with you shortly, Andrea wants to have a word with me' or 'Can you just let Delroy and me talk in private for a while'.
- Children and young people sometimes deliberately pick a time when your attention as an adult is partly elsewhere. Foster carers and residential workers often find that a child starts to talk during a shared domestic activity, such as washing-up, or when adult and child are driving somewhere. Some children and adolescents do not want full eye contact and the fact that you keep your eyes on the kitchen sink, or the road ahead, is an advantage.

Making sense of communication can be especially difficult when children and young people have severe learning or physical disabilities. Practitioners need to be confident in using sign and image systems, although with great care, to ensure that you do not over-interpret what the child communicates. A joint project by Triangle and the NSPCC addressed the gap in many signing and image systems for children to communicate about personal safety or experiences of abuse. They developed a booklet to help in this area entitled *How it is*. The materials are available to download from www.nspcc.org.uk/Inform/informhub_wda49931.html (go through *Resources for professionals*).

SCENARIO: KITTY

Kitty is 4 years old. There is strong suspicion that she was sexually abused by her grandfather when he cared for her on a regular basis. The evidence was not certain, but Kitty's mother was worried enough to agree that her father-in-law would no longer come to their home and that Kitty would never be left alone with him at any family gathering. Kitty has said very little in the nursery but, when she draws, sometimes she does a figure on the paper then scribbles all over it. Today she whispers to you, 'No more Grandad'.

Questions

■ **What sense might you make of this observation?**

■ **What should probably be your next step?**

You will find a commentary on page 114.

Use open-ended questions

Concerned practitioners need to resist feeling, 'But I must find out everything'; children are people and not cases. It is your responsibility to hear what they want to tell you, in the way that children want to tell it. You need not feel responsible for gathering significant amounts of information. If something worrying has really occurred, then there will be a time later for exploration in more detail, led by a social worker in a child protection investigation.

Sensitive conversations with children and young people will be supportive, and effective, so long as you avoid cross-questioning or leading questions.

■ A long sequence of questions unbalances any conversation – not only a sensitive exchange. The pattern puts pressure on children or young people to confide more details than they may wish. Some children may agree with a persistent adult questioner just to end the conversation.

- Leading questions tend to be guided by guesses or unsupported suspicions ('Did Daddy do this to you?') and will distort the disclosure made in the conversation. Children, and adolescents, too, may start to say what you appear to want to hear.
- When police officers are trainers on safeguarding courses, they often focus on the problem that leading questions can contaminate evidence, in the minority of cases that reach court. However, a more general point is that cross-questioning is experienced as oppressive by children.

You can avoid cross-questioning by appropriate and kindly use of language.

- Depending on what the child tells you, you might ask an encouraging question that is part repetition of what a child has just said. If a child says, 'My big cousin is nasty to me', you could follow with, 'Nasty in what way?'
- A child might whisper, 'Somebody hurt me' and you ask quietly, 'You say somebody hurt you?' (in a questioning tone of voice). You often do not have to ask the more specific question, 'Who hurt you, Daria?' This kind of gentle questioning is called reflective listening.
- Depending on the flow of the conversation, other open-ended questions might be, 'You say you were frightened?' or 'What has happened to make you cry?' You can also simply encourage a child by your open and attentive expression and simple questions like 'Yes?' or 'Anything else you want to tell me?'

Dealing with feelings

It is important to avoid telling children or young people how they are feeling: such a response is too directive and also disrespectful. Be attentive to their words and actions, rather than try to guess their emotional state.

- Listen to what children say about how they are feeling: 'I'm cross with him', 'She makes me cry and she doesn't care' or 'He says I'm a bad girl, that nobody will like me anymore'. Show empathy and support for the child, with comments such as, 'You're feeling cross now?' or 'I will always like you, Mario. Please tell me what has happened'.
- It is not for you to criticise the person who has hurt the child. In some cases, the abuser is a loved relative and the turmoil of mixed emotions is part of the problem. You can still reassure the child with more general support such as, 'Tania, nobody should make you this upset' rather than laying blame with, 'Your uncle is a bad person'.

As you listen, you may feel anger, shock or distress. But you cannot assume that the child necessarily shares your emotions. Children may feel all of these and more, but you can only find out by listening and by gently watching their expression and body language. It is also important that a child or young person does not feel overwhelmed by your reaction. It will have been hard for them to tell; children do not need the additional burden of feeling that now they have shocked you. You do not have to pretend to have no emotional reaction at all; that would be unrealistic and confusing to the child. But strong emotions, that trouble you, need to be expressed to a fellow-professional, later.

Children who disclose troublesome secrets need reassurance from the adult, but you should not give commitments that you cannot honour. You cannot promise a child that you will keep disclosures about abuse as a secret; you have a responsibility to take such concerns further. But you must be able to reassure them their experience will not become general knowledge in the setting or local neighbourhood.

Consult and make notes

As the person in whom the child confided, you are responsible for making notes on the conversation as soon as possible, and certainly with no more delay than later in the same day. If you work in a team, then the CPO should help you, especially if this is the first time you have faced the task (see also page 177). You will need to think through what you saw as well as heard.

- Your impressions and opinions can be valuable because you know this child. But support them with your reasons, for instance, 'I believe Sandy is very upset. When he said to me "My big cousin is nasty to me", Sandy was twisting his hair around one finger – the way he does when he is really distressed.'
- Your responsibility is to take seriously what the child or young person said to you. But you are not trying to assess the exact truth of what you have heard; it is therefore important that unsupported assumptions do not go into your written account. There is a difference between taking further the concern of, 'Delia told me that her evening sitter shows her "naughty pictures"' and the unsupported conclusion that, 'Delia's sitter is definitely abusing her.'

It is very unlikely that children will lie about abuse. They are far more likely to have difficulty in telling you, especially if the person harming them is part of their family or a respected authority figure. But it is possible that a child may give an account of only part of what is happening from a complex and troubling situation. So, the assumption that the child has told you the whole truth in one conversation could be a harmful conclusion to draw.

It would be bad practice to assume that children who disclosed abuse, especially unlikely claims (from the adult's perspective), are probably lying. However, it is also poor practice to take the naïve view that children and young people never lie about abuse. There have been cases when children have been bullied by one parent into making false accusations against the other parent, as part of vicious custody disputes. It also has to be accepted that older children and adolescents have sometimes made false allegations against teachers, foster and residential carers. Some children have not really understood the consequences of such claims. Others appear to have been so distressed or angry, as a result of their own disrupted experiences, that they are keen to spread that emotional damage.

When parents or other adults say something

Worries that may have child protection implications can arise because of what an adult tells you. There are several possibilities:

- Parents may speak with you about their own child. The concerns may relate to that parent as an individual, to a partner or other family member, or to other people involved with the family.
- Alternatively, parents may express concerns about another child in your setting, or that parent's deep worries about the other child's family life.
- Parents may voice direct concerns that something is amiss. Alternatively, what they say in passing could act as a warning for you, because it links with other incidents or information, unknown to this parent.
- Parents, or other adults who visit your setting, may communicate concerns or wish to clear up issues about the actions of a practitioner or volunteer.
- Concerns might be raised by one of your colleagues, a volunteer or another professional who regularly visits your setting.

Taking a positive approach when an adult tells you something of concern has many features in common with good communication with children.

- Listen with care to what you are being told. Give this adult your full attention and ensure that you understand what is being said to you.
- Ask open-ended questions as you would when listening to children or young people. You might repeat part of what the adult has said, but with a question implied by your tone or a few words of

SCENARIO: LONGMEAD PRIMARY SCHOOL

Staff and parents are keen for the children to learn to swim and groups are walked to the nearby leisure centre. Several children say that they do not like the swimming coach, that he is 'horrid' and 'shouts all the time'. There is an incident in which two parents, who are helping with the group, get into an argument with the coach about his insistence that tired children continue to swim widths without stopping. Their concerns are raised in a meeting but the head takes the view that, although the coach can appear sharp and rather impatient, he is successful in getting children to swim. Plans are raised that the eldest children form a swimming team for a gala and that the coach will give them extra tuition. Parents start to say that their children do not want to have extra lessons from this swimming coach.

Questions

■ **What do you judge are the main issues in this situation?**

■ **What do you think should happen now?**

You will find a commentary on page 115.

encouragement. You might reply, 'So, you've seen Marsha's mum hit the child a lot recently?' or 'You're really anxious about the baby. Please tell me more about what worries you.'

■ You do not have to work out the truth of what you are hearing. You should take seriously what you are told, even if what the parent says seems unlikely. Do not dismiss it, even if you feel this parent is a gossip, or dislikes the accused person.

An adult may ask you to keep what they say a secret, or ask that you promise to keep their name out of any further enquiries. You cannot make either of these commitments. Remind a parent of your setting's policy and obligation to pass on any concerns about children. But you may also be able to reassure the parent that your next step will be to talk with the CPO for your setting or service. You will not phone social services without any further consideration.

A parent (or a member of staff) who raises many child protection worries that prove to be unfounded needs to be challenged in a private conversation. There may be a number of possible explanations. For instance, this adult may believe an unrealistically high estimate about the prevalence of child abuse. Alternatively, a parent or colleague may be seeking attention through raising concerns. Frustrations with such a person should not be handled by automatically disbelieving them.

Commentary on the scenarios

In each example, the commentary offers possibilities and suggestions. No commentary can act as detailed guidance for an actual situation that you face.

Ciaran (page 74)

Option one

There are negative consequences to accepting the head's instruction, as passed on by the CPO. There is a strong chance that Ciaran will stop confiding at all, if he is blocked in this way. There is already concern about his home situation, so this possibility could raise, rather than reduce, the level of risk for Ciaran and his sister. In some schools, STAs are not shown the same respect as other team members and this different status may be a complicating issue here. But also the head may not understand that good practice in child protection shows respect for children's choice over disclosure.

There also needs to be consideration about contact with the parents. From Ciaran's comments there is concern that he and his sister could be at risk and that steps may need to be taken within child protection. But it could be very distressing for Ciaran if the one person in whom he has confided is made inaccessible.

Option two

Now there is a possibility that a more positive consequence could emerge for Ciaran. If you speak up, rather than passively accept the instruction, you are behaving professionally as an STA and are keeping Ciaran's interests to the forefront. The CPO needs to deal with the head's demand, explaining how she and you will work together. In the meantime, for Ciaran's sake it is important that you and the CPO find a way of working which respects Ciaran's choice. If a compromise is unavoidable, then perhaps ask Ciaran if the CPO could be present for a conversation.

All team members should be enabled to deal with possible disclosures so that a child is not 'passed on' from the person to whom they have chosen to speak. It is appropriate that the adult explains to a child or young person when and why the information has to be shared with somebody else.

Monica (page 80)

It is respectful that practitioners follow the family diet. However, partnership with parents has boundaries set by your responsibility for children's well being. There are health risks when a diet removes many sources of nutrition and young children have different nutritional needs from adults. Babies and toddlers have become very ill; some have died from extremely restricted diets.

It would be appropriate to attempt at least one other conversation with the mother. The childminder needs to get across that she is concerned professionally about the current and future well being of both children. But if there is no progress, then it would be necessary to see if the mother is willing to listen to informed advice from another professional, perhaps the health visitor responsible for the baby. If there is still no progress, it would be appropriate for the childminder to talk with the local childminding advisor about the situation.

If Monica's mother acts on her threat to find another childminder, this conversation should definitely take place. It is important that this family does not get 'lost'. If Monica's long-term childminder is rejected by the mother, that action raises the level of concern. The childminder and advisor might decide that a referral to social care services was the only safe way forward.

Sergio (page 80)

This kind of behaviour is not usual for a 4-year-old and should not simply be dismissed. The team has coped by reducing Sergio's opportunities for inappropriate behaviour, but they have not dealt properly with his actions. The team has also generated a spurious cultural explanation that needs challenge. It is not acceptable for practitioners to stereotype any national or ethnic group.

Without further information, it is not possible to know how Sergio has learned that it is acceptable to impose on women in this way. He may have observed inappropriate touching or heard adult conversations that are dismissive of women. At the moment, the concerned practitioner does not know. As a new arrival to the team, this practitioner needs to find the confidence to raise this problem, most likely with the CPO for the setting. If that person is equally dismissive, then the practitioner needs to go to the manager.

There need to be firm boundaries set for Sergio's behaviour, with an explanation that is suitable for a 4-year-old. The team needs to act in a consistent way to monitor that his behaviour does change. There also needs to be a proper conversation with his parents about the behaviour, the legitimate concerns that it raises and how the setting is now dealing with Sergio's actions. Any further steps would depend on the parents' reactions.

Rory (page 81)

Rory's parents are fully responsible for him when he is at home and they have to balance their home and work commitments in a way that keeps their son safe and happy. Rory's mother needs to be reminded that the nursery is responsible for tracking injuries to the children. It is also fair for Rory's key person to say that toddlers need careful watching and to be engaged in safe activities.

It may be possible to have a friendly conversation about work-life balance. But it is not for the nursery to be apologetic about their hours; Rory's parents accepted the time boundaries to the service. The family may need a different kind of childcare, probably a live-in nanny, if their work commitments continue at this high level. Depending on the relationship with Rory's mother, the key person might be able to talk around a greater involvement of Rory's father. But it is not the nursery's responsibility to sort out frustrations between the adults.

If Rory continues to have many minor accidents at home, this is a situation in which it would be very useful to be able to talk in general with an advisor or a social worker who will accept conversation without formal referral.

Yvette (page 81)

You may disapprove of Yvette's style of dress. But that is not club business unless her clothes are unsafe for play, in which case a conversation with her mother could be about practical clothes. An exception would be if Yvette's tops had an image or slogan seriously inappropriate for a young girl.

Yvette's comments about Martin would probably be at a lower level of concern without the incident with your male colleague. (Female readers should bear in mind that men are as alert to out-of-the-ordinary movements on their lap as females are to deliberate groping.) It is important not to link the two strands together by any assumptions about Martin. If something untoward has happened in Yvette's life, it is not certain that Martin is implicated. A conversation with Yvette's mother could include a comment that her daughter seems enthused about 'Martin' and imply a friendly question about his place in the family.

It would be wise to be alert to Yvette and notice if her behaviour suggests an inappropriate intimacy with male practitioners or boys in the club. If the same kind of incident is repeated, then the club team will need to talk with her mother about their concerns. Any further steps will depend on her reply.

The club team may need to develop clear boundaries that children are welcome to be close, to sit next to practitioners but not on their laps. The comments about physical contact on page 195 allow for sensible house rules about older children.

Marsha (page 81)

It would be right to intervene in the play, following the lead of the other child. Marsha could be helped to comfort the baby appropriately and you could make non-critical comments about how careful everyone has to be with babies.

Since there has already been contact with the social worker, it would be appropriate to share this observation, either in the upcoming meeting or to integrate into the written report that the playgroup should contribute to the child protection inquiry that is underway. Everyone has to take care not to over-interpret children's play and conversations. But this incident has the look and sound of a child imitating what she has observed.

Sally (page 85)

It is good practice to listen to this mother's concerns and ensure that you understand what she is saying, including an invitation to 'say some more' about Sally's play with dolls. It would not be appropriate at this point either to agree or disagree with the perspective, nor to the mother's request. You should thank her for telling you her concerns and say that you will talk with your team.

Sally's mother has not made an allegation as such, but her worries need to be taken as seriously as if they were expressed by a practitioner in the team. There needs to be an internal discussion about the dynamics of the group room run by Richard and Jessica. Much will depend on whether there have already been concerns about Jessica's style with the children. It will be important to hear Richard's view before he leaves. If he has been silent about poor practice from his room colleague, then any nursery senior team should find out the reasons that Jessica's unacceptable style has not been challenged properly. Again, depending on the situation, this may be an occasion when supervision, clear direction, even the early stages of disciplinary warnings may be necessary.

It is important that you get back to Sally's mother within no more than a few days. If there is an issue of poor practice, then this problem will not be resolved by moving one child. If you feel reassured that Sally's comments are not imitated from Jessica, then there may be reason to have a further conversation to help her mother consider the possible source.

Fazila (page 92)

It should be possible to join in Fazila's play through imagining, 'what can we do?' to make matters better for the doll. If Fazila makes the direct link to her own situation, then you can follow her lead.

Depending on your relationship with Fazila's mother, it may be possible to share this play as a way to highlight her daughter's feelings. If friendly support and suggestions for Fazila's mother fail to make much difference in the care of her daughter, it may be necessary to explore possibilities of family support that she would accept. If friendly persuasion does not bring any improvement, then you will need to explain to Fazila's mother that you wish to refer the family, because of your concerns about her daughter.

Olwyn (page 96)

As the practitioner you are faced with a number of concerns, some of them vague. It is time to bring in the CPO, not only because Olwyn's teacher does not seem to be taking your concerns seriously. It is inappropriate to assume that any out-of-the-ordinary behaviour can be explained away by disability.

Olwyn's behaviour has changed in terms of her habit of masturbation and the incident in the toilets raises concerns. You need to gather your thoughts, and make notes, with the help of the CPO, including what, if anything, Olwyn said to you about what happened in the toilets today. If the boys have been involved in inappropriate activity, then their behaviour must also be addressed.

You need to untangle the strands around Olwyn's tendency to masturbate in the classroom and the conversations with her father. The CPO should be able to support you as you think and talk through this aspect. If the behaviour were something different, for instance if Olwyn chewed her nails, do you think you would find the conversation repetitive rather than creating a sense of unease? Is there something about how the father speaks to you and, assuming you are female, in what way is the gender difference an issue? Is it a conversation that should happen out of the hearing of other children and yet this father starts talking in clear earshot of Olwyn's peers?

You need to be more specific about what feels wrong about the new driver. This unease and your other concerns need to be raised fully in a conversation with, ideally, both of Olwyn's parents. The CPO will probably decide whether it makes more sense for you to take that meeting, with her or his support, because you are Olwyn's STA. The decision may be that the class teacher also needs to be directly involved, as well as informed about the next step.

Cameron (page 100)

It seems likely that something has happened to confuse and distress Cameron. It is tempting to consider his mother's new boyfriend as the source of risk. But Cameron has also recently spent three weeks with some of his mother's friends.

Cameron's mother seems unable to consider his emotional needs, so possibly he would not confide in her, or his worries might have been dismissed.

The school needs to tackle the issues with Cameron's mother. One issue arises from his refusal to go home with the boyfriend and this strong reaction needs to be addressed with Cameron's needs to the forefront. Today, Cameron's teacher should telephone Becky and ask her to come for her son. It is almost certain that she is the only person who 'officially' can take responsibility for Cameron at the end of the school day.

Cameron's comment about people holding his 'willy' needs some exploration, if he is comfortable to talk, perhaps with the male teacher, with whom he has already raised the question. Another possibility would be to ensure that Cameron's class soon has a general session on appropriate touch, raising issues that concern Cameron, but in a way that does not put the spotlight on him.

The school needs to keep descriptive notes of Cameron's words and actions and of conversations with his mother that attempt to explore the situation. Without reasonable reassurance from such conversations, the concerns about Cameron may have to be taken further. But so far the information is vague.

Kitty (page 104)

Any conversation with Kitty needs to be gentle and avoid leading questions. You could reflect back her comment with a question in your tone or add something like, 'No more Grandad? Is that a good thing, Kitty?' When Kitty scribbles over a figure, you could ask a non-specific question such as, 'Do tell me what you've done to your drawing.'

It is important not to assume that all of Kitty's play is related to the alleged abuse and to support her as you would any 4-year-old. It will be appropriate to keep notes of Kitty's progress and careful descriptions of play and conversation. Much of this observation could be shared carefully with her mother. If the grandfather has been denied access to the family home, it seems likely that social care services have been involved. Depending on the current situation regarding child protection and Kitty, the CPO (or key person) might also need to continue to share relevant information with the social worker. Kitty's mother will understand that this careful professional communication will be ongoing.

Longmead Primary School (page 108)

The head should take more seriously the consistent feedback from the children. It is a very negative message for children that their emotional distress about the swimming coach has been dismissed. Even if the coach proves to be no more than bad-tempered and insensitive, the children should be supported by the head in tackling his disrespectful outlook and actions.

The parents' concerns have also been dismissed and this is a poor approach to partnership. If the head insists on the extra coaching, it is likely that some parents will withdraw their children, out of appropriate concern, and the whole situation will sour school-home relations in a much broader way.

Equality practice and safeguarding

Daily practice can bring situations that are not straightforward to resolve and which present competing priorities arising from concerns about equality. It is expected that the laws and guidance about child protection will be put into practice with active respect for all sources of diversity. However, concerns for equality and respect for traditions of any kind cannot overrule the obligation to protect children and young people.

> **The main sections of this chapter cover:**
> * **Key issues for gender and disability**
> * **Cultural background and faith**
> * **Cultural traditions that challenge protection**

KEY ISSUES FOR GENDER AND DISABILITY

Equality practice applicable to all groups in society requires that safeguarding does not rest on unacceptable or unsafe assumptions.

Male practitioners

Considerably more wariness and outright suspicion is expressed about men than women in paid or voluntary work involving children. Male team members are also, in some settings and services, given informal (if not official) job descriptions that differ from those of their female colleagues. There are some men working in early years who do not undertake any personal care of children. The rationale for this differentiation is sometimes that at least one parent has objected to a man changing a baby or young child. But sometimes the rationale is that men are more vulnerable to allegations of abuse, so, the argument follows, a different role is needed to protect this male practitioner.

On the basis of reliable statistics, sexual abuse is the only area of child abuse or neglect in which men predominate. Otherwise, the stance 'most abusers are men so . . .' is ill-informed. They do not outnumber women in terms of emotional or physical abuse or neglect. Furthermore, although most identified sex abusers are male, most men do not sexually abuse children or young people. It is hard to see reluctance to employ men, or willingness to give them a different care role from female colleagues, as anything other than gender discrimination against males.

Problems arise because an 'everybody knows' atmosphere has developed in which parents may express unease about a male childminder, or male

116

colleague, in a nursery or school team. Media reports also focus on the statistically less frequent dangers to children, such as abduction and murder by non-family members. Child homicides by parents tend to be perpetrated about equally by a child's mother or father. However, it is more often males who are responsible for the murder of a child if the act is committed by someone other than the child's parents.

Effective partnership with families has to acknowledge any unease, but problems have to be resolved by reassuring parents about the checks made on all practitioners before they join a team, or are allowed to work as a childminder or foster carer. Good standards of care and personal contact with children have to apply to all members of staff. Nor can any problem of parents' worry about men be solved by creating a situation in which all practitioners keep their distance from children. Such a practice undermines children's well being (see page 193).

Some settings are concerned that male practitioners may be especially vulnerable to false allegations about sexual abuse from children, young people or their family. Again, it is hard to see how a different job description for men is the best response to unacceptable behaviour from service users. Poorly supported allegations are made about other kinds of abuse and neglect, against female as well as male practitioners. Settings and services need a robust approach to allegations that prove to be false, irrespective of whoever is accused (see page 168).

Family preferences

Issues about male practitioners in the team can also arise because a child's family feels strongly that females should undertake any personal care. This stance may be linked with the family's cultural tradition or faith, but is not limited to parents whose identity would be classified as minority ethnic group. Ideally, any team needs to have thought through this potential dilemma before they are faced with a direct request for a female carer. Settings have made different decisions, but my considered support goes to those who take a full equality approach.

The head or key person, if the child has already started in the setting, needs to explain that all team members have the same role. So it is not possible to restrict a male practitioner from appropriate caring contact with any child in the setting. Families can use the childminding service if, for whatever reason, they want to be sure that only a female will be involved in the personal care of their child. Otherwise, settings create problems for daily practice, especially if one family's request is granted, on the basis of faith or minority cultural background, but other families are deemed not to have a good enough reason.

If you want to find out more

+ Consult the briefing papers under *Statistics* www.nspcc.org.uk/Inform/ informhub_wda49931.html (go in through *Resources for professionals*)

+ Elliott, Michele (ed) (1993) *Female sexual abuse of children* London: Longman

+ Lindon, Jennie (2005) *Equality in early childhood: linking theory and practice* London: Hodder Education (especially the discussion and scenario on page 119)

The vulnerability of disabled children and young people

Many people hope that disabled children and young people will be relatively safe from abuse or neglect. It is often assumed that high standards for their care, and support for their family, will be available to safeguard children. Unfortunately, they can be more vulnerable than their peers for the following reasons.

- Children may need more personal physical care because of physical disabilities, or they continue to need help at an older age because of severe learning disabilities. Such care can, of course, be offered with respect and consideration. But disabled children are vulnerable to anything from poor standards to deliberate abuse of their need for intimate care.

- Unsupported and exhausted parents, or other carers, may snap under the relentless pressure of a very high need for care, with no respite, especially when their sleep is constantly disturbed.

- Intrusive medical procedures, necessary for some conditions, may leave children with an underdeveloped sense of their own privacy or bodily dignity. Abusive behaviour by adults or young people may not appear to be out-of-the-ordinary or worthy of complaint.

- Children can have a high number of carers because of their condition or because they attend different specialist facilities. The risk is then that children learn intrusive attention by relative strangers is a 'normal' part of their life.

- Children and young people may not have developed a conceptual framework for making sense of what is done to them: appropriate and inappropriate touch, a sense of personal privacy and their right to express preferences. Limitations may be less related to the actual disability than to how carers have shaped the experience of the child or young person.

Children and young people can be made vulnerable in a situation where there is no key adult responsible for closely monitoring the child's overall care. Good practice guidelines for working with children and their families have regularly stressed the importance of a lead professional, as well as a child's committed parent, to avoid a patchwork of care and support. Good standards of practice in care will support disabled children just as much as their peers.

The impact of disability

The details of a child or young person's disability may complicate their ability to disclose what is happening to them.

- Children and young people with learning disabilities may have difficulty in telling a trusted parent or carer that something is happening to them that is wrong.

- Children and young people with severe communication disabilities may have difficulty in communicating that they are in physical pain, arising from non-accidental injury. There has been more general concern that profoundly disabled children and young people often experience chronic pain that goes unrecognised by their carers. This situation complicates the interpretation of behaviour patterns that are explained as part of their disability.

- A high level of physical disability may literally make it harder for children or young people to resist an abuser, who ill-treats them physically or sexually.

- The care and education of some disabled children and young people may mean that they are in a residential setting, perhaps some distance from home. They can be vulnerable to institutional abuse in a closed community, with very limited opportunity to disclose to family or other people external to the setting.

- When children's care and educational arrangements cause them to be isolated and less able to make friends easily, they can also be vulnerable to wanting to please their carers and less likely to object.

- Some forms of abuse may actually cause disability or serious ill health, or worsen an existing condition. An abusive or potentially abusive situation may be difficult to distinguish from the child's condition.

Risky assumptions by adults

Parents, practitioners and other professionals may hold unchecked beliefs, some of them offensive, that put children and young people at greater risk.

- Adults may assume that nobody would abuse a disabled child or young person, because they cannot believe that someone would be so cruel. In the case of sexual abuse, they may reject the possibility that anyone would want to become sexually involved with a disabled individual.

■ Behaviour and communication that would usually raise concerns may be pushed to one side. The assumption may be that any 'odd' habits are part of the disability or sexualised reactions are 'normal'.

■ Adults may fail to communicate with children about appropriate physical touch, using a vocabulary of words and signs (see also page 222). They may feel uncomfortable talking with disabled adolescents about sexual feelings and behaviour. Reluctant practitioners and parents may decide, conveniently, that sexual awareness is irrelevant to disabled young people.

■ Consequently, children have neither been enabled to judge and reject dubious behaviour from someone else, nor to make real choices about their own actions and preferences. The mistaken assumption may be that children are within a protected environment, so abuse cannot possibly occur.

■ When bad practice has been allowed to grow, practitioners feel that maltreatment matters less and that disabled children or young people are unaware or soon forget.

Consistent practice in safeguarding

Good equality practice meets reliable child protection when the same basic procedures are followed for disabled children and young people as for any individuals about whom concerns have been raised.

■ Any assumptions arising from disability need to be checked rather than assumed to be correct.

■ Appropriate support needs to be given to the children or young people so that they can better communicate about their experience and express their wishes and preferences.

■ Careful decisions need to be taken when a child or young person needs an interpreter to support communication. The individual's specialist teacher or residential worker may appear to be the obvious choice. However, this is an unwise choice, if there are already concerns that practitioners may be implicated in the abuse, or are very reluctant to consider the possibility.

■ Some disabled children or young people cause trouble for their peers through physical bullying, or inappropriate sexual activity. An environment of risk is created from mistaken beliefs that disabled children would not act in a bullying way, or could not become young abusers.

SCENARIO: HELENA

You run a holiday support group for carers of children with disability. 5-year-old Helena has recently started to attend with her childminder. Helena has mild learning and physical disabilities and her family is still distressed that their daughter is not 'normal'. Her parents seem to find it hard to place boundaries on her behaviour. Helena's childminder follows the family line that 'the poor little girl' cannot be expected to behave like other children.

Helena has a soft voice and sweet smile, but you are beginning to think that she deliberately hurts other children under the cover of giving them a cuddle in play. A couple of incidents also make you consider that Helena is adept at 'setting up' other children, so they break the group rules and get into trouble. You want to address the situation, without over-reacting. You want to be realistic about the ways in which Helena's disability may genuinely limit her understanding.

Questions

■ **What would concern you for the child in this situation?**

■ **What might be complicating factors for practitioners to consider?**

■ **What should probably be your first step now?**

You will find a commentary on page 140.

If you want to find out more

✤ Miller, David (2002) *Disabled children and abuse* www.nspcc.org.uk/ Inform/informhub_wda49931.html (go in through *Research* and *Child protection research briefings*)

✤ NSPCC (2003) *'It doesn't happen to disabled children' Child protection and disabled children* www.nspcc.org.uk/Inform/informhub_wda49931.html (go in through *Research* and *NSPCC Research briefings*)

CULTURAL BACKGROUND AND FAITH

Practitioners are possibly most anxious about making a wrong decision when there are differences of ethnic group, faith or cultural background. Good practice depends on well-informed problem solving and complex situations can require tough decisions.

Awareness of and respect for diversity

All practitioners need a broad base of knowledge to make sensible and properly supported judgements. The idea of what is 'normal' is certainly not explained just by what you know from your own childhood experiences of your family, or those of your friends. All practitioners, whatever their own cultural and ethnic background, have to make the effort to extend their knowledge of family traditions and ways of raising children and adolescents.

■ An awareness of cultural diversity in approaches to childcare has to be part of a more general awareness that adults vary in how they deal with children and young people, in the family and other situations.

■ Some parents may be less demonstrative than you in their dealing with children. Less overt affection does not necessarily mean that an adult cares less about a child; people have different ways of showing that they care. Alternatively, you may feel some parents are too emotional with their children, for your taste and upbringing.

■ None of these differences may relate to cultural traditions but are more linked with particular families and their personal style. However, if you do not share a culture with a parent, or know that you differ in religious beliefs, it is easy to assume that the different patterns arise from that group difference. This explanation may, or may not, be valid.

■ Cultural tradition is a strong influence on how parents raise their children and treat sons and daughters. All families are affected by the social and cultural environment in which they live. Culture is not something that 'happens' only for people within minority ethnic groups or faiths.

TAKE ANOTHER PERSPECTIVE

Think carefully about three or four families whom you know well and who share your own cultural background (or faith, if you prefer). These may be families you know through work or through personal contact.

■ If someone from a very different background met these families, do you think it would be accurate to take them as representative of your culture (or faith)?

■ In what ways could it be misleading to generalise from these families without further experience?

All professionals need a firm foundation of knowledge and to avoid believing 'I know all about. . .' on the basis of information taken from a very small sample. Knowing a few families with a particular cultural, national or faith background does not provide a safe basis for broad knowledge about this group. Practitioners whose national background is English or Welsh would be unimpressed by assumptions that they were much the same as people from any country picked from Europe. Yet people sometimes believe that contact with a few families from the continent of India is enough to be able to talk about 'Indian families'. There is a tremendous diversity in culture, faith and social status existing within the large group of families within the UK who are of Indian origin. Practitioners are not helped by the slap-dash tendency in some written materials to talk about Africa as if it were a single, small country. In fact, Africa is a huge continent with many distinct countries that vary between, and within, themselves in ethnic group, language, cultural traditions and faith.

MAKE THE CONNECTION WITH . . . BEHAVIOUR UNDER STRESS

A broad base of knowledge needs to grow from different sources. It is especially important to take care **not** to develop your beliefs about any culture or faith from contact with families who are under stress. When experiencing some form of crisis, families do not usually behave in the way that is normal for them in calmer times, let alone typical of the social group, culture or faith to which they belong.

Patterns of childcare

It is regarded as common family practice in the UK that mothers take the primary responsibility for children, although there is much more variation in this pattern than a couple of generations ago. There is also considerably more informal sharing of care than is often acknowledged, between friends and within families whose country of origin is the UK. However, in some cultures, for instance families from a range of countries within Africa and the Caribbean, it is more usual that the care of children is shared between relatives, who are probably female.

Within these same cultures, it has been accepted practice to leave some or all of the children with the extended family, while one or both parents go elsewhere in search of work, sometimes at a considerable distance. This pattern was continued by some West African families in the UK who sought long-term private fostering for their children while they worked or completed studies. A reverse pattern is also accepted in some cultures, in which children are entrusted to a relative living in another part of the country or another country altogether. The aim with this arrangement is to offer a better life to the child, or young person, who leaves the immediate family home.

SCENARIO: NATASHA

Natasha is just 4 years old and her family came to England from Jamaica when her mother was still a child. Natasha lives with her mother and two aunts. Other relatives live within two streets of her home. You have become increasingly concerned because neither you, nor Natasha, ever knows who will pick her up from nursery class and some days it is up to half-an-hour after the end of nursery before anyone arrives. Natasha always recognises the person and seems content to go but has said to you, 'I wish Mummy or Auntie Tess would pick me up.'

This week the arrangements for Natasha have become even less predictable. On two mornings you found her in the main school playground when you came to work, an hour before any child should arrive. You spoke with the aunt who arrived in the afternoon and she said, 'I can't help it. I have to get to work and you're here anyway aren't you?'

In the middle of the week, the school caretaker strikes up a conversation with you about Natasha. He recounts, 'They live three doors down from us. Poor little sod, nobody watches out for her. One evening she was wandering on the pavement in her nightie until one of them shouts out the window at her. A lot of weekends she knocks on the door to come in and play with our two and that's fine by us. So, the wife phones up and half the time Natasha's Mum doesn't even know she's gone and the aunties think my wife's odd for calling anyway. These people don't know how to look after kids properly. Now my wife is home with ours . . . .'.

Questions

■ **What are the main issues in this situation?**

■ **What do you think should be the next steps?**

You will find a commentary on page 140.

Delegating the parenting role across any extended care system depends on a high level of trust in the commitment and kind intentions of the subsitute parent(s). If that trust is abused, then the child or young person's family may not be close enough to realise the dangers. A longstanding cultural tradition within the UK, for some social groups, has been to entrust children as young as 7 years of age to non-family adults for considerable parts of the year at a location sometimes far from home: the boarding school system. Some children seem to have enjoyed, or at least tolerated, their experience of residential care and education. But this practice has continued in some families despite children's protestations that they are not at all happy. Alternatively, some children have simply not spoken of their feelings about the separation, believing that there was no other choice for them.

Legislation and guidance about safeguarding children and young people does not specify the details of exactly how they should be raised. The laws set a template that requires respect for family life and parents' decisions, from whatever basis, so long as those decisions do not damage children's development and well being.

■ It would be an unacceptable assumption for a practitioner to criticise a shared-care family system on the grounds that 'it should be the mother' who provides care. On the other hand, any way of organising family life must work for the safety and well being of the child. A shared-care system can fail children just as some mothers, or fathers, in sole charge have neglected their children.

■ Any professional involved with families should be concerned about the quality of care for children in the extended family, any private fostering arrangements and also any kind of residential accommodation where children and young people live away from the family home for extended periods of time.

MAKE THE CONNECTION WITH . . . FOCUS ON THE CHILD

The public inquiry led by Lord Laming reported on the events that led to the death of Victoria Climbié and made clear cut recommendations. In section 16.10 of that report, it was clearly stated, 'The basic requirement that children are kept safe is universal and cuts across cultural boundaries. Every child living in this country is entitled to be given the protection of the law, regardless of his or her cultural background. Cultural heritage is important to many people, but it cannot take precedence over standards of childcare embodied in the law.'

One of many failures in professional contact with Victoria was an assumption by the social work team that the harsh behaviour of her great-aunt was 'normal' for the family's cultural background.

If you want to find out more

✤ *The Victoria Climbié Inquiry* (2003) Part Five Working with Diversity
www.victoria-climbie-inquiry.org.uk

Willingness to challenge assumptions

Careful attention to equality practice is part of general good professional practice across childhood and into services for adolescents. Effective safeguarding practice has to integrate a willingness to address unsupported assumptions, yet in ways that enable practitioners to reflect and re-think.

- It is unacceptable and inaccurate to assume that particular kinds of families are more, or less, likely to abuse or neglect their children. Reviews of child protection have made it crystal clear that damage, as well as safe upbringing and treatment, occurs in every possible social, cultural or faith group.
- It would be a racist outlook to dismiss a family with, 'these people don't take care of their children' and the view should be challenged by colleagues, senior staff or advisors. Such practitioners are expressing bigoted attitudes, regardless of their own cultural identity, or faith, and the specific identity of 'these people'.
- Good quality practice for equality may be a particular struggle for practitioners when there is ill-feeling within a local neighbourhood on the basis of ethnic group, cultural background or faith. The necessary challenge of decent professional practice is to step aside from a poisonous atmosphere, however long-standing.

Practitioner outlook and anxiety

It is crucial to approach each child or young person and their family as individuals, alongside a commitment to understand more about this family pattern. Practitioners often need support in exploring their concerns when they do not share a cultural or faith identity with the family. In particular, some practitioners may be so anxious about an accusation of being racist, that they fail to express even serious concerns. No practitioner should have to think through complex, sensitive issues on their own. A senior practitioner, the designated child protection officer (CPO) or an advisor (see page 73) should help you to reflect on the situation, including your own uneasy feelings, and the basis of your concerns.

The inquiry into the death of Victoria Climbié (2003) raised the reluctance of some professionals to express concerns about a child when they did not share the same ethnic group identity and skin colour as the family. An atmosphere that creates such fears does not represent good equality practice and, in this specific case, was one of many contributing factors in the avoidable death of a young girl. The Laming report also raised a different, although related, issue about the discomfort faced sometimes by professionals from minority ethnic groups. Practitioners may feel judged as unsympathetic to families, with whom they 'should' have much in common, and maybe 'should' protect against an ignorant majority community. The obligation of accurate knowledge, compassion and professional objectivity with detachment is a requirement for everyone.

SCENARIO: ABBAS

Abbas is 10 years old and attends your primary school, with his sister Nneka, who is 7 years old. Both children appear happy, well cared for and attend school regularly. You and your colleagues have become aware that Abbas seems to carry a great deal of responsibility for Nneka. He accompanies her to school and home each day and deals with any messages for her class teacher. Abbas stays on the school premises if his sister has an after school activity, but has declined chess club for himself, with the explanation that he has to get Nneka home and organise a meal. You have also heard through the parent grapevine that children who invite Abbas round to tea always have Nneka as well. There seems to be no option, even at the weekend.

You and your colleagues are concerned that you do not appear to criticise Abbas' parents, although you feel that he is carrying undue responsibility for a 10-year-old. There is no direct cause for concern about either child, although a few comments from Nneka have made you wonder if Abbas has sole responsibility well into the evening sometimes. This year Abbas will move on to secondary school and the transition will involve a much longer daily trip for him, if he still brings Nneka to primary school; it is a walk that involves crossing two main roads. You wonder whether to raise the issue with his parents and in what way.

Questions

■ **Do you have any concerns about either child in this situation?**

■ **What might be the complicating factors for practitioners to consider?**

■ **What should probably be your next step?**

You will find a commentary on page 141.

Genuine knowledge

Team leaders in any setting, as well as professions such as social work, need to be clear about appropriate experience and knowledge. For example, practitioners of Caribbean origin will not automatically be better equipped than a 'white' Scottish colleague to relate to a Somali refugee family. Practitioners whose country of origin is China will not speak the same language as every family from that very large country. It would be appropriate use of a team member's skills, if that person shared a fluent language with a parent, who was otherwise ill at ease or limited in what could be expressed in English. However, practitioners need to speak up if they find themselves expected to have unrealistic levels of knowledge on the basis of culture, religion or simply their skin colour.

MAKE THE CONNECTION WITH . . . REFLECTIVE PRACTICE

Good intentions do not justify practice that is unsound on equality grounds and unsafe for protecting children or young people.

It is not good practice to assume that any 'black' practitioner, loosely defined, will somehow understand and be the best person to work with any 'black' family. There is far too much variety within such a broad definition. A 'black' practitioner may well have empathy with others who have experienced ill-treatment as a result of racism based on skin colour. But this likely shared experience does not provide detailed knowledge about another person's culture or faith and certainly does not guarantee a shared fluent home language.

'Black' practitioners will not necessarily have more understanding of every 'black' family, any more than 'white' practitioners will have a greater insight of any given 'white' family. You have to ask why should anyone expect this level of empathy?

Unchecked beliefs can be wrong and may put children at risk. Ill-informed assumptions might be bigoted on the basis of ethnic group or faith, but are not inevitably so. Any beliefs about a family need to be checked through discussion and support for practitioners in any setting or service. For instance, a practitioner might assume a lone parent will be without any family back-up, yet some lone parents have an effective network of family and friends. In contrast, perhaps another practitioner assumes, without asking, that the struggling Indian mother will be fine 'because all Asians live in an extended family, don't they?' But this mother may be on her own without any possible family support, or feel for some reason that she cannot access help from family and friends.

- You need to be ready to ask yourself, 'What is my basis for assuming this?' or 'What makes me so sure?' and accept similar questions from colleagues, the CPO or a support worker.
- The same process applies if concerns are dismissed with, 'It's about partnership. We're respecting the faith of families who attend this nursery' or 'I share this cultural tradition and you don't understand anything about it.' Questions such as, 'but what is the impact of this practice on the young person?' have to be asked or replies such as, 'so please explain to me the reasons I should not be worried about . . .' given as a response.
- All teams, or confidential professional meetings, need an atmosphere in which colleagues have the mental and emotional space to backtrack in a constructive way. They should not have to choose

between defensive silence and going on the verbal attack, because their stance has attracted heavy criticism.

If you want to find out more

✣ Lindon, Jennie (1999) *Understanding world religions in early years practice* London: Hodder and Stoughton

✣ Lindon, Jennie (2005) *Equality in early childhood: linking theory and practice* London: Hodder Education

✣ *The Victoria Climbié Inquiry* (2003) chaired by Lord Laming, especially *Part Five Working with Diversity* www.victoria-climbie-inquiry.org.uk

CULTURAL TRADITIONS THAT CHALLENGE PROTECTION

The 'handshake' between equality practice and safeguarding can create a delicate balance. You should not reject other ways of child rearing because it is not your culture's way, but neither is a practice made acceptable because it is associated with a long tradition. Children from a wide variety of different cultural backgrounds can be, and have been, damaged by their family's actions or inaction. Some traditions are regarded as justified and necessary by those who follow them, despite the risks for children or young people.

Hitting children

If you listen to everyday conversation, or discussion on radio or television, you will hear adults speaking who believe that it is fine to hit children. Some would rather avoid this action, but are puzzled about what else to do. Some adults express what sounds like enthusiasm and persistently link the right to hit children with the need for discipline. (Supporters tend to prefer the word 'smack'.)

The case against hitting children

There has been a long tradition within the UK, and in other countries around the world, of an adult right to hit children. Beliefs run deep within cultures and are sometimes justified from tenets of a faith. A strong counter-tradition developed over the last decades of the 20th century within work with children and young people, as well as an approach to family life.

■ The core of the argument is a moral stance. UK society does not approve of adults settling disputes and imposing their wishes through

129

SCENARIO: ANN-MARIE

This 3-year-old girl has attended your nursery for nearly five months. Her parents were initially doubtful about the nursery's behaviour policy and expressed vague reservations based on their Christian faith. Her father has since made several comments that children need more discipline than the nursery provides, for example that, 'You don't understand. Children need firm guidance and our daughter is very wilful.'

Ann-Marie came in last week with severe bruising to her bottom, which became obvious because she winced when she sat at the table to play. In reply to a gentle question, Ann-Marie said a few words about an 'accident on the stairs'. When you asked her father about the bruises, he confirmed that Ann-Marie had slipped on the stairs but was otherwise evasive, saying, 'I don't know, she was coming down too fast. We've told her so often to be more careful.'

Ann-Marie did not return to the nursery for three days, by which time she no longer seemed to be in pain. Today you notice red marks on Ann-Marie's palms and she is unwilling to explain what has happened beyond that she was 'very naughty'. At pick-up time Ann-Marie's mother is initially apologetic about an unspecified 'accident' to her daughter. Then she blurts out, 'Anyway my husband says you should respect our beliefs and what we do in our own home. We've got a copy of your equality policy. Respect us then!' And she rushes off with Ann-Marie.

Questions

■ **What would concern you for the child in this situation?**

■ **What might be the complicating factors for practitioners to consider?**

■ **What should probably be your next step?**

You will find a commentary on page 141.

physical maltreatment of other people. In law, this behaviour against adults is called assault or domestic violence; it is wrong to treat young citizens in this way.

■ The practical links are that there are respectful and effective alternatives to hitting when adults need to deal with children's behaviour, or when an adult is scared by a child's unsafe actions that often arise from ignorance of the risk.

■ Hitting gives children the clear message that physical means are an acceptable way to settle arguments or express anger and frustration. Adults are setting a bad example through their behaviour.

■ Supporters use bizarre phrases such as 'a gentle smack' or 'loving tap'. But hitting children is rarely calm and gets easily out of control. A disturbing rationale underlies claims that hitting can be an expression of affection.

Adults, as parents and practitioners, need to consider their attitudes as well as their actions. Childhood experiences can muddle adult thinking, as people struggle to reconcile the fact that parents, whom they love, raised them in an era when it was socially more acceptable to hit children. Times have changed and some adults have to address their feelings of 'my parents smacked me and it didn't do me any harm!' The questions have to be, 'What good did it do me?' and 'Was there really no other way that I could have learned how to behave?'

The law and hitting children

Legislation throughout the UK has largely removed the option of using corporal punishment (hitting and other forms of direct physical discipline) on children and young people in all public establishments and registered services. For some years, official guidance allowed childminders to hit children with parents' permission. Revised regulations (2002 in Scotland and Wales and 2003 in England) corrected a situation that was unacceptable to childminding organisations and many practitioners themselves. In Northern Ireland, avoidance of physical punishment in non-school settings is still a matter of guidance and not regulation.

National governments in the UK have still not introduced the same legal protection against assault for children that exists for adults. Many other European countries have taken this legal step, often alongside public education campaigns to create a climate in which adults make the effort to guide children's behaviour in non-physical ways. An anomaly has remained for families in the UK because law in each of the four nations still allows parents, or other family members such as a step-parent, to hit their children and adolescents. For many decades this exception had been the right for parents to inflict 'reasonable chastisement'.

TAKE ANOTHER PERSPECTIVE

The legal loophole for parents to hit their own children exists because of a court decision made as long ago as 1860, when a 13-year-old died as the direct result of a beating by teachers at his school. The judge presiding over that case created the legal precedent that punishment of the boy was unacceptable and beyond 'reasonable chastisement'. So, this concept, still active in the early 21st century, was established to make it clear that killing children was going too far in terms of chastisement.

Through much of the 20th century, parents who were judged to have overstepped the boundary of an acceptable level of punishment could be prosecuted for wilful assault and causing unnecessary suffering under the Children and Young Persons Acts (1933 for England and Wales, 1937 for Scotland and 1950 for Northern Ireland). The burden of proof remained with the prosecution to establish, beyond reasonable doubt, that a parent's actions went beyond the limits of lawful punishment. Many parents have been excused legally for repeated attacks on their children, including using implements.

In this first decade of the 21st century, domestic violence between adults is regarded as unacceptable. Safeguarding law and guidance recognises the damage that such aggression in the family inflicts on children (see page 248). Yet UK governments feel justified to determine legally acceptable ways to raise a hand to non-adults in the same domestic environment.

In 1991 the UK central government signed the United Nations Convention on the Rights of the Child 1989. Several of the articles within the Convention aim to secure children's rights to be protected from physical or mental violence. The UN Committee on the Rights of the Child (which monitors the Convention) has recommended prohibiting physical punishment in families and the active change of social attitudes that support it. The Committee has stated several times (1995, 2002 and 2006) that the UK government approach to limit, rather than remove, this parental right was a failure to comply with the Convention.

There have been significant campaigns aiming to bring all children under the same legal protection against assault as adults. But by 2007 no part of the UK has taken this final step. Changes that have taken place in the 21st century include the following:

- The Criminal Justice (Scotland) Act 2002 provides the concept of 'justifiable assault' when parents, or others in a parental role in the family, hit under-16s. The Act lists various forms of attack that are not acceptable under the law. However, if parents hit their 17-year-old, it becomes the crime of assault.

- The Children Act 2004, for England and Wales, replaced the phrase 'reasonable chastisement' with 'reasonable punishment' and offered the alleged protection that adult actions should not be so violent as to leave a visible injury or create lasting physical or mental damage. In effect, parents are permitted to use physical punishment up to the level of common assault.

- A clear stand has been taken in Wales against permitting parents to hit their children. The Welsh Assembly cannot change the law, but openly supports bringing children under the same legal protection against assault as adults.

- In June 2006 (when the Assembly was still suspended), Parliament in Westminster brought the laws in Northern Ireland in line with the legal situation for England and Wales.

MAKE THE CONNECTION WITH . . . YOUR GROUND RULES

Any setting will have a ground rule that nobody hits anybody within the boundaries of your 'territory'. Sensible teams, childminders, nannies and foster carers also support children and adolescents to use words: to tell another child to stop or to resolve common problems that need negotiation within play.

Regardless of the legal situation about parents and hitting children in their own home, practitioners can take a firm line of 'not here'. Even if a child has passed from your responsibility to that of their parent, or other family carer, you cannot ignore the situation if that adult hits, or otherwise roughly handles, a child within your hearing and sight. Doing nothing gives the message that you agree with the action, or are only confident to take children to task for hitting each other.

It is important, ideally right at the time, to go up to the adult and child, say something like, 'Please don't do that. We have a firm rule in nursery/my home/club that we never hit each other.' You can immediately follow with something appropriate to the circumstances. It might be that you realise the parent is in a terrible hurry, or that the child was being rude and uncooperative. You are pleased to help now or later, but any hitting has to stop. One point of establishing a friendly working relationship with parents is to ensure that a sense of fellow-feeling comes across as genuine. But your professional role is also to be ready to discuss other ways of dealing with the same behaviour.

If you want to find out more

✤ *Children Are Unbeatable* – an alliance of organisations and individuals seeking to bring children the same legal protection as adults, 94 White Lion Street, London N1 9PF Tel: 020 7713 0569 www.childrenareunbeatable.org.uk

Female genital mutilation

Female circumcision, in any of its forms, has been illegal in the UK since the Abolition of Female Circumcision Act of 1985. The recognition that this practice is a form of physical abuse led to its being described as female genital mutilation (FGM). The practice is also known as female cutting.

WHAT DOES IT MEAN?

Female genital mutilation: the removal of part or most of the external genitalia of a girl or young woman as a cultural ritual to ensure purity for marriage.

FGM appears to have become established many centuries ago in parts of Africa and the tradition remains strongest in some countries within that continent. FGM is also practised in communities within several countries in the Middle East and Far East (as described from a European perspective). FGM is a strongly held cultural tradition and has travelled with communities that have relocated elsewhere, including the UK. Many, but not all, of these communities follow Islam. Religious leaders of these social groups often insist FGM is a requirement of faith. However, considerable numbers of Muslims around the world reject the practice, saying there is no basis in the Qur'an for what is a cultural, not a religious, tradition. Some Christian communities, for example in Egypt, are also committed to the tradition.

The cultural pressure is strong to perform FGM on girls before they become young women, because it is seen as the way to ensure that daughters are chaste and therefore marriageable. Families living in the UK have been able to find some doctors who are prepared to circumcise their daughters and some traditional circumcisers have operated illegally in this country. Otherwise, mothers or grandmothers have taken girls abroad to obtain the operation. The Female Genital Mutilation Act 2003 made it additionally illegal for any residents of the UK to take girls to any other country for this purpose.

The practice of FGM was made illegal in the UK because the procedure results in considerably greater mutilation of the female genital area than the usual circumcision procedure for males. Girls either have the clitoris cut, or suffer the removal of all the external labia, and almost complete sewing up of the vaginal opening (infibulation). The circumcision itself can be very painful, since traditional circumcisers do not necessarily use pain relief. Girls can bleed dangerously and be left with pelvic infections, gynaecological problems and later difficulties with childbirth.

The issue of FGM is one in which child protection concerns are in inevitable conflict with the wish to respect cultural traditions of a community. It is an important reminder that respect for any cultural practice must not override concern for children's well being. Nor is respect for cultural tradition a more important concern than that of equality: the procedure is judged as violence towards the girls, a matter of gender discrimination. Child protection teams who face this issue also need to offer support for those families and girls who wish to break with the practice. They are likely to face hostility from their community and pressure that the girls will no longer be pure for marriage.

Early years practitioners are less likely to encounter the practice, since girls from the relevant communities are most likely to experience FGM from between 4 to 10 years of age. Any concerns about unexplained injury and pain should be dealt with as possible abuse, in line with good child protection practice. But it is also important that schools, and out of school provision, are very aware if girls talk about an impending 'holiday' in ways that suggest concern.

Male circumcision is not regarded as an automatic child protection issue, since the procedure does not cause equivalent damage to boys. In previous generations, the circumcision of baby boys was more common in the UK on the grounds of easier personal hygiene, but this practice has now been discredited. Prevailing medical opinion is now that male circumcision is inappropriate, unless there are physical reasons that justify the removal of a boy's foreskin. Some Jewish and Muslim groups regard male circumcision as an important religious and cultural rite. This practice is not illegal and protection issues would only arise if the ritual was undertaken in ways that threatened the baby or child's health or well being.

If you want to find out more

✤ *Foundation for Women's Health, Research and Development* www.forwarduk.org.uk 765–767 Harrow Road, London NW12 5NY Tel: 020 8960 4000. An organisation supporting women and communities to resist pressures for female genital mutilation and forced marriage.

✤ A range of papers and reports on the UNICEF website www.unicef.org

Forced marriage

The tradition of arranged marriages has operated in many countries and cultures for a very long time. The approach of assisting young people towards a suitable match, for themselves and their families, also has a long tradition in some social groups within the UK. A pattern of introduction and encouragement, with the option that young people can decline a partner or series of recommendations, creates a system of arrangement of or assistance towards marriage.

Forced marriage has no such flexibility and is the term used when young people have no choice whatsoever. In child marriage, children younger than the legal age to marry in the UK (16 years in England, Wales and Scotland, 17 years in Northern Ireland) have been promised in marriage to someone and know they will have no choice once they become of age. Families, and sometimes other members of the local community, combine to coerce, physically threaten, attack and in some cases imprison or abduct the young person; this is usually a young woman, but sometimes it may be a young man.

Forced marriage is regarded in the UK as an abuse of the human rights of the young person concerned. At the time of writing (2007) there is not a specific law against the practice, since physical attack, false imprisonment or abduction are already illegal actions to take against another person, regardless of any family connection or deeply felt cultural justification, for what is actually a form of domestic violence. Forcing the bride to have sex within the marriage is judged to be rape. Children and young people are also directly protected in the UK by child protection legislation up to their 17th (Scotland) or 18th birthday (England, Wales and Northern Ireland).

Practitioners who work with older children and young people have a responsibility to recognise that forced marriage and child marriage is a protection issue. Again, the key practice point is that explanations on the basis of interpretations of faith, cultural tradition, family honour, or privacy do not outweigh the safety and rights of the child, or young person, resident in the UK. Schools and colleges need to be fully aware of circumstances that give rise to concern, such as disruption of attendance, concern about an impending trip abroad and any of the signs of possible physical and emotional abuse described in chapter 3. School and college teams are responsible for making effective inquiries if a child or young person goes missing. They must take matters further, to social care services or the police, if there is no believable explanation for the pupil or student's absence.

WHAT DOES IT MEAN?

Arranged marriage: when the two parties meet through the actions of family but have genuine choice, and veto, over the suggested partner(s).

Forced marriage: when a young person (or adult) is coerced into marriage and alleged consent is not therefore valid, since it is given under duress.

Child marriage: when one or both of the partners coerced into a future marriage contract is younger than the legal age for marriage.

If you want to find out more

✤ *The Forced Marriage Unit* (FMU) of the Foreign and Commonwealth Office www.fco.gov.uk Admiralty Building, London SW1A 2RA Tel: 020 7008 0151 For help and advice about individuals and general information.

✤ The Forced Marriage Unit *(2005) Dealing with cases of forced marriage, practice guidance for education professionals* www.fco.gov.uk/Files/KFile/ Dealing%20with%20cases%20of%20Forced%20Marriages.pdf

✤ Teachernet home page on Forced Marriage www.teachernet.gov.uk/ wholeschool/familyandcommunity/childprotection/usefulinformation/ typesofabuse/forced_marriage/

Safeguarding and religious faith

Any hope that children would be automatically safe within faith communities does not stand up to the weight of evidence. Serious child protection issues have arisen that have tainted a wide range of faith groups and religious leaders.

Faith and the risk of abuse

Significant risks arise when the well being of children and young people is judged less important than the reputation of the religious or community leader who is alleged, sometimes with very good reason, to be an abuser.

- Members of faith communities who feel under threat from people who do not share their beliefs can be especially keen to close ranks. Representatives of a range of different religions have insisted on dealing with any problems within their own internal systems, until pressurised to take a more transparent approach.

- Pressure has been put on children, young people and their families to take the matter no further, because of the likely backlash on the community. Similar risks have also arisen around domestic violence.

- Interpretation of faith values and key scriptures can be used to justify the chosen priorities and even to vilify the child or young person. In some cases, serious cruelty and sexually abusive treatment has been justified on the grounds that the child or young person is sinful or evil.

- Such an atmosphere provides a safe haven for individuals who would abuse children and young people wherever that adult lived, worked or worshipped.

- Involved professionals who share the faith or community allegiance can be forced into a choice between personal and professional loyalties. Professionals who do not share this source of identity may be anxious that they will be accused of ignorance or outright hostility to the faith or cultural group.

Scandals within the Catholic Christian church and the Protestant Church of England have arisen from the preferred solution of moving the alleged abuser to another parish, or to a post in which it is claimed he will have no contact with children. (The abuser always has been a male in reports of which I am aware.) This option is an unacceptable response to the actual abuse of children, or risky adult behaviour like accessing child pornography. Additionally, the promised 'no contact' has sometimes failed to be upheld. See for instance the editorial news item about the Church of England in *Caring*, Summer 2007, www.ccpas.co.uk

Children and young people are at risk from any combination of a closed community, powerful social position and values that consider adults to be the more important individuals in an uncertain situation. The incidence of abuse or neglect within a given faith does not, of course, support the stance that everyone who shares the religious beliefs would tolerate ill-treatment of vulnerable individuals. However, concern cannot be brushed aside because the identity of a group is based on faith, or a combination of cultural background and faith.

- All religious groups and leaders are obligated to address safeguarding of children and young people within their community as a whole.
- They should make proper checks on individuals who are responsible for activities for children and any form of religious education offered by the faith.
- Many faith groups, and separate sects within a world faith, have developed or accepted guidelines and clear policy about action that is needed to protect children.

Faith-based abuse and spirit possession
Some sects and church groups within the Christian faith believe that it is possible for children to become infected – possessed – by an evil spirit, or to become a witch. The accepted solution is to perform a ritual of exorcism that involves actions that are physically and emotionally abusive of the child or young person. This tenet of faith is strong in some Christian groups whose country of origin lies within parts of Africa. However, families who originated from the Caribbean and 'white' English families have also been involved in documented cases.

Some involved adults genuinely believe that what they are doing is mandated by their faith and in the best interests of the child, whom they believe to be possessed. However, the process is a welcome option for adults who dislike and resent a child, or regard them as unacceptably different in some way. Spirit possession offers a useful external explanation for what the adult insists is bad behaviour, and justifies abuse and neglect of the child. This dynamic was one of the many appalling events experienced by Victoria Climbié before her death.

The DfES 2007 guidance (see below) about safeguarding children from this kind of abuse makes the clear statement that, 'Child abuse is never acceptable in any community, in any culture, in any religion, under any circumstances' (page 3). Safeguarding practice should not change because family faith may be an issue.

- Practitioners in all services for children and young people should be aware of injuries, unexplained accidents or fearfulness shown by children towards particular adults. It is part of good child protection practice to take notice if children seem to be treated significantly differently from others in the family, or individual children seem convinced that they are 'bad' or 'unwanted'.
- Listen to your feelings of anxiety if a child, about whom you are already concerned, talks unhappily about an impending trip or holiday. Practitioners should be alert for any children going missing for a period of time, because some are taken abroad for the exorcism ritual.
- Effective working between services and professionals should include sharing information about places of worship and individual faith leaders about whom there are growing concerns. Effective local and national initiatives (such as that of the CCPAS, see below) have to make sustained contact with the groups in question, dealing with concerns about children whilst giving the very clear message about what constitutes a crime against children in the UK.

If you want to find out more

✤ DfES (2007) *Safeguarding children from abuse linked to a belief in spirit possession* download from www.everychildmatters.gov.uk or www.teachernet.gov.uk/extendedschools

✤ *Churches' Child Protection Advisory Service* www.ccpas.co.uk PO Box 133, Swanley, Kent Tel: 0845 120 45 50. Information about child protection and faith groups. CCPAS is a Christian-based independent charity that has developed materials which may be useful for other faiths and organisations.

✤ Muslim Parliament of Great Britain (2006) *Child protection in faith-based environments: a guideline report* www.muslimparliament.org.uk/ Documentation/ChildProtectionReport.pdf

Commentary on the scenarios

Here are possible suggestions for the scenarios given in this chapter.

Helena (page 121)

Disabled children can behave in ways that hurt or distress other children, as well as being secretive about their behaviour. A sentimental approach does not help children, nor does a reluctance to address their behaviour out of pity.

It is right to be careful about over-reaction, but observations made during the days should give you a firm basis for a conversation with Helena's childminder, who is the key carer in the working relationship at the moment. You definitely do not want to label any child as a 'bully'. However, it is important to address Helena as a girl who may well need some clear guidance on how to behave. She will not be helped by a lack of boundaries, either now or in the future, and adults have a responsibility to look towards what is likely to block Helena's friendships with other children. Her peers will become annoyed if she appears to 'get away' with actions that would be stopped if another child behaved in that way.

If Helena's childminder is open to considering another perspective, then the discussion and support might extend to including the parents. It will be useful for you to have information about appropriate support groups, but that step will depend on what happens in the short term.

Natasha (page 124)

There is cause for concern about Natasha, since the care arrangements seem to be unpredictable and potentially unsafe. All carers within her family need to understand that nursery hours are not elastic and that children must be handed safely to a member of staff. It also seems that the nursery team may have been too flexible in allowing a wide range of family members to pick up Natasha. The nursery teacher needs to talk urgently with Natasha's mother and be very clear about what is acceptable and what is unsafe regarding this 4-year-old. If the school has a breakfast club, it may be possible for Natasha to arrive in time to join that facility. But any change must be properly discussed and no child must be simply left in the playground.

The information given by the school caretaker raises further concerns. The nursery needs to gain some idea of the reliability of this information before discussing anything with Natasha's mother. The lack of supervision, if true, is outside nursery time, but the staff can have the same concern that a neighbour might feel. If Natasha's mother is unresponsive to a careful conversation about her daughter's supervision, the nursery could look for a low-key conversation with another professional, perhaps in the social work team. It is unlikely to be at the stage yet for a referral.

It is appropriate that the caretaker should share information relevant to the children in nursery class or the main school, but it is inappropriate for him to talk dismissively about 'these people'. His line manager, possibly the head of the school, needs to talk with him about respect for families and needs to tell him that sweeping statements are unacceptable and unprofessional.

Abbas (page 127)

It is appropriate that the school team resist making judgements about Abbas and his family. 10-year-olds can be very competent and, in many cultures, older children take safe responsibility for younger siblings. The staff may feel regret for Abbas that he cannot have an independent social life, but that would not be a basis for intervention. It would be possible to look at practical issues, such as can Nneka come to chess club as well, so that Abbas may enjoy this activity.

It would be possible for Abbas's or Nneka's class teacher to talk with their parents about making practical arrangements for Nneka when her brother goes to secondary school. Perhaps there could be a friendly offer to see about linking Nneka up with another family who walk in from the same direction. Such an arrangement would have to be a clear agreement between the families; the school team will have to be careful about not taking responsibility outside their sphere. An alternative might be possible if the primary school has a breakfast club.

The children appear well and healthy, yet there is a level of concern that Abbas may be responsible for his sister into the evening. The school do not know for sure; there may be other people in the home. The class teacher, after discussion with the CPO, might look for an opportunity to raise the issue within a meeting with the children's parents.

Ann-Marie (page 130)

Neither partnership nor equality policy mean that settings should accept actions from parents that place children at risk. It is important that family faith is shown respect, but that does not extend to acceptance of cruel treatment of children, apparently justified through religious beliefs. The nursery team, led by the CPO, also need to be aware that suspicions are not in themselves firm proof. If Ann-Marie's parents are hitting her, it is also important that nobody in the nursery assumes that their behaviour is typical of other families who follow their faith, or sect within the faith.

141

The nursery needs to keep records of what has happened and the reactions of Ann-Marie's parents. Part of the written record will be to put in descriptive terms the reason that pain from bruising became 'obvious'. The team will be aware that UK law still allows parents to hit their children, within limits. It is not the nursery's task to try to work out the precise legal position. However, if Ann-Marie's injuries are the result of being hit by one or both parents, such treatment has definitely left a visible mark.

There needs to be a proper meeting with Ann-Marie's parents to express the serious concerns of the nursery arising from recent incidents, and listen to what the parents have to say. Unless concerns are put to rest, it is likely that the CPO will need to make a referral for Ann-Marie's protection.

An effective safeguarding process depends on clear policies and linked procedures for daily practice with children and young people. Policies and procedures matter, but a guidance document, however well written, cannot actually do the safeguarding job. It requires people to behave in ways that protect.

> **The main sections of this chapter cover:**
>
> ⭐ **Policies and procedures for safeguarding**
>
> ⭐ **Safety and security**
>
> ⭐ **Child protection and written records**

POLICIES AND PROCEDURES FOR SAFEGUARDING

Laws define the legal framework for safeguarding, and guidance explains how practitioners and services need to operate in order to implement the legal requirements (see chapter 1). Settings and services are expected to have written policies on key aspects of good practice, and child protection is definitely one of those areas. A written policy is usually a statement of commitment. Then the procedures are the defined steps that enable policy to be put into practice on a daily basis: actions to take, with a sequence of actions, when that makes sense and any details about what should not be done.

Key issues to cover

Some documents for safeguarding combine a policy statement followed by more detailed procedures. It is, however, useful to distinguish between the different aims of a policy and procedures. Your policy makes a succinct statement and should ideally fit a single side of A4, certainly no more than two pages, and states:

- who you are: the name of your organisation or kind of service and the main aspects of what you offer to children, young people and/or families
- the importance of child protection and your safeguarding responsibility, with brief reference to the main laws and guidance for your part of the UK
- the responsibility of everyone within a setting or service to be active in safeguarding and the prevention of abuse or neglect

MAKE THE CONNECTION WITH . . . HEALTH AND SAFETY

You do not, for instance, wait for children to have accidents in your setting, before you decide on the best procedures for first aid or dealing with a medical emergency. Everyone on a team should know the basics of first aid and be fully informed about the special health needs of individual children.

The parallel of health and safety highlights the obvious fact that a policy and written procedures do not create effortless, immediate solutions. A well-written health and safety policy does not, in itself, keep children and young people either healthy or safe. The actions of people create and maintain a suitable environment and their skills are necessary to deal with incidents, either predictable or utterly unexpected.

In the same way, a well-considered policy and procedures on safeguarding can create a positive environment for the task of protection. But the behaviour of the responsible adults will determine the end results for children and young people.

The NSPPC booklet *Stopcheck* (see page 150) has a useful 'Checklist' for spotting a risky project that has a slapdash approach to safeguarding children and young people. One of the realistic warnings is 'a child protection policy that is gathering dust on top of a cupboard', as well as worrisome patterns such as minimal supervision of children, or of staff and volunteers, or lack of guidelines for dealing with concerns about children or the behaviour of adults.

- in broad terms, how you will meet that obligation, for instance through safe recruitment to the team or active support for children and young people
- that the safeguarding commitment works together with other policies, such as equality, your policy on behaviour and partnership with parents.

WHAT DOES IT MEAN?

Policy: a policy lays out the key principles and values that guide this aspect of practice

Procedures: provide details of what will be done, or steps that will be followed

Your procedures will be longer, although it is unwise to create such a lengthy document that people rarely read it. Your procedures make clear your responsibilities, as an individual or members of a team, and that everyone is accountable for their own actions. Procedures have to be clear about the following points.

- The obligation to respond appropriately, and in a timely way, to any concerns, whoever raises them. Some procedures include a brief summary of signs that should concern practitioners, or refer to a guidance document.
- The steps that should be taken when there are concerns, perhaps with a flow chart (similar to that on page 72), and the boundaries to the role of a familiar practitioner or the designated child protection officer (CPO) in a team.
- Details of the service(s) – name(s) and telephone numbers of those who should be contacted or consulted locally.
- Some procedures build in specific guidance about how to behave if a child or young person discloses an abusive experience.
- How child protection is supported by other procedures, such as written records or dealing with allegations of abuse or malpractice.
- Effective safeguarding includes helping children and young people to learn skills of personal safety. A school, for instance, might make commitments linked with the curriculum, whereas childminders or an after-school club might explain their ground rules around internet use.

Putting good intentions into practice

No procedure, however well-drafted, will make every decision for you. The most experienced professionals in child protection still need to make carefully considered judgments. There will always be a level of anxiety when dealing with concerns about the well being of children or young people. So, good teamwork and easy opportunities to discuss work issues will be the essential support for practice in child protection. Practitioners who work alone, such as foster carers and childminders, need easy access to a fellow-professional (see page 75).

It is also important to recall that the 'team' of people who have responsibility for the same child, or young person, can be an extended system. Some disabled children cannot reach services, or get home again, without the driver of their special transport. The 'school run' by local taxi firms is necessary in many areas where pupils or students live beyond the reach of public transport. Some families are judged in need of this kind of extra support to ensure school attendance.

SCENARIO: HEATHER

You have recently joined the staff of a small private nursery school. Heather is nearly 4 years old and has been attending the school for six months. She is an articulate girl and has started to talk with you about what she has done at the weekend or the previous evening. In a conversation with you yesterday, Heather described a film she had watched on television that you know did not start until 11.00 pm. You said to her, 'You were up very late, Heather. Did Mummy know you were watching that film?' Heather replied, 'Oh, Mummy was with John. They were in the bedroom, doing . . . well, you know what'.

Today, you notice that Heather is playing with Jack in the home corner. When you look more closely, you realise that Heather is sitting astride Jack and bouncing up and down. She is making grunting noises that sound very like orgasm. At that moment Heather's key person goes into the home corner and lifts the child off Jack, saying, 'None of that, Heather. Don't be silly.' In a coffee break later, the other practitioner explains, 'I should have told you. We have to watch Heather. She tries that sort of stuff with the little boys. Poor kid, it's not her fault. Goodness knows what she sees at home. But we can't have it here.'

Questions

■ **As the new arrival to this team, what is your impression of their approach to child protection?**

■ **What are your concerns about the children in this situation?**

■ **What would be a sensible first step?**

You will find a commentary on page 185.

Professional discussion and reflection

Policy and procedures need to be easy to understand for all the team, including any volunteers. Details must effectively be shared with all the adults involved in the setting or service, not only those practitioners who work directly with children or young people. In any setting there needs to be a whole team approach, bringing in all support and administrative staff.

Part of the induction for a new team member must include a proper discussion about child protection policy into practice. However, it is essential to continue to talk around safeguarding issues within an established team. Everyone needs to be sure about, 'this is what is meant by that point.' If you are drafting a policy for the first time, it is a good idea to set a date for review that will take place a few months ahead. You will need a full discussion about whether all the procedures are clear to everyone and if there have been unexpected confusions or consequences. Childminders and foster carers are expected to have simple policies and practical procedures for child protection. Helpful discussion for these practitioners often arises within their professional support network.

MAKE THE CONNECTION WITH . . . REFLECTIVE PRACTICE

Good practice in safeguarding and protecting children and young people has to be reflective. Practitioners are dissuaded from being reflective when they believe, or are told, that they have no choice about a specific 'do' or 'don't' in practice. Any advice from a fellow practitioner, or advising professional, should be received with courtesy and taken seriously. However, it is important to recall that such advice is often at the end of a long filtering process.

It is necessary for all practitioners to find the confidence to ask for the rationale behind a specific 'do' and certainly to ask, 'Which law?' when they are told that a specific 'don't' is 'illegal' or 'against the law'. Children and young people are not well protected if practitioners, who deal with them day by day, feel they cannot ask questions after a blunt announcement of, 'It's child protection policy'. Every trainer, advisor or writer does not reach the same conclusion about some of the dilemmas that are hard to resolve within child protection.

Practitioners have to be professional, bringing any inconsistencies into open discussion and not hiding behind comments such as 'We were told to . . .' or 'You can't win; everyone says something different.' See the example about physical contact on page 192.

Policy and procedures for child protection are not isolated from other aspects of your work. For instance, in full-day early years settings it is important that children get out with staff on regular, local trips and practical risk assessment ensures that children are safe. A nursery policy would be clear that children visit public places such as the library or the park, but are never taken to a private home. But good practice on outings also includes that the organisation of an outing has the child's interest at the centre. Practitioners should engage with babies and children; it would be bad practice if adults talked endlessly with each other, or on their mobile phones.

Communication with service users

Parents and other family carers need to understand that you have an obligation to address serious concerns about children. Open communication about the policy is not only an issue for early contact. A written policy and procedures should continue to be available for parents, or other adults, to read on request.

Written policies or procedures should ideally be available in the main languages spoken in your neighbourhood. For some settings, this task may be straightforward, but if you work in a diverse area that has many languages and written scripts, the translation task will be daunting. Some parents, or carers, will not be literate or may be very reluctant readers; the same issue may arise with some practitioners or volunteers.

Practitioners should be ready to explain the key points of policy in straightforward spoken language, and more than once, when necessary.

- Every team member, or the individual childminder, has a commitment to children's welfare and safety. Part of that responsibility is an obligation to follow up any concerns about a child or young person.
- The preferred route will be to discuss any worries first with the child's parent or other family carer. In the same way, the setting would welcome that parents directly raise any concerns they have with their childminder, the child's key person or class teacher. In a group setting, parents can talk with a senior team member or the CPO, if they prefer.
- Private family matters are kept confidential. But, if there are serious concerns, then practitioners are obliged to make a referral to social care services.

LOOK, LISTEN, NOTE, LEARN

Gather some examples from local, public material about services for children and young people. Look at the ways in which different leaflets, brochures or websites for settings cover the ideas in this section.

- How does the material explain child protection to users of the service?
- What words and phrases are used? Do they appear clear to you? Discuss your examples with friends who do not work in your profession.
- What meaning do they take from the materials?
- Are there any phrases which are unclear to anyone outside the profession?

Children and young people, not only their parents, are also users of services. Practitioners should be:

- ready to give a clear explanation, in appropriate language, to older children and young people when they join a setting or service;
- sensitive to the different ways in which this communication unfolds, depending on the age and understanding of a child or young person;
- willing to make any safeguarding policy available for older children and young people to read on request;
- able to take part in open discussion with older children and young people when they question rules that they are told are for their own protection.

TAKE ANOTHER PERSPECTIVE

In what ways do you discuss safeguarding issues with older children or young people in your setting or service? Are you or some of your colleagues reluctant to talk about policy with those individuals whom the material is designed to protect?

Look at *Kidscheck* (2005) www.nspcc.org.uk/Inform/informhub_wda49931.html and search by title – an audit tool developed by the NSPCC for use with older children and young people in settings and services.

Consider, with your colleagues, how you could use this resource in your school, club, leisure facility or residential home. If you work as a childminder or foster carer, consider how you could use the materials.

Look at The Child Protection in Sport Unit (2003) *Standards for safeguarding and protecting children in sport* www.thecpsu.org.uk. The Communication standard includes listening to the views of children and young people. These standards were developed jointly by the NSPCC and Sport England.

If you want to find out more

A short internet search brings up a wide range of documents that will help you to draft a policy or revisit your existing procedures.

For group settings:

- Read one example of a child protection policy on Teachernet www.teachernet.gov.uk and search for 'child protection policy'

✥ See other possibilities on www.nspcc.org.uk/Inform/informhub_ wda49931.html (go through *Resources for professionals* and *NSPCC reading lists*)

✥ NSPCC – *Stopcheck: a step-by-step guide for organisations to safeguard children* (2003) Leicester: NSPCC Consultancy Services. Useful for small organisations and explores the thinking behind a policy as well as suggested details. www.nspcc.org.uk/Inform/informhub_ wda49931.html and search for 'Stopcheck'

✥ NSPCC *Firstcheck: a step-by-step guide for organisations to safeguard children* (2006) Leicester: NSPCC Consulting Services. A pack that can be purchased, suitable for larger organisations.

For home-based child carers:

✥ NCMA *Safeguarding children: a guide for childminders and nannies* (2006) London: NCMA and NSPCC (for England and Wales) www.ncma.org.uk/download/safeguarding_children.pdf. The National Childminding Association also has outline policies to download from the site – go through Downloads to Sample Policies.

✥ The Northern Ireland Childminding Association (2002) *Child protection – policy and procedures. A good practice guide for registered childminders* Newtownards: NICMA www.nicma.org

✥ Scottish Childminding Association (2004) *Safe and secure* Stirling: SCMA www.childminding.org

✥ British Association for Adoption and Fostering – see information on www.baaf.org.uk/info/lpp/fostering/index.shtml

Childhood memories of practitioners

Memories of personal experience of childhood abuse or neglect, which may include a practitioner's own distress or that of a sibling or close friend, can be revived by working with an abused child and family, or through training workshops on child protection. A proportion of early years and out-of-school practitioners are still in their late adolescence or early adulthood. Deeply unhappy memories may still be fresh and perhaps undisclosed to anyone so far. The CPO of a setting or of a college needs to be aware of this real possibility, but the situation can also apply to practitioners who are mature in years. All professionals have to consider, preferably with support:

▪ in what way their own difficult experiences (not just abuse) are relevant to their work;

▪ to what extent details are shared, with whom and how;

- how they will seek help for unresolved problems or distress, that can otherwise affect their work.

It is good professional practice to raise personal issues within supervision, in confidence with a link worker or childminding advisor. Anyone can use a helpline, like that of the NSPCC (0808 800 5000), to talk about troubles arising from abuse. The following points can help, whether you offer support or are yourself working through memories of childhood abuse.

- Practitioners who themselves experienced childhood abuse or neglect should neither be regarded as too close to the subject to help a child, nor as the ideal key worker because of their own experience. There should not be an automatic decision in either direction.
- If your feelings about your own experience are still raw, especially if you have not disclosed your experience until this time, it would be professional to accept generous support as you work with a particular child and family. In a setting, there would be a good reason for the CPO to take the lead in this situation.
- If you have strong and unresolved feelings about your own abuse, then the professional step is to seek help. An advisor or the CPO will not be in a position to offer proper counselling, if that is what is really needed. Students should be encouraged to access the college or university counselling service.
- If you were given support as a child and your abusive experience is part of you (an unhappy memory but resolved in some way), then there is no reason why you should not continue to be the key person with this child and parent.

Sorting out personal from professional

In any helping relationship it is crucial to keep your own experiences in perspective. Practitioners' personal experience of abuse (or of bullying) does not give them a shortcut to insight on this child's experience now. You have some understanding of how this child, young person or parent might be feeling. But it is never wise to say, 'I know exactly how you feel' because nobody can.

- Any discussions about possible action must focus on the individual child and family. Do not be tempted towards a particular course of action because it helped you, or because you wish somebody had taken that approach.
- Supportive discussion with parents needs to be open and not run to swift conclusions. Just because your own child had a very unpleasant experience with a sports coach, does not mean that the uncertain

problems of this young adolescent are related to his attendance at a sports club.

■ It is very unlikely to be appropriate to let a parent know about your personal experience, whether in the past or more recently. The risk of any kind of personal disclosure, not only about a sensitive issue like abuse, is that a supportive conversation may easily lose its focus on the other person and become a discussion about what happened to the practitioner.

■ You might decide to make a personal disclosure with colleagues, because you feel your knowledge could help them understand the current situation. However, bear in mind that the consequences of sharing a highly personal experience can be unpredictable.

SCENARIO: OWEN

In a conversation over lunch at your centre, 3-year-old Owen is talking about the new baby that will soon be born. Owen is talking with affection, 'I pat the baby in Mummy's tummy. Her tummy's very big and knobbly. I see it in the bath'. Your colleague asks Owen with some surprise, 'Do you and Mummy have a bath together?' He replies, 'Oh, yes. We have wet cuddles in the bath.'

You have never been concerned about Owen or his family but your colleague talks with you later. She says, 'Don't you think we should report this? People shouldn't have baths with their children. It isn't right.' She shudders and looks very uncomfortable.

Questions

■ **Are you concerned about the child in this example?**

■ **Do you have any other concerns and if so, what might you do?**

You will find a commentary on page 186.

SAFETY AND SECURITY

Determined adults who mean children harm, and who are socially skilled, may work their way into a position of trust. Unfortunately, slapdash systems make their task so much easier. On the other hand, proper checks, together with effective supervision and team working, will do a good job of safeguarding.

Vetting and barring

Organisations and services are obliged to make official checks on anyone who will be in a position, paid or unpaid, that brings them into close contact with children and young people on a regular basis. The organisation itself is responsible for ensuring that they do not allow anyone to be in such a position if they are disqualified from working with children or young people. Settings and services are also obliged to pass on the details of anyone whose behaviour makes them unsafe to be in contact with children or young people. Guidance explains the kind of misconduct that would be relevant and the authority which keeps this database in different parts of the UK. See the references on page 158.

The checking process applies to any organisation and setting, including the home-based services of childminding and foster care. Agencies that supply nannies are recommended to make the relevant checks of people who apply to go on their books. Parents can apply for a check on an individual whom they wish to employ as a nanny, but making this check is not compulsory.

The system operates to vet applicants by name through checking that they are not on a database of individuals who are barred from contact with, or taking responsibility for, children or young people in any role, paid or voluntary. Individuals may be barred for two main reasons:

- They have come to the attention of the police for behaviour that makes them unsafe to be with children or young people. Examples would include the use of child pornography, inappropriate conduct of a sexual nature or behaviour that put a child at risk of physical harm. Individuals may not only be barred because of specific criminal convictions, but also for being cautioned over relevant offences.

- Their conduct in a job was seriously unacceptable and led a service or organisation to submit their name to the relevant authority to be placed on what is currently often a different database from that held by police.

The vetting and barring process is similar across the UK. Each system checks whether a named person has behaved in ways that mean they are barred from 'regulated activity': in this case close contact with children or vulnerable young people. The process removes a negative; it cannot tell a potential employer whether the person is suitable for the job or voluntary support. Vetting works alongside, and not instead of, a thorough process of recruitment. Additionally, the vetting process is not a check for identity fraud, since it accepts the personal information given in order to run a name, or names, through the databases.

Changes in the system
During 2007–8 the vetting and barring system in England and Wales will be overhauled, following the Safeguarding Vulnerable Groups Act 2006: a

WHAT DOES IT MEAN?

Vetting: the process of making a series of checks to ensure that someone can safely be allowed to do something.

Barring: the process and agreed basis by which someone is not allowed to do something.

Regulated activity: the specific involvement, paid or voluntary, that is covered by this vetting and barring process.

new law passed in response to recommendations from the Bichard Inquiry (see page 14). The aim is to create a single list of named individuals who have been barred from working with children and young people. The new database will replace the separate lists operated by the Department of Health (the Protection of Children Act List) and the Department for Education and Skills List 99 (this part of government is now known as the Department for Children, Schools and Families). This list will be aligned with another database relevant to working with vulnerable adults. The 2006 Act also introduced an Independent Barring Board that will decide who should be placed on the list, rather than leaving this decision to the varying standards applied by different government departments.

The Scottish Parliament also took account of the Bichard Inquiry and passed The Protection of Vulnerable Groups (Scotland) Act 2007. This law will integrate the different sections of the vetting and barring system in a similar way to the law in the rest of the UK. All the new legislation aims to make it easy to share information appropriately about unsafe adults across the UK and address the risks that arise from both the mobility of individuals and inadequate data sharing.

Most of The Safeguarding Vulnerable Groups Act 2006 also applies in Northern Ireland. During 2007 the Province was developing a statutory disclosures agency. Cross-border issues are a serious concern for Northern Ireland, since unsafe adults move between the Province and Eire. Child protection professionals in both countries are working hard to get their vetting systems coherent and enable communication between teams across the border.

Recruitment and induction

Vetting checks can only highlight individuals whose past behaviour has brought them to the attention of the police or who have been reported for professional misconduct. Thorough recruitment procedures are therefore crucial and the basics for any service include the following.

- Use application forms for everyone, including volunteers. A prepared, standard form ensures that the same questions are asked of everyone. The application process also then links properly with the interview.
- If applicants have difficulty with literacy, then they can seek appropriate help. Under some circumstances, that may be offered from within your service. But it is non-negotiable that a written record is created for any application.
- Take up at least two written references and follow them up by telephone. Explore any doubts about the people whose names are given as referees: what they say or how you are required to contact them.
- Many people legitimately use a mobile phone for their work. But you need to make an independent check, most likely through a landline, to be reassured that applicants hold the position, or previously worked for the organisation, that has been claimed.
- Look carefully at the curriculum vitae of any applicant and reassure yourself about any unexplained gaps or swift changes of job. Verify any qualifications by asking to see original certificates.
- Ask for proof of identity, preferably something that contains a photograph, or request a National Insurance number.

An effective recruitment process is only part of good practice to ensure that adults are safe and supportive of children and young people day by day in their practice. All settings and services should have an introductory process, usually called induction, which eases new staff or volunteers into what good practice means here.

- Policies and related procedures are discussed in terms of what they mean in practice, and not left simply as a task of, 'please read through these'.
- Friendly conversation also invites a new team member to ask questions along the lines of, 'Does that mean that . . . ?' or to check, 'In my last job, I was told not to . . . How do you handle that situation here?'
- Such exchanges can be useful because a reflective colleague can revisit key policies. Questions from a new member of staff also sometimes reveal a misunderstanding established within the existing team.
- Paid staff should have a written job description but that will not cover every single detail. Everyone needs to be consistent and clear about guidelines on good practice, for instance about taking a positive approach to children's behaviour, their physical care or trips out of the setting.

▪ Staff should know how they will be offered continued support, whether through informal conversation as well as regular supervision, and that it is good practice to ask rather than assume, when you are uncertain. Anyone involved in your service or setting needs to recognise that poor practice will be challenged, as indeed good practice should be encouraged.

WHAT DOES IT MEAN?

Induction: the process of introducing someone new in a setting, service or specific role to the details of their work.

Students and volunteers

The induction process is usually organised for paid staff. Such support is sometimes overlooked for regular helpers like parents or for students on work placement. It is unlikely to be appropriate to take non-staff through a full induction process. But everyone involved with children and young people has to keep within the good practice boundaries. It is irrelevant for children, or young people, that someone is volunteering or present only for a short placement.

▪ Students, parent helpers and other regular volunteers should be given an explanation of what they are expected to do and the limits to their responsibilities.

▪ Clear support may be necessary to explain what is legitimate discussion and what is gossip, or breaking of confidences overheard in the setting.

▪ Volunteers can be welcome and may be crucial for the running of some community settings. But no setting should ever tolerate bad practice from a volunteer on the grounds of 'We can't make a fuss, she's giving her time.'

▪ Poor practice from volunteers will not always be abusive or neglectful. Team members may need to explain, for example, that it is not alright to insist on table manners that are culturally very specific.

Recent changes in legislation have made it clear that vetting checks should also be made for unpaid volunteers when they are going to be involved on a regular basis. A working definition of 'regular' is when, for example, a parent helper will listen to children read three or more times each month, or another volunteer is pleased to run a regular basketball game. It is expected that these voluntary helpers will be asked to go through the vetting process, but will not experience the full interviewing procedure that is necessary for job applicants.

Vetting is not judged necessary for irregular support such as accompanying a group on outings or helping out at a concert or fete. The key difference is that for such activities the volunteer or parent helper will not have close, unsupervised contact with children or young people.

Ground rules for other adults

Many services have a range of adults who legitimately visit the setting or premises. Recent safeguarding legislation has not changed existing good practice for protection and basic security for everyone.

Some regular adults are, of course, parents or other family relatives of children and young people who attend the provision. The result of good practice in partnership with families is that practitioners get to know parents and other family carers as individuals. Safeguarding practice certainly does not require you to return to a suspicious attitude towards parents with 'not beyond this point!' notices. A friendly yet working relationship will mean that practitioners should be aware if there are any family members (adults or adolescent siblings) who have problems, such as drug or alcohol use, which mean they could pose a risk.

Other visitors to a setting, such as a medical practitioner or an educational psychologist, may have a professional reason for their presence and it is reasonable for a setting to assume that their professional organisations have undertaken proper checks. Other people have a legitimate involvement in your practice, for instance, members of the management committee or school governors. Any visitor, however well known, should cooperate with standard security, such as signing in and out, and wearing a visitor's badge. Even regular visitors of this kind should not have unsupervised access to children or young people.

Settings may also receive requests for other people to visit, for instance to learn about innovative practice. It is good practice, and respectful of children and young people, that you keep a record of and limit the number of visitors. It is very encouraging when people are keen to find out more about how you work. With prior warning and discussion, the young users of any facility can be involved in making the visitors welcome. However, team leaders and practitioners must not lose sight of the needs of children or young people and that the setting is also their nursery, school or club. A steady stream of visitors, however well-meaning or peaceful, is a disruption of daily life.

SCENARIO: ANSEL

Your class of 9-year-olds starts each morning with a circle time, in which children can 'show and tell' any item of interest from their own lives. Today, Ansel stood up and told the group that his father had gone away to a special hospital this week and explained it by, 'You know, because Dad drinks so much'. Ansel continued in a matter-of-fact tone, 'But Mum says it's a waste of time, 'cos he's such a boozer.' The other children look mildly surprised yet interested.

You know that Ansel's father has a serious problem with alcohol and there have been several incidents in the playground, when he became verbally, but not physically, aggressive while drunk. It seems fair that Ansel should share something of importance to him. But you are concerned about his father's reaction if he hears about the announcement. You are also concerned about the meaning of this news. Is Ansel's father now getting effective help, or has he become worse and does that raise safety issues for the school?

Questions

- **Do you have any concerns for the child in this situation?**

- **What is unclear from the information so far? What more might you need to know and understand?**

You will find a commentary on page 186.

If you want to find out more

✛ The Office of Public Sector Information www.opsi.gov.uk provides information (full texts and shorter explanatory notes) about legislation in all four nations of the UK and Bills that are in process.

✛ The Bichard Inquiry Report www.bichardinquiry.org.uk

✛ *Safeguarding children and safer recruitment in education* (2006) www.teachernet.gov.uk Statutory guidance for England applicable from January 2007, but much of the advice is appropriate across the UK, including a set of examples (on pages 111–13) about volunteers and the need to vet.

High risk people in the neighbourhood

The system for vetting and barring works to reduce significantly the possibility that unsafe adults gain a position of trust with children or young people. However, risks may also arise from people who live in their local neighbourhood. Good practice for protection means that children and young people steadily learn, with sensible practical support from adults, how to keep themselves as safe as possible (see page 200). But there are also limits placed on the free movement of people who have been convicted of serious sexual offences against children or young people.

Individuals who have previously harmed children can be judged a continued risk when they leave prison. Their names will be on the sex offenders register, which means they will be required to notify their local police when they move into an area and keep the police up to date with any change of address. Some individuals may be required, on release, to live for a period of time under supervision in a hostel for people who have served their sentence but are assessed as still posing a risk. Sex offenders cannot, of course, undertake any kind of regulated activity. But they may also have other restrictions on their behaviour, for instance that they do not go near any services for children, including public facilities like an open-access play area.

Local panels operate with the police to manage information about known sex offenders who pose a risk to children or young people. In England, Wales and Scotland this panel works with MAPPAs: the multi agency public protection arrangements. In Northern Ireland the panel works within MASRAM: the multi agency sex offender risk assessment management system. These panels, like the police, can decide to disclose information about a sex offender in order to safeguard children. The obligation for child protection overrules the privacy of the individual on the sex offenders register. This discretionary disclosure may be made, for example, to the head of a primary school because a person known to target children is now resident in the neighbourhood.

A safe setting

In the second half of the 1990s, several frightening, and sometimes tragic, incidents raised awareness that some mentally disturbed individuals target settings with children. Nurseries, pre-schools or primary schools cannot turn themselves into fortresses and it is important to realise that incidents such as the murders at Dunblane primary school, in 1996, are very rare. A realistic, everyday balance has to be found between access and sufficient security.

Practitioners are responsible for keeping children and young people safe. It is good practice to be ready to reflect on questions such as:

■ Have we (or I, if you work alone) achieved the right balance between friendly access to the setting or service and enough security?

159

LOOK, LISTEN, NOTE, LEARN

In the United States legal changes to ensure public disclosure of known sexual offenders followed the rape and murder of Megan Kanka in 1994 by a convicted paedophile living close to her home. Different states in the US have their own version of what is called 'Megan's Law'. In the UK, campaigners for public disclosure have proposed the change as 'Sarah's Law', following the murder of Sarah Payne in 2000 by Roy Whiting, who had already attempted to abduct other girls. The media coverage of the campaign often overlooks the fact that discretionary disclosure about sex offenders already exists in the UK. Also, a decade of public information in the US has not reduced re-offending and appears also to have motivated a proportion of sexual offenders to go missing.

Look at these references (they are relatively short) and discuss the main points with colleagues or fellow-students. Reach these papers from www.nspcc.org.uk/Inform/informhub_wda49931.html and search by 'Megan's Law'.

- Fitch, Kate (2006) *Megan's Law: Does it protect children? (2)* London: NSPCC.

- Fitch, Kate and Sutton, Diana (2007) *Sex offender management: children's rights, Megan's Law and the Child Sex Offenders Review*

- Who are the security systems protecting? Have we explored the right balance between genuine protection of children or young people and anxiety about allegations against staff?
- Do we use opportunities to enable children and young people to take an active part in keeping themselves safe?

Who is here today?

Any setting that takes responsibility for children or young people needs to have an efficient system of registering who is present today and what happens when a child who is expected does not arrive. Completing a register does not have to be a tedious process and can be a combination of self-registration followed by a thorough adult check to complete the written record.

However, safety also includes the following:

- Adult alertness, plus secure physical boundaries to a setting that mean young children cannot crawl or wander off the premises without anyone realising they have done so.

- Settings for older children need to be organised so that children cannot run away from school or club, or be removed, without an adult realising very swiftly.

- Even open-access facilities can fairly request older children or young people to say 'hello' when they turn up and 'goodbye' when they choose to go.

- Settings for children have to manage the personal aspects of transition times. Children must pass explicitly from the responsibility of a parent to the practitioner and then the reverse. Older children and adolescents will increasingly manage their movements independently.

You want to welcome parents and children, yet avoid making it easy for people who have no business in your setting or home simply to wander in.

- Explain how you handle security to parents when they first come to your setting with their child. Stress that taking care over fastening gates and closing doors properly is for the safety of their children: a shared responsibility. Adults who are legitimately in a building still go via reception or the office.

- Practitioners who work with older children, for instance in an after-school club, should teach them about safe behaviour at the door: checking who is there, fetching a practitioner and not simply opening the door to anyone.

Closed circuit television (CCTV)

Some group settings such as nurseries and schools consider whether to install CCTV. This system may offer additional protection if your neighbourhood has problems arising from adults who are under the influence of alcohol or drugs. Alternatively your setting may be in an area with a high burglary rate. Cameras for security against intruders are likely to be positioned close to the entrances to your buildings, not in group rooms. However, some companies now promote an internal CCTV and webcam system as part of child protection for nurseries.

Serious issues are raised by the practice of recording children and staff on a continuous basis. You could use this section as a basis for discussion, whether or not you are currently working in a setting that uses the technology.

It is said that cameras will provide greater protection to children, because it will be possible to see, or to dissuade, adults who mean harm.

■ But, if abusive adults get through proper checks, it is very unlikely that they will be so foolhardy as to ill-treat children in front of the CCTV.

■ The system cannot be secret; any setting is obliged to inform everyone who uses the premises, including staff, parents and visitors, by a clear notice that CCTV recording takes place here.

■ It is risky to delegate the protection task, even partially, to technology. A good leader manages and monitors by walking about the setting, not by sitting in the office watching the screens.

It is claimed that the recordings will avoid false allegations of abuse, because a setting will be able to prove that nothing untoward has occurred.

■ It is possible that a parent might be reassured by a tape recording, when there has been a specific misunderstanding.

■ However, parents who are convinced their child has been abused within the setting may not have a particular incident in mind. They may assert that anything happened off camera, or that someone has tampered with the tapes.

■ All recordings must be stored in a secure place and not be held indefinitely. Settings would need a very good reason to keep tapes for more then three months. So the system cannot counter accusations about less recent events.

I have yet to encounter any company marketing this kind of CCTV that discusses the impact on children, other than to assert that being watched by camera is for their own protection. Guidance is unclear about the rights of children to know they are being watched remotely and also recorded. However, the Information Commissioner's Office (ICO) has stated that school pupils, and not only parents, should be informed and consulted over the use of fingerprinting technology for borrowing library books or cash-free lunch purchases. Any setting that installs this kind of CCTV needs to conform to laws about data protection. For example, some equipment enables a watcher to zoom in on individuals. This system generates personal data and the user will have to register with the ICO.

Webcams
Similar issues of privacy and lack of informed consent for young citizens are also sidestepped when the CCTV monitoring is linked to a webcam facility for use by parents of children attending a nursery.

These systems are marketed to early years settings as a way to reassure parents that their children are safe and happy. Parents are given a password that enables them to log onto the website and the rationale is that parents can join in their child's day while at their own place of work. However, parents are not spending time with their children; they are watching a screen. Parents are best reassured by practitioners who welcome them – sometimes at short notice – and who share the child's day through conversation and generous displays of photos.

There is nothing in the webcam system to ensure that parents only watch their own children. There is no protection of confidentiality that they will not talk about what they see of another child's frustrations or difficulties. Intermittent watching is unlikely to provide the context, and parents should not be informed about the private life of other families so that they can make sense of what they viewed today. There is no way, other than asking for responsible behaviour, to ensure that a wider circle of adults, for instance work colleagues, do not watch the webcam images.

If you want to find out more

✣ Information Commissioner's Office www.ico.gov.uk. Look at the section for Employers and go to the CCTV option.

✣ The ICO *Code of Practice* was being revised over 2007. www.ico.gov.uk/upload/documents/library/data_protection/detailed_specialist_guides/cctv_code_of_practice.pdf

Use of photos
Computer technology and digital photography may be very useful for those working in a nursery setting or at home as a childminder. Photographs that have been taken using a digital camera may be displayed on a laptop at the end of the day, or very soon after the images were taken.

SCENARIO: HAPPY DAYS NURSERY

This private nursery and others within the same chain have promoted access to the nursery webcam facility as a way for parents to join in their child's day. The baby room team has reached an awkward position with one parent.

Darren's mother uses the viewing facility a considerable amount. She phones several times each day from her office to instruct Darren's key person that his nap is being allowed to continue for too long, or he is not being given enough attention, compared with other toddlers. At pick-up time this afternoon she comments on the behaviour of another toddler, whom she has watched, and seems to expect to hear an explanation from the practitioner. Another parent, also in the room, comments sharply, 'Excuse me! My son is none of your business. The point is to watch your own baby.'

Questions

■ **What issues arise from situation? Do you have concerns of any kind?**

■ **What would be a sensible next step?**

You will find a commentary on page 187.

Practitioners are sometimes confused about the use of photos because, during their training, some were told not to use images showing a child's face in their student portfolio. This situation is different from visual displays within a setting or your home as a childminder.

There is usually no problem with images that remain in the setting and document in a visual way what a child or young person has done.

- It is appropriate that you involve children in choosing between photos and in taking photos as well. It is a matter of respect not to insist on an image that, for any reason, a child or young person does not want on display.

- If you work for services that operate from shared buildings you should not leave photos on public display, but may use a photo album, large scrapbook, or room dividers, all of which may be locked away when the service is not operational.

- Photos should not leave your setting, except to go home with children, unless parents (and older children or young people) have given their informed consent. Photographs, or other visual images like video recordings, are personal data and so their use is determined by laws on data protection.

■ You would not usually put images of younger children on a website, unless the composition of the photograph excluded their faces. Children's faces should be obscured in photography in a natural way, not by blanking out their features. Older children and young people might be happy to be seen, but it would not be good practice to have a photo and a name that identified an individual.

LOOK, LISTEN, NOTE, LEARN

Some nurseries, schools and after-school settings have developed their own website: as a means of giving information about the setting and promoting their services. You need to consider carefully what materials are put on the site.

Check on both the formal or informally understood guidelines in your setting or service about the use of photos, whether for a website or in general.

Look at these two sources. What ideas could apply to your own practice?

■ Briefing paper from the NSPCC *Using photographs and images of children on websites and other publications*. www.nspcc.org.uk/ Inform/informhub_wda49931.html and go through *Resources* for *professionals* and *Child protection fact sheets*

■ Advice on Teachernet about use of photos and other images www.teachernet.gov.uk/wholeschool/familyandcommunity/ childprotection/usefulinformation/photosandvideos/

Dealing with allegations about practitioners

Any group setting, daily or residential, should have clear procedures for dealing with allegations, from whatever source. Childminders and foster carers also need to be clear about the steps they must take in response to allegations.

Listen and understand

When you first hear about an allegation, then your main focus should be to:

■ Listen carefully to what you are told by a child, a parent or another practitioner. Ensure you understand the details but do not leap to conclusions.

■ The allegation may be about your own actions or the behaviour of another practitioner or volunteer. Childminders or foster carers may hear an allegation arising from their own behaviour or that of family members who are also living in their home.

▪ Discuss the matter with appropriate people who are more senior than you, or in a position to help you find a sound perspective on the matter. A practitioner working in a setting should speak with the CPO. If the allegation is about someone else, then one of these senior team members should discuss the matter with the practitioner or the volunteer in question. Childminders or foster carers need to contact their advisor or link worker promptly.

▪ Follow the procedures set out by your setting and ensure that anyone involved – parent, practitioners and other professionals – realises that you are acting in accord with agreed guidelines. Steps will include writing up the allegation and what is done at each stage of the process.

Sometimes there may have been a misunderstanding and a parent, or other adult, accepts there is a credible explanation for the behaviour that they questioned. Simple details should be entered into the written record in the same way that you would write up a parent's account of a child's injury, when the matter was satisfactorily explained.

Who needs to know?

Unless there really has been a complete misunderstanding (and still write this up), the details of an allegation of abuse or neglect must not be kept within the setting or service. If you are the leader or manager, then it should be clear who should be told about the allegation within your line management and other relevant bodies, such as a management committee or school governors.

Allegations must be passed to the relevant body that inspects and regulates provision in your part of the UK. This body has to be told of any issue that could affect the validity of your registration, including if a child protection investigation, started by a social worker, raises doubts about the behaviour of any member of your team. The same obligation to inform will arise if the allegation, or an investigation, raises questions about the safety of your premises. Other than these circumstances, it is not appropriate for the inspection or regulatory body to be told about child protection concerns; the referral and the responsibility belongs to social care services.

It would not be good practice for a visiting professional to report a concern, for instance to the social work team, without first speaking with the practitioner or setting manager. The only exception would be if this individual genuinely felt a conversation would put a child or young person at risk and that the situation was therefore an emergency. Nor would it be good practice for the local educational department, or similar body, to deal with an allegation without informing the setting or practitioner who had been accused. Apart from the right to defend oneself against serious allegations, the leader of a setting, with the CPO, needs to make their own investigation of what is alleged to have happened.

Whistle blowing

Some concerns will be expressed by practitioners who are part of the setting or service, or temporary members of the team, such as students or volunteers. The term whistle blowing is used to describe reporting any serious concerns – not only child protection – within the practitioner's own setting or service. The phrase usually means taking steps beyond talking with the person or people directly involved. Some people who whistle blow have felt obliged to take their concerns up the hierarchy or outside their setting, because they believe that ordinary procedures of expressing concern have not worked or have been ignored.

Whatever the level of concern, most practitioners are understandably reluctant to allege that something is dubious about a colleague's behaviour.

- Feelings of loyalty mix with fears of the consequences: 'What if I am wrong?' Guidelines on whistle blowing often state that the focus needs to be on the well being of children or young people and 'What if I am right to be worried?'
- Practitioners feel in a difficult position if their concerns arise from something they were told in confidence. Again, the key issue is whether it is right to keep that confidence. What is the likely impact on the safety of children?
- It is better to express a concern at an early stage. Then it may be more straightforward for appropriate action to be taken. Any concerns about what worries you, in what way and for what reasons need to be expressed clearly.
- Keep a personal note of who you told and when, especially if you feel your concerns were belittled.
- Practitioners may be concerned about possible repercussions, especially if the team member is of a higher status or apparently more experienced. Unfortunately, even junior team members can be regarded as culpable at a later date, if they saw bad practice and failed to say anything, whether or not they were actually involved in abusive or neglectful actions.
- Be prepared to raise your concerns again; either that the situation has worsened, or that the practitioner in question has not kept a

commitment to change the actions or approaches that were challenged.

It is the responsibility of senior practitioners, managing or governing bodies and any involved advisors to ensure that whistle blowers are not put at a disadvantage by their actions. No team member should believe that loyalty to colleagues or the actual setting overrules safeguarding. If practitioners victimise the whistle blower, then their behaviour should become a disciplinary matter.

WHAT DOES IT MEAN?

Whistle blowing: raising serious concerns about actions or methods in ones own setting or service; it is not always about safeguarding issues.

Take appropriate steps

If there is clear evidence or serious reason to suspect abuse or neglect, then procedures for dealing with an accused practitioner have to follow the same pattern as that of suspected abuse by any adult. Depending on the severity of the accusations, a practitioner would almost certainly be suspended while further enquiries were undertaken. Colleagues may find the allegations hard to believe; and everyone has to remember that suspicions may be unfounded. Depending on the nature of the allegation, childminders or foster carers may have their practice temporarily suspended and children or young people will be transferred to other carers.

Any investigation should be undertaken promptly for the well being of a child. But it is unacceptable for practitioners to spend weeks, even longer in some cases, with a serious allegation hanging over them. Childminders and foster carers can feel especially isolated under these circumstances. However, practitioners working in a team may be placed on leave of absence, or in a large setting given duties that do not involve contact with children. This disruption cannot be allowed to drag on indefinitely and the practitioner should be kept informed of the progress of the investigation. If allegations prove to be unfounded, then equal effort should be made to ease the practitioner back into work and to reinstate the practice of a childminder or foster carer.

Unfounded or false allegations

Unfounded allegations may arise because of a misunderstanding or a premature leap to an unsupported conclusion about behaviour or an event. However, some allegations can be called false, because there never was any basis for the claims.

SCENARIO: JOAN

A practitioner in your children's centre has been suspended following complaints. There are claims that Joan regularly humiliated and threatened children. Colleagues objected to her use of harsh punishments, such as shutting one child in a cupboard and making another child stand out in the rain.

This afternoon you watched a group of children play out what seem to be some of their experiences. The child who played Joan was shouting insults at the others and threatening, 'It'll be the wooden spoon for you!' The game came to a close when the other children all leapt on 'Joan' and shouted, 'You're going to prison now'. A letter was sent to the parents, explaining in brief that the member of staff had been suspended, pending an investigation. But there has been no conversation with the children.

Questions

■ **What should catch your attention about this situation?**

■ **What should probably be your next step?**

You will find a commentary on page 187.

TAKE ANOTHER PERSPECTIVE

A small minority of practitioners have behaved in an appalling way towards children and young people. But there are a growing number of cases of practitioners wrongly accused by older children, adolescents or parents.

The case of Christopher Lillie and Dawn Reid, who worked as nursery practitioners in Newcastle Upon Tyne (England) in the early 1990s, is a sobering reminder that allegations destroy lives. Both these practitioners were accused of sexually abusive actions that were dismissed as completely without foundation in a court. Some years later, in 2002, they won a libel action against the city council arising from an inquiry report that made the same false allegations, supported by professionals who continued to insist that abuse had taken place.

Professional organisations for teachers are increasingly concerned about the consequences of false and sometimes malicious allegations against their members. There are equivalent, although less publicised, problems for practitioners who work with vulnerable children in residential or foster care.

WHAT DOES IT MEAN?

False allegations: claims about the behaviour of someone that prove to be untrue when the factual evidence is fully explored.

Malicious allegations: false claims made with the intention of causing harm and distress as a direct result of what is said.

A high proportion of adult fears underlying the anxiety about physical contact (see page 192) arise from false allegations about abuse. The fear is also sometimes about malicious accusations. Strictly speaking, the two are not the same, although 'false' and 'malicious' can become entangled in practice and create a poisonous atmosphere, sometimes leading to personal tragedy. Everyone needs to know that allegations, like disclosures, are taken seriously. But, equally, it is necessary that everyone also knows that false allegations made by adults, children and young people are not simply brushed away. Evidence of malice, defined as the desire to vilify or take revenge on another person, is an example of reprehensible behaviour that needs to be tackled in its own right.

False allegations from children or families sometimes draw attention to serious problems that need to be addressed. However, appropriate support has to be offered alongside actions, whether serious conversations with a young person or documented meetings with parents. It must be made very clear that it is an unacceptable strategy to use accusations to gain attention or attract some help.

When fellow-professionals make allegations that prove to be unfounded, a great deal depends on the details of the case. It is crucial not to discourage an expression of serious concern, nor to punish genuine whistle blowing.

- It is one situation when a practitioner turns out to be mistaken, but expressed concerns appropriately and behaved professionally while the matter was being investigated. However, even under positive circumstances, the manager and CPO will need to work hard to re-establish trust and team working.

- It is a different situation if a practitioner has ignored appropriate confidentiality or shows a pattern of poorly supported accusations against one or more colleagues. The manager needs to consider disciplinary steps for anyone who excuses unprofessional behaviour with, 'better safe than sorry'.

Disciplinary procedures

Allegations of serious bad practice by a practitioner become part of a child protection investigation when there is evidence that the person has:

- behaved in a way – by action or inaction – that has harmed a child or young person or made it very likely that harm could result;
- committed or possibly committed a criminal offence against a child or young person, in which case the police would also be involved;
- shown such poor practice that this person is unsuitable to work with children or young people. Then it is necessary to inform the relevant authority to place the name on the appropriate database (see page 153).

Serious misconduct would lead to dismissal but, whatever the details of the situation, proper procedures have to be followed for disciplinary matters. This aspect of the process runs parallel to a child protection investigation, and might be put on hold until the evidence of the case is clearer. However, it will never be satisfactory to use dismissal as the only way to deal with practice which has put children at risk. Likewise, voluntary resignation is certainly not the end of the matter, if a practitioner's actions have been abusive or neglectful.

Addressing unsatisfactory practice

You might be reassured that a practitioner's actions have not been as serious as abuse or neglect, but that their practice falls short of good standards. Senior team members should address relevant issues promptly: through supervision or broader staff discussion. Examples of situations that need to be challenged are given below.

- A practitioner has been lax in informing parents about incidents between children in the club that led to injury and failed to mention a child's accident.
- Two nursery practitioners working in one room have already been told not to use their mobile phones while they are on duty. A parent has questioned why a student was left alone with the children, while both members of staff were in the corridor, each talking on their mobile phone.
- The key person did not check properly whether this mother had given permission for her child's photo to appear in a feature about the school in the local newspaper. Apart from the fact that it is for parents to give or withhold such permission, some parents are in hiding from violent partners.

■ A parent's comment reveals that a practitioner does personal shopping during trips with children and drops bags at her home on the way back to the centre.

Clear directions about a practitioner's behaviour should be written up after the supervision session in the practitioner's file. If practitioners do not heed warnings and persist in bad practice then they might eventually be dismissed. However, proper procedures will have to be followed to avoid accusations of wrongful dismissal. A senior practitioner may, for instance, have to ensure that a certain number of clear verbal and written warnings have been given to a practitioner. Check out your own procedures; they will be relevant whatever the unacceptable practice, not only alleged child abuse. A similar written process should be followed if childminders or foster carers need to address their less-than-good practice with the childminding advisor or link worker.

Communication with children

When children have been ill-treated by practitioners or volunteers it is important that their experience is recognised. They need to know that responsible adults took notice and have taken action on the children's behalf. They might be reassured that the behaviour of a volunteer was wrong and this person will not be allowed to come to the centre anymore. If there has been long-term or organised abuse in a setting or service, children may need specialist input, supported by the care of practitioners whom they know and who were not involved. Children and adolescents need to be reassured, more than once, that they, or their peers, have been tricked by adults whose behaviour was wrong and in no way justified, for example, by tough training regimes for a sport.

Communication with parents

It is better to be ready to talk with parents when there has been a problem. The local parent grapevine operates at speed and dealing properly with questions is the only way to increase the chances that accurate information is passed around.

In the early stage of an investigation, staff might be told to say that complaints have been taken seriously and are being thoroughly checked. It is important that practitioners do not allow themselves to be drawn into gossip. If a practitioner is dismissed, then it is wiser to give an explanation, otherwise parents will naturally speculate about the reasons. The head or manager should consult the management committee, school governing body, or other line management, about how best to phrase any communication, spoken or written by letter.

SCENARIOS

Consider the following questions. If possible, bring together the views of your colleagues or fellow-students.

■ **What would concern you about this situation?**
■ **What should probably be your first step now?**

You will find a commentary on each scenario on page 188.

Aaron

Aaron is 3 years old and attends the community drop-in session that you organise within the local children's centre. On his left hand, he has an extra finger, which is loose. Aaron does not seem to be worried and his childminder has explained in the network support group that the family is waiting for surgery to deal with the problem.

You have noticed that a childminder, new to the drop-in, seems to avoid being close to Aaron and has visibly shuddered when she looked at the boy's left hand. Last week you thought this adult deliberately ignored Aaron's outstretched hand when he asked to be helped to jump down from the climbing frame. Today, you overheard the same childminder talking with a parent, another regular at the drop-in. The childminder looked across at Aaron and said, 'It's horrible. That floppy thing gives me the creeps.'

Greg

You have heard an increased amount of noise from the room next to the one in which you work with your group of children in a day nursery. A student on work placement appears to have taken a dislike to one of the children. She always calls him 'Gregory O'Connor', although he is known as Greg to everyone else and children in this setting are not usually addressed by their first and family name. Over the last week most of her shouting appears to have been aimed at Greg and you thought you heard her mocking the child's accent with, 'Can't understand you – talk properly!'

Your colleague next door has been showing the student how to complete a developmental record on children. As you passed the door of that room you saw the student propel Greg into a chair and say, 'Right, Gregory O'Connor. Let's see all the things you can't do.'

Today the two rooms have joined together for lunch. You are chatting with Greg. The student ignores you, leans over to Greg and shouts very close to his ear, 'You shut up, Gregory O'Connor! No talking at mealtimes!' You say to the student, 'I was talking with Greg' and she just stares at you. The practitioner responsible for this room looks across but he says nothing.

SCENARIO: SOUTH ROAD INFANTS SCHOOL

A class of 7-year-olds was taught by a supply teacher for two days when their own teacher was ill. The supply teacher was unable to keep control of the class. The children were initially amused by the chaos but became increasingly distressed as the teacher screamed at them. Two children, who would not behave quietly, were chased out of the classroom and around the playground, leaving the main group alone. The teacher got into a wrestling match with one child over a book when the child would not let go. Then on the second day, the same child was slapped twice on the hands for speaking rudely to the teacher.

On the third day the class's own teacher returned and a few children spoke to her about the previous two days. With the support of the head, the teacher first talked with the whole class, explaining that she needed to find out exactly what had happened. She reassured the class that she was not blaming them. It was clear from some children's comments that they expected to be criticised for misbehaving with the supply teacher.

The class teacher and the head spoke individually with each child in the class to build an accurate picture of events. They told the whole class the next day that the supply teacher had behaved very badly, explaining that teachers are not allowed to hit children and this person would never be allowed back to South Road Infants. A report was sent to the agency that organised the supply teacher. The head decided to talk with parents if and when anyone raised the issue.

Questions

- **What do you judge are the main issues in this experience for the children?**

- **The head did not to write to parents. Do you agree with this decision?**

- **Are there any other concerns that you feel should be addressed?**

You will find a commentary on page 188.

If you want to find out more

✤ Department for Education and Skills (2007) *Safeguarding children and safer recruitment in education* www.teachernet.gov.uk/wholeschool/familyandcommunity/childprotection/

✤ Department of Education for Northern Ireland (1999) *Pastoral care in schools: child protection* www.deni.gov.uk and search by the title. Guidance that is 'strongly recommended' for schools, also covers dealing with allegations

CHILD PROTECTION AND WRITTEN RECORDS

The importance of good quality records for child protection runs alongside what should already be careful and attentive standards. When concerns are raised from outside a setting, practitioners should be able to make an informed contribution from their knowledge and descriptive records of the child or young person's physical well being, development and patterns of behaviour.

MAKE THE CONNECTION WITH . . . PERSONAL INFORMATION

Vulnerable children and young people especially need attention to the detail of their lives and this cannot be achieved without keeping records in residential and foster care. Items such as a birth certificate and informal documentation of the kind that would usually be held by a child's birth family need to be stored carefully. Looked-after children and young people need good care taken of their personal information and keepsakes, with their involvement.

Children can experience many changes and part of the whole safeguarding process is that adults create a safe place for items of personal value that might otherwise get lost forever. When children do not have a family to keep a record of childhood events, then someone else needs to respect and store photos, drawings, certificates from school, birthday cards and all the other items that are very important later for adolescents and adults who have spent time in care.

When child protection becomes a possible issue, then good standards in written reports apply in the same way as any recording. The following guidelines for reflection apply to most kinds of records. The basic questions to consider are:

- **what** you need to record;
- the reasons **why** you are recording this information;
- good practice in **how** you record;
- issues of confidentiality of reports and of appropriate access to them.

These general issues apply to all kinds of records: log book, diary, accident book, serious incident book, medication records, descriptive record of a child's progress, diet or health and so on. Any record needs a date for each entry and a clear signature of who has written this entry, even if you work alone as a childminder or foster carer. Children and young people move on to another setting or form of provision and earlier records may need to be accessed, read and understood. Separate individual records need to be kept, even for siblings. Otherwise it can be hard to track clearly what has happened to a particular child or young person.

Different kinds of information

In terms of writing up child protection concerns, it helps to distinguish the following kinds of information.

Directly observed evidence

What you can honestly describe as events you saw and words you heard. This information is in the first person: your own observations. In making it clear and writing it up accurately you may still need to take care in keeping distinct what you observed and the sense you make of it – your supported opinion and interpretation.

Evidence from reliable sources

Some information is relevant that you did not hear or see for yourself; you judge that the person(s) describing an event or concern are reliable. You may trust them because they are fellow professionals, but that would not be the only standard. Another child or young person might be reliable from your experience, whereas an individual fellow professional, or any adult, might have an outlook on events or people that unsettles your view of them as reliable. So you need to be clear of the grounds for judging somebody as a reliable source on this occasion.

Opinion

The important theme running through good written records is that they are honest, distinguish the source of what is presented as factual and explain the reasoning and support for professional opinion. Some practitioners are still told that reports must only be 'factual' and that they must not write about their 'opinions'. This ruling is neither helpful nor workable.

Well-supported opinions are of value for professional discussion as well as written records. But there always has to be the sense of 'for these reasons. . .', 'because. . .' or 'from my knowledge of. . .'. Opinions are potentially dangerous if they are mixed with directly observed evidence and the boundaries are unclear. Can you give a straight answer to the question, 'In what way(s) does my opinion add to my factual description and help to understand what has happened?'

Hearsay

The key points in the definition of 'hearsay' in the *Shorter Oxford Dictionary* are: 'founded upon what one has heard said, but not within one's direct knowledge' and 'report, rumour, common talk, gossip'. Hearsay might include comments such as, 'Of course she hits the children. People are always hearing screams from that flat' or 'All the girls in this school know you don't go in the stock cupboard with Mr Brown'. Hearsay can come with an aura of certainty, but reliable details are hard to distinguish from rumour because of the sense that, 'Everybody knows . . .'.

Hearsay information should not be immediately dismissed as unreliable gossip. There will be important factual content in some hearsay, but it has to be identified. If the content of hearsay raises concerns, there would need to be some exploration, for example, of who is included in this 'everyone'? What has happened to build this certainty? Can anyone contribute a more direct 'I saw' or 'I heard' or even 'So-and-so told me that . . . had happened to her'.

A clear narrative

It can help to hold four basic questions in your mind: Who? What? Where? and When? These are sometimes called the 4 Ws and are useful shorthand. The following examples use 'I' and 'we' but practitioners need to follow the style of writing requested for their own records. Sometimes, the preferred style is to step back from the personal, for example, 'Mrs Singh told a practitioner (name) that . . .' or 'In the conversation with Tania's elder brother, it was made clear that . . .' with the information of who (named practitioner) had that conversation.

Clear source of information

Sometimes you will write up what someone else has told you, perhaps a parent or concerned older child. Then make it clear in your report that you are documenting what somebody else says they saw or heard. Only quote somebody else's words if you are sure that this is accurate. Certainly, do not edit a child's words, or those of an adult.

If you are uncertain, show that you are recording the broad message. If what was said is open to more than one interpretation, then this ambiguity has to be left in an honest way. For example: you may not have direct experience that 'Emma's parents are having awful rows'. More accurately, what you are reporting is that 'Emma's next-door neighbour (name) spoke with me on (date) to say that he is "very worried" because he hears "all these screaming matches" through the wall between his home and the Davisons'.'

Description of events and concerns

Does your concern focus on a pattern of behaviour or changes in a child's more usual reactions? Then what have you seen or heard, and when?

Support your observation with an explanation of your reasons for concern. For example, perhaps an older brother has been observed to hit and drag the younger sibling he picks up from nursery. Who saw this incident? When did it occur? What happened before the blow was struck? Where were the siblings when the elder struck the younger one? Has there been more than one similar incident? What action did you, or anyone from the nursery, take?

If a child's physical well being is in question, then be specific about your observations. It would be inadequate to state simply that, 'Fazila's parents neglect her'. A professional report has to offer full description, arising from, 'We have been concerned about the standard of Fazila's care from her family because she wears the same clothes, including underwear, for over two weeks at a time. Fazila has become distressed because other children do not want to sit next to her and say that she smells. Fazila is in regular pain with her teeth, which we have mentioned on three occasions (dates) to her mother. To our knowledge the child has not yet (date) been taken to the dentist. Fazila is usually very hungry on Monday mornings and eats several helpings at breakfast. Her hunger seems to lessen as the week goes by . . .'. And so on.

Intuitions and feelings

It is good practice to include in your written record details of how you reached a conclusion, not simply the judgment itself. If you know you frequently use words like 'obviously', then get into the habit of answering the question of, 'what is so "obvious" to me?' and 'why am I making that link?'

Sometimes it will not be easy to put your finger directly on what concerns you. It is important to pursue strong feelings of unease and a colleague may be able to help you identify an observational basis for an intuitive feeling (see page 75). This observation can then be written into the report. If you cannot identify the factual basis, then you should not write vague comments such as 'Nobody in Liam's family seems to care about him'.

Sometimes your uneasiness may be fuelled by what does not happen. For instance, perhaps a child's mother rarely seems to react to situations; she neither shows happiness when the child is excited or sympathy if the child is distressed. You would not conclude from this pattern that the child was necessarily subjected to deliberate emotional abuse. An equally possible explanation is that the mother is severely depressed, which is a cause for concern in itself and a family problem that needs appropriate support services.

Visual facts of injury

If a child has injuries, then make an accurate record of the nature and extent of the bruises, cuts or other marks. Use the body outline figure (see page 86) to sketch the location of any injuries. Do not draw any conclusions that you are unable to support, especially guesses about the possible cause of any injury. For example, you might write that 'there were four bruises on Aled's upper arm and one under the arm'. You should not claim that the marks are probably from a fierce grip on the child's arm, unless you directly observed that physical attack. A series of small, round, inflamed marks on Aled's back might be cigarette burns. But what independent evidence do you have? Unless you have some basis for this statement, for instance that the child told you, then do not go any further than a factual description of the injury in your report, with the area marked up on the body outline.

Do not feel under pressure to go any further than is appropriate given your role.

* Practitioners should use only the body outline and a written description; you should not be asked to take photographs.
* Assessment in a child protection inquiry sometimes involves photographic evidence, gained later and within the investigation. But everyone who is part of such an inquiry must be highly aware of children's dignity and their right not to be subjected to intrusive or unnecessary investigation.
* Practitioners will not always be in a position to see children unclothed. Babies and very young children need a level of personal care that involves changing their clothes. Some disabled children continue to need a high level of adult support with personal care.
* School-age children may have reason to change for games. But some early years and out-of-school settings do not have routines that make it likely practitioners will see a child in less than lightweight summer clothing.
* You would not, of course, pressure a child to remove clothing. But you might ask a question if a child rubs her leg, as if in pain. If children tell you that something hurts, it is wise to ask, 'Can you show me where the pain is' or, 'Please point to where it hurts'. Younger children do not always have accurate words for parts of the body and a word like 'tummy' is often non-specific.

Details of an explanation

Write down, as literally as possible, any explanation that the child gives about the injury. Use the words and terms that are familiar to the children or young people. If their words for parts of the body are unusual, then put the correct term in brackets afterwards.

After a conversation with parents and other family carers, make notes of your conversation, even when what they say reassures you. For example, your observation of a minor lacerated area on a child's leg might be supported with the note that: 'Sian and her father both said that the family dog bit her on Saturday evening. Mr Evans told May (key person) that he took Sian to A&E that night. The doctor cleaned the wound but said that no stitches were necessary.' On the other hand, it is appropriate to express a professional concern through a description of inconsistent explanations of the same event, or changing stories.

Professional written style

Records and reports need to be legible, accurate and professional.

- Correct spelling, appropriate punctuation and basic grammar really do matter. The spellchecker on a word processor is useful, but you still need to read a draft carefully. It is a common mistake to have a word correctly spelled but it is not the word you intended to use.
- If you do not work with a pro forma, then make it easy for anyone to follow the flow of your report. Ensure that any narrative about a child or family goes in the right order, with dates or times next to the incident in question.
- Use headings and consider a series of bulleted points for a series of incidents or concerns. This layout is easier to absorb than a long, unbroken paragraph.

More experienced practitioners should be ready to help colleagues improve their style. Feedback needs to be constructive, so avoid non-specific criticism, such as, 'Your report is far too muddled'. Any help given needs to focus on why this draft is 'muddled'. For instance, the practitioner needs to be told, 'You have identified well that you have three main concerns about Tom. But the report is hard to follow because your concerns appear in bits throughout the report. And your descriptions are often separate from the dates you give. Let's start with your worry about Tom and the games he tries to play with Shoshana.'

Keeping a record of accidents

Parents should be used to your normal practice of keeping a record of any accidents that happen while their child is in your care.

- Each accident should be written up promptly with details of the child, or young person, on a separate page of the log, or on a separate sheet that will then be placed in the accident record file.

- The record should include the date, time and location of the accident, any equipment that was part of the event and a description of what happened.
- There should also be a clear description of any immediate action taken to care for the child or young person and of any issues arising, such as a risk assessment about time or place.
- There will not always be significant issues; sometimes accidents just happen. Often the appropriate action will be to remind children about 'one at a time on the slide' or similar ground rules.
- The form should be signed by the practitioner who observed the accident or who was first to go across to the child. The form should be shown to the child's parent that day and that adult also signs the form. On the same day, the information goes into the accident file.
- A similar system can operate using a form to complete for 'accident on arrival', when a parent or other family carer lets you know that the child has a bruise or sore spot arising from an incident at home.

There are advantages in also setting up an appropriate spreadsheet. (With many thanks to Buckingham's Nursery School in Leek for this explanation of their spreadsheet system.) The information is entered under different headings: date and time of the day, the base room or class of the child, where the accident happened and any equipment, the sex and name of the child, the practitioner involved and whether a risk assessment followed. The type of accident is also entered under a small number of possible categories, for example: TSF (trips, slips and falls) HC (human collision), CSG (cuts, scratches and grazes) and HI (head injury). More serious incidents, such as breaks or fractures, will need other categories. The spreadsheet technology then enables a senior practitioner or head of centre to look for patterns, such as how often an individual child has accidents or whether there are more problems at particular times or places.

Timely recording

You should write up your notes about children and young people as soon as possible after your observation or conversation, preferably the same day. If a situation with a child or parent has become very emotional, then it may be more sensible to make brief, personal notes right after the event. Give yourself time to calm down, especially if the incident happened at the end of a day or shift. But return to the notes and write them up for a proper report no later than the next day.

In general, the longer you leave it to make your written record, the greater the chance that you will forget details. Another real possibility is that you start to lay your interpretation over events. Prompt recording is especially important in child protection. Risk to the child may unfold quickly in some situations. But also if the case reaches court, then professionals giving evidence are often asked to be specific about exactly when they made their notes. Records written up days after important events are far less credible than those promptly recorded.

It is very unlikely to be appropriate to make notes while you are talking with a child, young person or a concerned adult. Writing down becomes a channel of communication that interferes with listening, looking and talking. It is also very likely that a child or young person would feel a practitioner was more concerned about a written record than attending to what is being said. (How do you feel, as an adult, if you consult your doctor, and he or she makes notes in a file or directly onto the computer screen at the same time as you are talking?)

The most usual situation for disclosure (see page 98) would be that you take the first opportunity to note down what you have heard. A possible exception may arise with older children and young people, most likely those who are already looked-after and have a general understanding about how such matters work. You might make a careful decision to ask an adolescent if it would be alright to make notes now. You would ask on the basis of signs that this conversation is serious and detailed, but you would accept 'no' as an answer.

Professional notes

It is accepted that practitioners sometimes need to make more speculative notes, for instance, about ideas for how to help a child or information that is of uncertain relevance for the moment. Check whether your setting or service has a specific guideline about professional notes. General good practice is that professional notes should be kept in a safe place and must meet the standards for good quality records. Such notes are not a justification for unsupported speculation or offhand remarks about a child or family. Professional notes must not be used as a means of maintaining a secondary or secret file and they should not last indefinitely. After a maximum of two to three months, the notes should either be integrated into the main file or shredded.

Confidentiality and information sharing

Generally speaking, children, young people and their parents have the right to expect that information about them does not leave this setting or service, either through written or spoken communication, unless they have given their permission through informed consent.

This obligation needs to be revisited when anyone – adult, child or adolescent – shares a confidence with you, or you become aware of a situation that could put children at risk. Wherever possible, you gain that

WHAT DOES IT MEAN?

Informed consent: when anyone, child, adolescent or adult, is given sufficient information to be able to make a genuine decision to say 'yes' or 'no' to a request.

person's consent to talk with another professional or service. If that permission is refused, then you need to be sure about the compelling reasons that mean you cannot follow the refusal of consent. Briefly, these reasons include factors such as when the impact of a serious family problem, the actions of practitioners, what is happening to this child or a child's behaviour towards a peer means that your silence will place children at risk. These will be times when practitioners need to talk with someone else for a second opinion, within their own setting or in a careful way outside those boundaries (see page 73 for possibilities).

The wishes of a child or young person should be treated with the same level of respect as those of an adult. It is also good practice to record the reasons for your decision: to share information, and whether this step is with informed consent, or not to share information at the moment.

Access to records

Parents should have straightforward access to the records of their own children and adolescents (usually up to 18 years) in childcare, educational, health and other family services. However, parents do not have right of access to their child's file when a child protection investigation is in progress and not necessarily once the work is complete.

In general, it is good practice to share with children and young people what is written in their own files. This sharing will be through conversation and young people signing some of their own records in residential care. It is expected that any under-18s should be able to see their own records so long as access is not likely to harm someone else and they can, or can be helped to, make a written request, if that is required by this setting or service.

If you want to find out more

✤ Data protection is the responsibility of the Information Commissioner's Office www.ico.gov.uk. The website gives the regional offices around the UK.

✤ *Information sharing: practitioners' guide* www.everychildmatters.gov.uk/_files/ACB1BA35C20D4C42A1FE6F9133A7C614.pdf

Contributing to an assessment

Good quality reports will support your professionalism and show social care services that you have a vital contribution to make to the process of child protection.

At some point you might have to present a summary of your report on a child to a group of other professionals, perhaps at a case conference. In a meeting, it is not usually appropriate to work your way through the written report; a copy will have been provided as part of the papers for the meeting. Practitioners who attend case conferences need to be ready to talk through the main points of a child's record or the report. You will cover the following:

- the nature of your concern about the child or young person, placed in the context of development;
- information supporting your concerns, if you have them;
- what you have done in your setting with the child and parents;
- any changes, for better or not, that you have observed in the child.

The contribution of any practitioner is not going to be the final word on whether a child is being abused. Your input will be part of informal early enquiries or a more detailed investigation. Your contribution may support the need to worry about a child, or may place isolated concerns in a more positive context.

Assessment frameworks

When there are concerns about a child, or plans are already underway for family support, your knowledge will contribute to the detailed assessment undertaken by professionals such as social workers. Each part of the UK has (or in Northern Ireland is developing) a framework for assessment that is to be used under these circumstances. It is possible that the CPO of a setting might contribute directly to this assessment but individual practitioners would work through the CPO.

- The Common Assessment Framework is used in England and Wales and an online version, the e-CAF, is being piloted in a few authorities throughout 2007. This framework, presented in the format of a triangle, encompasses three broad areas: the child's developmental needs, the parenting capacity of the primary carer(s) and the family and environmental factors.
- In Scotland the Integrated Assessment Framework (IAF) , sometimes referred to in full as the Integrated Assessment Planning and Recording Framework, is also laid out as a triangle and worded from the perspective of the child or young person. The three sides of

this triangle are: How I grow and develop, What I need from people who look after me, and My wider world.

LOOK, LISTEN, NOTE, LEARN

Print off the assessment framework relevant to your part of the UK. Look at the summary triangle and consider what kind of contribution you could make from your professional knowledge.

■ **The Common Assessment Framework (CAF) for England and Wales www.everychildmatters.gov.uk/_files/F71B9C32893BE5D30342A2896 043C234.pdf The CAF form can be downloaded from www.everychildmatters.gov.uk/resources-and-practice/TP00004/**

■ **The Integrated Assessment Framework for Scotland is described in** *Getting it right: proposals for action* **on www.scotland.gov.uk/ Publications/2005/06/20135608/56144 and in** *The assessment triangle* **– information from the Scottish Institute of Excellence in Social Work Education on www.sieswe.org/opencontent/ assessment/index.html**

■ **In Northern Ireland there is the plan to develop a Single Assessment Framework described in the SSI report at www.dhsspsni.gov.uk/ oss-child-protection.htm**

Commentary on the scenarios

Each commentary offers some possibilities. You and your colleagues may raise other ideas and perspectives.

Heather (page 146)

Heather's conversation and pattern of play are not usual for a 4-year-old girl. A new member of staff needs to raise her concerns, ideally first with Heather's key person. If that conversation stalls, then the issue needs to be taken to the CPO. It is not sufficient to deal with the situation just by telling Heather to stop. Practitioners may be concerned about family privacy, but the child's words and actions have brought her home life into the nursery. Other parents may also become aware of Heather's play, when their own child says something.

The CPO will need to deal with the immediate situation and with the apparent confusion in the team about how to react to out-of-the-ordinary behaviour from children. Heather's key person, or the CPO, has to speak to Heather's mother. It may help to start with a phrase like, 'I feel uncomfortable raising this matter. But I need to talk to you about what Heather sometimes does in her pretend play.' (This phrase helps you get into the conversation and is not a distracting apology – see page 77.)

It is feasible that Heather is imitating what she has seen and has not been sexually abused through direct contact. But it is irresponsible for adults to behave in such a careless way that they are highly likely to be observed by children. Responsible adults stop sexual activity if a child wakes up and wanders into the bedroom – as they do in a family home. If Heather is poorly supervised late in the evening, she may watch inappropriate material on television.

Heather's mother may accept that she has been irresponsible. If there are changes for the better, then Heather's key person should be able to track those improvements. If the situation does not improve, or events suggest that Heather is more directly involved, the CPO should make a referral to social care services.

The nursery team, led by the CPO, need to consider whether to speak with Jack's parent(s). If something is said, it would be along the lines that a child in the nursery makes inappropriate physical contact with other children. Jack did not seem distressed, but the practitioner is aware that he may mention the event.

Owen (page 152)

Some parents have baths or showers with their young children and Owen is only 3 years old. This pattern may seem odd to anyone whose family style is less intimate in this way. Owen seems perfectly happy and there is nothing in what he says that raises concerns, given other knowledge about the family.

Your colleague's reaction does need some exploration in a confidential way. It is possible that her family was more reticent about bathing. But her words and the shudder raise the possibility that she experienced inappropriate or abusive attention around bathing routines as a child. Practitioners need to use opportunities for support so that personal experiences do not overwhelm their professional judgment about risk and protection.

Ansel (page 158)

Practitioners are sometimes taken aback at what children choose to share within circle time. Boys and girls often feel confident to speak up about personal and family matters and regard the event as confidential. It would be appropriate to follow the boy's comment with something like, 'Thanks for telling us, Ansel. We all hope it works out well.' Given the nature of the situation, it would not be a time for inviting 'any questions from anyone?' But it is important that Ansel does not feel he has been inappropriate; this event is part of normal life for him.

Good partnership with families in this case would mean a closer relationship with the parent who is more reliable. So it would make sense to have a private conversation with Ansel's mother about the most recent family development. If Ansel's father later raises the circle-time announcement, you could say, 'The children share events that matter to them and your visit to the clinic was important for Ansel. But I stop children if they go into detail about family life.'

There may be no other action necessary, so long as the school is aware of Ansel's family situation and his mother is genuinely able to keep him safe.

Happy Days Nursery (page 164)

Partnership with parents means forming a close liaison about baby and child care. Staff should make efforts to ensure continuity between home and nursery, especially for the care routines. However, parents need to trust the staff in this shared care arrangement. Directing operations through the nursery webcam facility is not a feasible way to run this relationship. Darren's key person needs to talk with his mother about boundaries and trust. A warm welcome can be given for her to spend real time with her child in the nursery or pick him up early on some days.

The mother's comments about other children in the room with Darren raise one of the serious issues about nursery webcams. It must be made clear to this parent that the team respect the privacy of each child and family. They are pleased to talk about parents' own children, but will not respond to detailed questions about other babies or toddlers. This situation may well give food for thought to the nursery team about the webcam facility and privacy for all the children.

Joan (page 169)

There needs to be a conversation about Joan with the children and observation of their play is a natural opening today. The group needs to be reassured that Joan's behaviour was wrong and that she will not be allowed back. It may feel right to apologise to the children for the fact that nobody has had a 'proper chat' with them about what happened. Perhaps this observation adds further details about Joan's bad practice and should therefore be written and added to the relevant report.

Depending on the details and timing of the incidents, it may be that children need a chance to talk about the events. Alternatively, they may deal with their feelings effectively through the play. Within reason, the children should be allowed to play out their distressing experience. Practitioners could look for ways to intervene that could reassure children through the pretend play.

Aaron (page 173)

A practitioner responsible for a drop-in, even an informal session, should challenge poor practice. You need to talk with this childminder and express your concerns. If the practitioner feels uncomfortable about Aaron's disability, it is her task to deal with those feelings. It is not acceptable to show distaste and certainly not to be offensive in a child's hearing. This practitioner needs to understand why her reaction was emotionally cruel and her comment to the parent was unprofessional. There needs to be a clear commitment that she will change her behaviour towards Aaron; it is irrelevant that she is not his childminder. If she belittles your concern, you need to talk with the local childminding advisor, telling the practitioner that you will take this step.

It would make sense to raise the issue with Aaron's own childminder, to clarify if she has been aware of the situation. If so, then what has stopped her from saying anything? A possibility might be to raise the issues in the childminders' support group: both how to deal with difficult feelings about children and addressing the practice of a fellow-practitioner.

Greg (page 173)

This student's behaviour is unacceptable and needs to be challenged. She appears to have taken a dislike to Greg and her behaviour is emotionally abusive and offensive. Additionally, she seems not to understand good practice about developmental records or the importance of a social mealtime.

You need to talk promptly with your colleague who is responsible for this room. Why has he apparently said nothing to this student? Ideally, you would like him to speak now with a senior practitioner, with your support if that will help. If your colleague believes there is no problem, you need to disagree and explain that you now feel obliged to talk with the CPO or the head of your setting.

All group settings need an atmosphere in which team members can express concerns to a senior practitioner. In this case, a senior practitioner needs to deal directly with the poor practice and communicate with the student's tutor. There appear also to be issues of confidence for the practitioner, who should be guiding this student and has failed to address poor practice.

South Road Infants School (page 174)

The situation concerning the supply teacher's bad practice has been generally well handled. The children have been reassured and given a clear message about adults' responsibilities to behave properly. They have also experienced that their teacher and head genuinely wanted to hear from them what happened.

It would have been better for the head teacher to write to parents of the children in the class. Some will have talked at home about what happened and the story will travel along the local grapevine very fast. Parents should not have to tackle the class teacher or head to find out what occurred, nor should they have to depend on information from their children over a serious incident.

The head and class teacher would also need to check to what extent other staff had been aware that something was wrong in this class. Two days is a long time to assume that serious noise levels were a matter only for the teacher concerned.

6 Taking care of children and young people

The younger generation will not be raised in safety to adulthood exclusively through the steps of a child protection system. The term 'safeguarding' is useful because it includes a wide range of supportive adult behaviour. Practitioners, as well as parents, need to ensure they take good care of children and young people: safety without over-protection. Part of that task is to support children and young people as they learn steadily how to take care of themselves.

> **The main sections of this chapter cover:**
>
> ⁎ **Physical care and nurture**
>
> ⁎ **Skills of personal safety**
>
> ⁎ **Troubled relationships between peers**

PHYSICAL CARE AND NURTURE

Care really matters within the experiences of children and young people. They need to feel confident that familiar adults will meet their personal care needs and that those adults are pleased to be close, physically as well as emotionally.

Care-full and not care-less

Physical care routines are a vital means of communication with babies and young children and continue to be important for children and young people whose disabilities mean they still need help. A personal, communicative experience enables children and young people to feel they merit time and attention. Rushed, disrespectful care undermines emotional well being, but also puts children and young people at risk from more than inadequate nurture. Children may be less able to distinguish abusers – physical, sexual or emotional – who are keen to exploit children's uncertainty about their own worth.

Babies, children and young people should be able to get to know the small number of people who offer physical care. Children should not start to believe that any adult can appear and deal with their needs, regardless of whether they like or really know this carer. Consistency of care can be a serious issue that should be properly addressed when settings have a large staff group or depend on agency staff. Even if everyone's care is of a high standard, a child or disabled young person can experience a long list of people who attend to intimate care needs.

Practitioners responsible for the physical care of a child or young person will inevitably get to know how their body usually looks. You will notice whether a mark, bruise or other sign of injury is new, since you last helped this child with personal care. You become familiar with individual children and young people. But it is also important to realise, if you have not yet met the situation, that some striking differences on the skin are not a sign of physical abuse.

Children of African, Caribbean, Asian and Mediterranean origin sometimes have patches of darker skin that occur naturally: the medical term is congenital dermal melanocytosis. The darker areas are benign skin markings, but unfortunately can look like bruising to the inexperienced eye. These areas are a consistent slate-blue in colour, unlike genuine bruising that varies in shade and changes over a period of days. However, the similarity has sometimes raised concerns of non-accidental injury. Open communication will give parents, and their children, the opportunity to tell you that these differences in skin colouration are permanent.

Some children, from a range of ethnic groups, have areas that are without melanin and so have no pigmentation. The condition is called vitiligo and may not be noticed in lighter skinned children, until they have been in the sun. The permanently pale areas of skin are more noticeable when children have a dark skin colour. Practitioners who are unaware of the condition may possibly worry about old injuries. Vitiligo is not in itself a problem for health, except that these areas of the body have to be protected by sun block. Children may, however, feel self-conscious, when the different skin tones are obvious.

Dilemmas around physical contact

In recent years, many practitioners across different settings and services have become uneasy about touch within their daily life with children and young people. There has been concern over whether there have to be limits to physical contact on the grounds of child protection. Any problems and dilemmas must be resolved in ways that genuinely safeguard the younger generation.

Law, guidance and policy

Practitioners sometimes justify actions which severely limit touch by, 'we're not allowed to . . . it's the law' or 'we have to . . . it's child protection policy'. However, all relevant legislation across the UK places the well being of the child or young person at the centre of the safeguarding task. None of these laws, nor any national or official guidance, has banned physical contact between children or young people and practitioners in the relevant services and settings. Problems arise through interpretations of parts of

191

SCENARIO: MEADOWBANK NURSERY

A division has developed between staff in a large nursery about different approaches to the physical care of babies and toddlers. Two practitioners feel that very young children should be given time and attention for their personal care routines. The other two practitioners who work with the youngest children argue that everyone is supposed to focus on educational activities and that changing and feeding time is 'just care'. A situation has now developed where toddlers vote with their feet and go to the more caring practitioners to be changed and if they want any personal attention. Their colleagues now say that the children are spoiled and should not be able to exercise this kind of choice.

Questions

■ **What do you judge are the main issues around practice for this setting?**

■ **What should happen now?**

You will find a commentary on page 226.

guidance, conflicting directions from advisors, trainers and writers, and sometimes misunderstanding of that advice by practitioners or students. The main issues seem to stem from anxiety about what is 'inappropriate' contact and fear that caring touch, or direct physical contact to keep a child safe, could be misinterpreted as abusive.

Some, possibly many, schools have a policy, which may be formal or less obvious, of 'no-touch' between children and staff. Early years provision on a school site is sometimes told to follow the same ruling. Statutory guidance for schools in England (*Safeguarding children and safer recruitment in education*, page 7, 2006 www.teachernet.gov.uk) states, 'All education staff need to know that inappropriate behaviour with or towards children is unacceptable'. But the example given in this section is that it is an offence for an adult in a position of trust to start a sexual relationship with a student. There are no examples that ban a reassuring pat to a distressed young person, or accepting the hand of a child who wants to walk around the playground with you. The next paragraph states, 'It is not realistic to suggest that teachers should never touch pupils' and goes on to confirm that, 'staff in schools and FE colleges have the right to use reasonable force to control or restrain pupils in certain circumstances'.

I hear some practitioners use the words, 'You have to watch your back'. This phrase demonstrates the level of anxiety about allegations in some settings. However, no-touch rules do not avoid this situation, nor resolve adult fears. Individual practitioners and teams need to take a thorough, problem-solving approach that focuses on children's well being and not just on avoiding unpleasant situations for adults, which may never occur. Otherwise safeguarding policy and daily practice is led by protection of staff (losing the 'child' in 'child protection') and paranoia. Worries and questions have arisen around several aspects of daily practice, which are now discussed in turn.

Friendly physical contact

Touch is part of friendly and full communication with familiar children and young people. Touch, that is accepted from or offered to children, is a way to express welcome, friendliness, shared excitement about a project or comfort and reassurance.

Young children need touch, yet there are nurseries which have established a cuddling policy or stated an age limit, for example that children older than 2 or 3 years are not to be allowed to sit on laps. On the other hand, some teams and individuals have a responsible approach to child protection and an equally strong focus on the full developmental needs of babies and young children. For many practitioners the answer to the question, 'Can we cuddle?' is a confident 'yes'.

Occasionally, it is possible to track the source of rules about limited physical contact. Sometimes, practitioners have misunderstood appropriate suggestions about the personalised care of babies or young children. For instance, it is not good practice to pat all toddlers to sleep, regardless of whether that is their preference. On the other hand, there are situations in which practitioners have specifically been told not to cuddle young children, or have been given training in how to pick up young children in ways that minimise physical contact. Some have definitely been given rules about sitting children on cushions on an adult lap, or that a child must never face inwards with their legs around an adult waist.

One reason given for unworkable, and occasionally bizarre guidelines, is that physical contact may be misinterpreted as inappropriate sexual touching of children. Nobody can work effectively in an atmosphere where practitioners assume parents, or young children themselves, are poised to claim abuse at the slightest excuse. A second reason given is that adults who want to abuse children sexually may gain access to provision. Of course, services need to be alert to this possibility but effective safeguarding cannot build on worst-case scenarios. Checks on recruitment must be thorough (see page 152) but, if dubious adults gain access to children, they will certainly not be dissuaded by a cushion rule.

The most pressing argument against restricting touch is the impact on the young children themselves. What sense can young children make of adults who pull back or look uncomfortable through their body language and facial expression?

- Children do not think, 'Never mind, it's their child protection policy'. They take it personally: 'she doesn't like me' or 'Nobody cares about how I feel' (and the emotion could be 'excited' just as much as 'upset').
- Children who are persistently deprived of affection can be emotionally at risk. The need for affection does not go away, so children are vulnerable to anyone who offers personal attention. They are then doubly at risk, because they have not built an understanding of how safe adults behave.

MAKE THE CONNECTION WITH . . . SAFE FAMILY LIFE

Withdrawal of physical contact by early years practitioners, in the name of child protection, creates an atmosphere of emotional deprivation. In short, it leads to behaviour that would properly raise concerns, if those adults were within a child's own family. In each of the frameworks for assessment of children in need (see page 23) there are aspects about emotional warmth in the family.

Children are at risk if their important adults are emotionally disengaged. The logical end result of the argument (sometimes heard), 'They are not our children and they should get their affection at home', would be to shut down this provision in order to protect children from the damaging experience of emotional abuse.

When children have experienced relaxed and generous physical contact within their early years, they make sense of the reduced level of touch that is likely in primary school – even before the recent adult panic. However, children may still be fond of their class teacher. Playground support staff can be important to children, and children will be hurt if an adult withdraws a hand that the child clearly wants to hold, or shifts away on a bench when the child has moved in close. During middle childhood, children themselves choose to limit touch to peers and adults with whom they have a close relationship. Adolescents are even more likely to restrict close physical contact to people they directly choose.

Of course, practitioners should be guided by children; it is inappropriate to demand affection or particular kinds of expression.

- Wise adults re-direct a young child, or a child with learning disabilities, who is still finding out about respectful touch and the private areas of other people's bodies. The same kindly guidance is needed if a child's sense of boundaries has been distorted by experience that was genuinely abusive.

- Children whose families tend to kiss on the mouth (hello or goodbye) can be offered kissing on the cheek, the hand or blowing a kiss. Otherwise, germs can pass round at lightning speed.

- Older children's emotional well being will be under threat if practitioners are denied even a light touch to the hand or shoulder. Another option is to sit next to an older child or young person and put an arm round the shoulder, known as a 'sideways cuddle'.

- Physical contact will be necessary for safety during some lively activities and games. Respectful ground rules are established when adults say what they are going to do, in order to help or to demonstrate. There should be no need to touch a child or young person in intimate areas of the body.

TAKE ANOTHER PERSPECTIVE

Some schools and nurseries have explored the possibilities of simple massage. Heather Piper (see page 199) has pointed to the irony that, at the same time as a panic about touch, there is great interest in a more organised pattern of contact.

Massage by adults of infants and younger children can be very positive and relaxing for both adult and child. Careful introduction of massage as something children of 4 to 5 years of age and older can do for each other has worked well. Massage sessions, explained and initially led by a practitioner who has been trained, can be an enjoyable addition to the day. However, touch should not be seen exclusively as something that is organised in a special session and involves expert training.

Residential and foster carers are professionals whose role has to include a large element of parenting. It makes sense to discuss thoughtful guidelines about contact that meet the needs of vulnerable children and young people. Practice can still recognise that abusive experiences mean some individuals may misinterpret touch or allege that practitioners have been inappropriate. Residential teams have ground rules that are genuinely needed to protect everyone, such as keeping the bedroom door open when a practitioner is talking with a child or young person. Foster carers might adjust routines, such as a story before bedtime, so that this enjoyable event happens on the sofa and not in a child's bedroom.

Physical care of children or young people

Misdirected anxiety about child protection has led to decisions in some settings that a practitioner must never be alone with a baby or child while attending to physical care. This ruling is achieved either by leaving the bathroom door completely open, locating the changing area in a main room, or imposing a rule that there must always be a second adult present. All these options, especially the second and third, raise the important issue of privacy for children.

The obligation to have a witness for intimate care routines in early years provision is presented as necessary by some trainers and writers on child protection. Yet this requirement needs to be challenged precisely on the grounds of safeguarding. An adult has been withdrawn from the other babies, young children or older, disabled children, whose safety and need for friendly company has now been compromised. The assumption is also that practitioners will be in a group setting; the requirement is obviously a non-starter for most childminders.

Most children in primary school are likely to be able to deal with their own toileting needs. However, it is part of normal life through middle childhood that girls and boys will occasionally have a toileting accident. Some schools have a ruling that staff do not help children at all under those circumstances. Children have to wait until their parent, or other family carer, arrives to change the child. Families are told, 'We are not allowed to change children', with the implication that powers outside this particular school have forced them to leave a child, often distressed and embarrassed, in wet or soiled underclothes.

This approach needs to be challenged when applied to children in primary school. However, some early years settings follow the same rule, adding 'it's child protection policy' to the claim that they have no changing facilities or expect that children are reliably toilet-trained, so the problem should not have arisen. There are also teams who have been told not to help children in the toilet, although 3- and 4-year-olds often cannot manage to wipe their own bottom.

There is nothing in any of the relevant legislation or guidance that justifies refusal to help with ordinary, basic physical needs. Any service that accepts responsibility for children should have the proper facilities to deal with normal events, including toileting accidents. There is no legitimate justification from child protection and writing this ruling into a policy does not make an unjustified stance immune from challenge. Furthermore, such rulings are discriminatory, since a proportion of disabled children will not be continent in childhood.

MAKE ANOTHER CONNECTION WITH . . . FAMILY LIFE

There is very good reason to challenge any behaviour from practitioners that would raise serious concerns, if those adults were within a child's own family. Practitioners have a duty of care as well as obligations about genuine child protection.

How would you judge parents whose normal practice was to:

▪ leave a child in wet or soiled underclothes for long periods of time?

▪ expect a child to deal with their own scrapes or bumps, to be handed a plaster without any contact and denied a hug or touch, even if they were very distressed or shaken by a fall?

Would you consider that the parents or other key carers in the family were safe, caring or responsible?

Minor accidents and intervention for safety

Anxiety about touch has also extended to reluctance to take care of children after accidents. Some primary school teams refuse to administer any kind of first aid. The excuse sometimes given is that children may be allergic to plasters or antiseptic first aid preparations. But this situation should be resolved the same way as any allergy: all the team know that particular children need different first aid treatment. Similar reluctance has been expressed about helping children with sun tan lotion, which leaves them open to the health risks of sunburn.

Practitioners need to use close physical contact when children plunge into an unsafe situation, or because they will not stop hurting each other unless an adult intervenes. Refusal to use touch could well be seen as neglect, a failure in the duty of care. It would also be irresponsible if practitioners let a child continue with a successful escape bid from the school grounds. On outings, a child or vulnerable young person who does not respond quickly to firm words cannot be allowed to run off into the distance, because practitioners fear to use physical contact.

TAKE ANOTHER PERSPECTIVE

Think about what would happen if some settings were honest with families about the unspoken rules. Parents would then read a policy that said something like:

▪ 'We are very anxious that you will accuse us of sexual or physical abuse of your children. We have decided to solve the problem by not touching them at all, not helping them directly if they have accidents (toileting or otherwise) and leaving them to get into danger or be hurt by other children. Rest assured we will not touch your children under any circumstances.'

How would that be received? How many parents would want the problem that worries teams to be solved in this way? When it is put this starkly, what team leader or manager would persist in this approach?

Of course, practitioners must use their greater strength wisely.

- Physical intervention is not the first option every time. For instance, it would be unacceptable to seize hold of a child because they did not immediately comply with a request to pick up a dropped item of litter. Firm words or an uncompromising look enable many children to re-direct themselves.
- Physical contact to stop children and keep them safe needs to be the minimum necessary: a touch rather than a grab, a containing hold rather than rough handling. Your use of physical adult strength has to be proportionate to the situation and to this child or young person.
- The safety of a familiar adult's arms is accompanied by the words that communicate, 'You are safe in my arms' or 'I will not let you hurt yourself.' Your informed judgment may be that this child prefers to calm down from an outburst in a cosy corner, aware of your watchful look from close by.

Practitioners who work with volatile older children need training in the techniques of safe physical restraint. Poorly understood, or wrongly applied, techniques of restraint can injure children or adolescents, especially when more than one adult is involved in the restraint situation. Adults can also sustain injuries themselves. This situation is especially pressing when children live with severe emotional and behavioural disabilities, as they may not respond to lower levels of physical intervention. Children whose experience has damaged their ability to cope with ordinary life may react unpredictably or become increasingly violent – to themselves or to others.

It is good practice to write up in an incident book, whenever you have needed to use physical means to intervene, physically guide in a firm way or restrain a child or young person. Any team needs to discuss the minimal level of intervention that could be seen as 'restraint'. For instance, daily life with babies and very young children is full of times when you gently remove little fingers from poking someone, or carefully untangle a couple of wrestling bodies. However, with younger and older children there is a good reason to keep an accurate note of out-of-the-ordinary intervention. Records also help to judge whether your strategy to guide behaviour is actually working; for instance, have you intervened less often this week to stop a child who bites when thwarted?

TAKE ANOTHER PERSPECTIVE

Children and young people spend many hours of their life in school and they need staff to create a friendly social atmosphere. Then, the younger members of this community feel confident to resolve some difficulties themselves. Children and adolescents will sometimes use physical intervention: a warning touch on the arm or actually holding back a peer who is displaying extreme emotion.

It is important that neither child protection nor behaviour policy prevents this kind of conflict resolution. There are serious problems if schools label all physical contact as 'unacceptable behaviour', whether from adult to child or between children themselves. The resulting atmosphere is nothing less than institutional; it is hard to see how normal community life can develop under such a definition.

If you want to find out more

✤ Boxall, Marjorie (2002) *Nurture groups in school: principles and practice* London: Paul Chapman Publishing

✤ Lindon, Jennie (2003) *Too safe for their own good? Helping children learn about risk and lifeskills* London: National Children's Bureau

✤ Lindon, Jennie (2006) *Care and caring matter: young children learning through care* London: Early Education

✤ *Safeguarding children and safer recruitment in education* (2006) www.teachernet.gov.uk

✤ Piper, Heather and Stronach, Ian (2008) *Don't touch! The educational story of a panic* London: Routledge

✤ NDNA Briefing paper, in partnership with SCOPE (2007) *Managing carer/child contact* www.ndna.org.uk

✤ Scottish Institute for Residential Child Care *The practice of restraining*

children www.sircc.strath.ac.uk/publications/Holding_Safely/
005Holding_safely_five.pdf

SKILLS OF PERSONAL SAFETY

Responsible adults need to support all children and young people to learn about how to keep themselves safe. A key point is neither to wait until something happens, nor to focus only on those children and young people whom you believe to be more at risk. Learning how to keep themselves safe, and being confident about what to do in doubtful or emergency situations, is part of growing up through childhood. Helping children learn is a continuing process over the years, certainly not something that is 'done' after using a story with nursery age children or one session about road safety at school.

A safe perspective on 'stranger danger'

When children or young people go missing, the news media tends to focus on abduction by strangers, with lurid headlines around 'every parent's nightmare'. Any avoidable death of a child is one too many, but abduction and murder by a complete stranger is very rare; it is this fact that makes the event so newsworthy. When children do not survive their childhood, it is far more likely that they have died from accidents (road or domestic) or the diseases that, despite medical advances, still sometimes kill children. To acknowledge these facts does not reduce the terrible loss for families who have been struck by a statistically unlikely tragedy. However, there are serious consequences when adults try to build rules for everyday life on the basis of rare events.

Prominent news items require practitioners and parents to admit that some adults intentionally harm children. But an honest message is that most adults are kind and caring. Saturation coverage, for example in the disappearance of 4-year-old Madeleine McCann (still missing at the time of writing), means that adults have to be ready to answer children's questions. There is sometimes concern that honest conversation undermines the 'innocence' of childhood. But, of course, children are not innocent in the sentimental way presented in some media discussions. Children are ignorant in the most positive sense of the word; there is so much they do not know. Children are learning about the world and they need an accurate framework in which to make sense of events.

Children are statistically more at risk from people they already know. However, the younger generation would not be supported by safety campaigns to make everyone afraid of their own family and neighbours.

The vast majority of parents and practitioners will protect children and some have placed themselves in direct physical danger in order to keep children safe. The genuine risks to children are best met by steadily coaching them in personal safety and life skills. In a similar way, the real dangers to child pedestrians and bike riders are met by teaching children how to be safe near and on the road.

If you want to find out more

✤ NSPCC (2006) *Child abductions: Key child protection statistics*
www.nspcc.org.uk/Inform/informhub_wda49931.html (and go through *Resources for professionals* and *Statistics*)

Learning about personal safety

Whenever possible, supporting children in personal safety should be a joint responsibility between practitioners and families. Like any other aspect of your work, parents have the right to be informed and consulted about your aims. Some conversations will appropriately be shared, with a child's involvement, because, 'this is an important subject that your mum/dad will want to discuss with you too'. It may also be important to ensure that parents understand subtle messages that you wish to communicate. For instance, you do not tell their children to be rude to every adult: strangers or familiar people. You explain that grown-ups do not deserve politeness, if they behave in ways that upset, worry or frighten children.

Older children and young people will begin to move about independently, starting with being at a slight distance from their responsible adult. Safety messages need to be considerate. Children can be unnerved when they gain the idea that danger lurks behind every bush and corner. It is irresponsible to make children or young people so anxious that they dread making even the simplest of outings on their own, or with friends. It is equally risky to create a situation in which some children or adolescents decide that adults make a huge fuss about things that never happen. These individuals stop listening to anything that adults say.

Safety from a strong sense of self-worth

Personal safety is supported by children's conviction of their right to feel and be safe. Children learn in an atmosphere of respect and trust: where their concerns are taken seriously and not dismissed as 'silly'. A great deal of supportive work with children arises through daily experiences, which are not in themselves a source of trouble or worries.

▪ When children are treated with affectionate respect, they learn about personal space and their rights over their own bodies, including a right to say, 'No'. Over time, you can talk about 'comfortable' touches, what makes children uncomfortable, 'happy' sitting distances and 'private' areas of the body.

- Children need to develop trust in their own feelings about appropriate behaviour. This confidence develops from positive experiences around touch and physical care routines. Older children then have a strong sense of 'not OK', when someone infringes on their wish for privacy, for instance when changing their clothes or taking a shower.

- Care over first aid, trips to the dentist and other health needs are further opportunities to build children's confidence and bodily awareness. Any health professional should talk with children, not over their head to the accompanying adult, explaining what they are about to do and definitely not claim 'It doesn't hurt' when any procedure clearly does cause pain.

- Older children can follow the idea of 'good' and 'bad' secrets. 'Good' secrets, perhaps better called 'surprises', are enjoyable because they will give pleasure to someone else ('What we've bought mummy for her birthday'). 'Bad' secrets make children feel uncomfortable or unhappy. They feel they should say something, yet an adult or young person is pressing them to remain silent against their wishes.

Children learn confidence through experience, including affectionate and trusting relationships, and respect shown for their feelings. You affirm children and young people when you listen to their intuitions or 'gut' feelings about people. You would not encourage unreasonable criticisms, but children's view that somebody is 'not nice' or 'creepy' is usually based on their observations. You can have an open-ended conversation with, 'In what way "not nice"?' or 'What does she do that you find "creepy"?' Sometimes the explanation will be innocent; perhaps a child has not understood that her uncle leans close because he is hard of hearing. But there are still alternative ways to solve this problem that avoid the uncle sitting closer than the child wishes.

Materials to support your messages

You need to recall that supporting the skills of personal safety extends over childhood and adolescence: avoid trying to cover too much at one time, or getting too complex for young children. Just as with any other aspect of how you support learning, make sure that any planned experiences or activities will connect in a meaningful way with what you are sure the children or adolescents already know and understand. You have a range of resources to draw on:

LOOK, LISTEN, NOTE, LEARN

Companies now market a range of devices to parents who are anxious about the safety of their children, or the independent mobility of their adolescents. These products include electronic wrist bands and badges sewn into a child's clothing that sound an alarm if the child goes further than a designated distance from the adult. Electronic tracking devices and GPS tracking using a mobile phone are offered for older children and young people who will go on adult-free trips. A microchip has been developed that is implanted under the skin and transmits the location of the child or adolescent via satellite or mobile phone technology.

Explore this issue by an internet search with the phrase 'child protection devices'. Look also at this short article www.safekids.co.uk/ChildProtectionDevices.html

Then consider the following questions, ideally with colleagues or fellow-students.

- Do you feel such devices are justified? Are some more acceptable than others?

- There are concerns that parents or other carers may delegate responsibility to the technology, and that it is far from 100 per cent secure. What do you think?

- If adults feel they need to track, should they tell children and young people what they have done? Should they accept being tracked in their turn?

- Stories, told from books or played out with dolls or puppets, may be a way of communicating simple points to younger children.

- During middle childhood many boys and girls relate well to story telling that works with a 'pause' in the story that enables discussion of, 'what might they do next?' You can also use a 'rewind' that goes back to 'what if . . .' the characters had made a different decision at this choice point. It is wise to ensure that such narratives do not suggest life is continuously risky, for these story characters, the familiar puppets or anyone else.

- Videos, DVDs, appropriate software, books and leaflets can be useful with older children and adolescents, but they do not do all the work for you. Any materials need to be accompanied by conversation at the time and at any later point when children or young people want to talk.

- Sometimes the storyline of a television series or drama, popular with enough children or young people in your setting, naturally provokes a conversation in which safety and risk can be a key issue for discussion.

During middle childhood, girls and boys become more able to talk around any of these fictional scenarios. Sensitive contributions by an adult bring in the perspective that it is not just 'stupid' people who get themselves deep into a risky situation. It helps children and adolescents to identify, in the plot, what made the character think it was safe enough to make the choice that they did. Were they embarrassed to say 'no' to something, concerned that peers might make fun of them, or too trusting for too long of someone who seemed 'nice' at the outset?

SCENARIO: SELENA

Today in your secondary school you have intervened in a shouting match in the corridor between several 15-year-olds. Once you had calmed the group down, it became clear that there was more going on than a temporary disagreement. Selena had been screaming at Ian to, 'leave me alone, you pervert-stalker!' and had called her peer several other offensive names. However, when it was obvious that you were willing to listen, two other students in the group recounted the events that had taken place over recent weeks, and a tearful Selena confirmed what they said.

Ian has been following Selena home and calling her on the telephone, despite being told to stop many times by Selena and most recently by her father. Selena had confided in her close friend, Jake, who had tried to talk some sense into Ian, but only succeeded in reducing the activity for a short while. Ian also follows Selena at school, stands very close and stares at her 'all the time'.

Selena had tried to engage the help of her class teacher. Selena's view is that this teacher 'just didn't want to know' and said to her, 'If you stop encouraging him, then he'll lose interest'. Selena is now angry, distressed and beginning to be scared. In the last few days she has received text messages bordering on obscene, and believes they are sent by Ian too.

Questions

■ **What would concern you about this situation?**

■ **What should probably be your first step now?**

You will find a commentary on page 226.

Rules to guide keeping safe

It is unwise to set up a 'don't talk to strangers' rule that is never discussed for possible exceptions. Older children, let alone adolescents, will start to move around without an adult, either on their own or in the company of friends. Situations will arise in which they need to feel able to ask a stranger for help. An equally unfortunate consequence of the focus on stranger danger is that it has made some people, especially men, wary of offering help to an unknown child or young person, who is lost or in distress. Caring adults need to consider how they offer assistance. But children are at an unnecessary additional risk, if potential helpers walk away for fear of being accused of attempted abuse or abduction.

Useful guidelines

Children old enough to be allowed to move from an adult's side and hand may become separated from a school group or their family in a large space like a museum. Children need to feel confident that they will not be left behind, and proper checking systems in a group must ensure that their trust is never shaken on this matter. Children need to have been told, more than once with a clear visual explanation, about going to the person at the reception desk, or how to recognise a member of staff in public places, such as a library or large supermarket.

Older children and adolescents will make local trips and some will use public transport to get to school. Adults need to take time to show children how to manage the underground or trains before they head off with friends. But even the most careful of boys and girls will get on the wrong bus or tram at least once, or otherwise go astray from their plan. They need to have a good sense of what kind of 'stranger' to approach. It will be wiser to seek directions from someone in a uniform: a play ranger in the park, public transport staff or a police officer. An alternative is to go into a shop and ask a member of staff for directions or the current location (essential in order to use a mobile phone to ask to be fetched). No guideline will ever be 100 per cent foolproof, so children need awareness that adults have to follow rules too. Even 'official' adults should not try to take a child out of the more public area where their help has been asked.

Adults have to follow rules too

You need to establish safety guidance in ways that do not put children at risk. For example, it is potentially unsafe to tell children that they must be polite to all adults at all times, or to insist that grown-ups are always in the right.

- You can encourage courtesy and consideration, but as a two-way process. Help children to understand that some behaviour from grown-ups is anything from mildly inappropriate to definitely unacceptable and removes any adult right to expect politeness.
- Children who are encouraged to follow adult requests need to understand that this guideline does not apply when what is asked seems wrong or makes the child feel very uncomfortable.

205

Children need to know that dubious people, like paedophiles, look 'just like anybody else'. They do not all wear dark overcoats and have menacing expressions. Children and young people need to assess risk based on people's behaviour and whether this seems right, now or later on. It is not a child's responsibility to sort out the 'bad' strangers or less known acquaintances from the 'safe' ones. On the contrary, it is the responsibility of all adults to behave properly towards children.

Children and young people need to be confident that rules for proper adult behaviour hold regardless of whether the children were involved in any misbehaviour; for instance, having wandered off from their school group on a trip. Rules for adults still apply even if children have accepted gifts from the adult or much older adolescent. In fact, the older person is in the wrong for putting pressure on a younger or more vulnerable person. Children are right to be wary of adults, or persuasive young people, who knowingly increase the pressure to behave in ways that would definitely concern their own family.

The right to defend yourself

You should encourage children to deal non-aggressively with their peers and teach them how to use their words, rather than their fists. But it is not safe to tell children that they 'must never hit anyone ever'.

- Older children and young people start to face situations when talking is not going to help and there is no friendly adult close. Children have the right to defend themselves in their neighbourhood from intimidating older children or adults. An effective defence includes yelling at and shoving somebody who will not allow escape through less noisy or physical ways.
- Such choices need discussion with children. You can teach children to shout out loud, push and struggle if they are attacked or grabbed. But do not encourage them in unrealistic estimates of their own physical strength; there is a time to run away, as fast as possible.

Children should never be left with the impression that they are totally responsible for protecting themselves. Adults carry the main responsibility: both in protecting children and in behaving in a safe and proper way. Children, and then young people, need to feel that they can make some decisions and keep themselves safe, but not that this ability is a burden. Some children have done their level best to protect themselves, have said 'no' to an abuser and tried to tell, yet have still experienced abuse. They should never be left with any sense that they failed; the guilt and responsibility rests with the abuser.

TAKE ANOTHER PERSPECTIVE

Older children and young people also must be given the message that it is wise to cease contact with someone whose behaviour is dubious. They need to feel sure that this action is a sign of strength, not weakness.

Older children sometimes feel that they can deal with an adult or adolescent whose actions have crossed the boundary towards inappropriate sexual touching, especially if that person appears mainly 'nice'. They may not realise that sexual abusers, like paedophiles, will increase the pressure until it is difficult to get away from the situation and it feels increasingly harder to tell.

Reflect on your knowledge of older children, or your own memories of adolescence. How can this age group inadvertently get involved with an unsafe person – in ways that look foolish, with the benefit of hindsight?

If you want to find out more

✤ *Kidscape* – materials about personal safety to download www.kidscape.org.uk

✤ *NSPCC* has materials in magazine-style leaflets like *Worried, need to talk?* on www.nspcc.org.uk/documents/worried_pdf_wdf36333.pdf

Safe behaviour on the internet

There is a breathtaking array of information on the world wide web. Children and young people need to learn appropriate search and study skills to gain the benefit of this huge resource. However, the same technology that enables access to reliable materials has also created space for some loathsome websites. In answers to surveys of their internet experiences, most children and young people have reported accidental encounters with pornography. However, many sites will not come up by accident and the more deeply unpleasant ones, those involving pornography or glorification of violence, would require deliberate searching. If young people start to use a club or home computer to access inappropriate materials, practitioners need to tackle the situation as unacceptable behaviour.

It is good practice in a setting or home to keep the computer in a communal area, so that adults can be watchful, without being intrusive. Practitioners in any setting or service need to share the interests of children and young people and be ready to query something on screen that looks dubious. Adults need to install reliable software to block inappropriate access but also realise that the results are rather hit or miss. Some programmes will prevent access to materials that are needed for study and yet fail to block off some offensive sites. Software may also be adeptly bypassed by children and young people who are considerably more computer literate than the adults around them.

Finding support from reliable websites

The current younger generation often look to the internet for self-help information and support groups, as well as face-to-face opportunities. You need to be aware of reliable organisations and their online support groups and chatrooms. Then you can pass information on to young people. For example:

▨ Young Minds have organised *Minority voices: don't fret, get on the net:* a resource listing on-line support groups www.youngminds.org.uk

▨ Older children and young people do not always want to ask adults, however familiar, about sex and relationships. Reliable websites work alongside adult input. Take a look at www.there4me.com, a site designed for 12- to 16-year-olds, with information to download, which also has an option to sign in and ask questions online.

Children and young people need to gain skills to judge information and certainly not to trust single sources, on the internet or elsewhere, especially if the group or organisation is unknown. An additional safety issue is that some websites encourage high-risk behaviour; for example, those that present eating disorders as a misunderstood life-style choice and sites that support self-harm and suicide.

Taking care in a public forum

The Child Exploitation and Online Protection Centre (CEOP) has documented the growing problems of children and young people being targeted by paedophiles by means of the internet. There is a large number of chatrooms, some linked with online games and social networking sites. The CEOP is active in tracking attempts to groom for abuse over the internet and has been part of significant international operations to break online paedophile rings. However in their Strategic Review for 2006–7 the CEOP team also highlight a growing problem of what they call self-generated risk: risky behaviour by children and young people themselves.

The CEOP report does not shift the blame from paedophiles to the young online users themselves. But they make the point that young people need to take responsibility and not put themselves, or others, at risk by providing a lot of personal information in a public forum. Another serious concern is the extent to which young people engage online in cybersexual behaviour: creating and posting sexually themed words and images, about themselves or other people.

WHAT DOES IT MEAN?

Self-generated risk: when the chosen actions of children or young people put them at increased risk, when the danger might otherwise be minimal.

Cybersexual behaviour: provocative words or images posted by young people through chatroom conversation, their personal blog or on social networking sites.

The CEOP review makes balanced points about safety online. Children and young adolescents can be naïve, although technologically knowledgeable, and adults need to build up the safety understanding. But there comes a point, as in all support for personal safety, when young people share that responsibility. The safety messages need to be given consistently from all practitioners involved with children and young people, accompanied by partnership with their family.

The main messages to get across to children and young people are:

- Be cautious about people you 'meet' within an internet chatroom. The text that people type in is not always the truth and often the fiction is about fun. But some adults enter chatrooms, where there will be children and young people, with the intention to trick and distress.
- Be wary about rude, unpleasant or suggestive messages. Do not respond at all, pull out of the exchange and let an adult know what has happened.
- Do not put yourself at risk by posting suggestive material about yourself: in a chatroom, a blog or social networking site. Neither should young people post this kind of information about other people. Offensive postings about someone else can also fairly be seen as cyberbullying (see page 211).
- Be very cautious about giving out personal details, including your home address or name of your school, which could identify you in the real world. Check any exchange of personal information with a trusted adult before you send anything, whenever the communication is with someone you do not know for real.

■ Never arrange to meet someone you have met online unless you go to a public place and are accompanied by an adult, such as your parent. Older adolescents might go with a trusted peer, but still tell someone about the plan. Be very wary of someone who puts pressure on you to keep this contact a secret.

SCENARIO: KIMBERLEY

You are the group leader for the 9- and 10-year-olds in your after-school-club. You have very clear rules about use of the computer and the internet in club time. This afternoon you have had a group discussion about wise rules for the internet.

Kimberley asks to speak with you after the discussion ends and says she is worried about her friend. Kimberley explains that this friend has met someone on line and is enthusiastic about meeting him. You check with Kimberley whether the 'friend' is really her and the reply leaves you sure that it is in fact someone else. However, Kimberley is being pressed by the other girl to be her companion when she goes to meet her on-line contact.

Questions

■ **What would concern you about this situation?**

■ **What should probably be your first step now?**

You will find a commentary on page 227.

Adults need to stress the safety message that children and young adolescents only use chatrooms that have a moderator: a real person who can go online to check the conversations. However, a popular chatroom has a significant flow of information. So, the moderator may only check automated data on whether users have had personal blocks set up against their name, by other users who object to the tone of their conversation. (Acting as a moderator in this kind of chatroom is a regulated activity under vetting and barring legislation – see page 152.)

Even if a chatroom does have a moderator who intervenes online, older children and young adolescents still need to follow the personal safety rule of not to continue talking with someone whose conversation (real or online) makes you feel uncomfortable. There is the option sometimes to step 'out' of a chatroom and have a private online conversation. Some advice suggests that children and young people should be discouraged from taking this option. Other experts take the view that a prohibition is unlikely to be followed and young internet users should be guided on how to take this option in safety.

Visual information

Webcams are video cameras linked to the internet and are a technological innovation that enable full communication over distances between people who know each other. But children and young people need to be reminded that the images are not only effectively public, but also an enduring record that can be copied and distributed. Personal safety online has to include extreme wariness about somebody who is unknown other than online and who is pressing for inappropriate behaviour through the webcam.

Generally, it is wise to do a self-check for anything that is written, said or done visually online: 'Would I do or say this in front of total strangers on my local high street?' The computer may be located in what feels like a safe and private place, but once something is launched online, it takes on a life of its own. Unfortunately, there are many examples in the media for young people of offensive and sexualised behaviour that is promoted as just a laugh. The risk is not only from paedophiles online; adolescents may encourage each other towards sexual exhibitionism that is deeply regretted later, when webcam or mobile phone images have been circulated far beyond their original intended audience. The prohibition about provocative or pornographic images of under-18s applies to adolescents too; even young people should not create indecent images and make them public.

If you want to find out more

✢ Carr, John (2004) *Child abuse, child pornography and the internet* London: NCH summary on www.nch.org.uk/uploads/documents/children_internet_report_summ.pdf

✢ Child Exploitation and Online Protection Centre ((CEOP) *Strategic overview 2006–7* www.ceop.gov.uk/pdfs/CEOPStrategicOverview2007.pdf

✢ www.thinkuknow.co.uk – advice about internet safety aimed at young people

✢ *Cyberspace Research Unit* general advice on www.internetsafetyzone.co.uk.

✢ Livingstone, Sonia (2002) *Children's use of the internet: a review of the research literature* www.children-go-online.net – go through *Reports* and then *Other related research and policy reports by Sonia Livingstone*

Sharing the responsibility to avoid risk

There comes a time when young people themselves, along with their friends, are on that list of 'It's everyone's job to make sure I'm alright' (the title of the review in Scotland, see page 17). Exploration around shared responsibility sometimes becomes embroiled in misunderstandings about attributing blame and guilt.

- Young people who put themselves at greater risk through their chosen course of action are not responsible for the unacceptable behaviour of an adult, or peer, who takes full advantage of that window of opportunity. (The person who breaks into your car to steal a laptop left on display is still a thief. But it is foolish to make it easy and inviting for criminals.)

- Adolescents of either sex deserve an atmosphere, at home and elsewhere, in which supportive adults help them pick up the pieces, when something does go wrong. However, young people are not on the path to a psychologically healthy adulthood, if they are encouraged to deny accountability when their own behaviour increased the level of risk or created unnecessary dangers.

- Adult support through adolescence has to be sensitive to the fact that young people sometimes do not foresee the consequences of their actions. Even apparently streetwise adolescents have areas of naivety. Young people have always been vulnerable to peer pressure towards risky behaviour and also tend to think that bad things only happen to 'old' people.

Advice and information

Studies and materials about safety for young people often fall into the separate groupings of alcohol, use of drugs and risky sexual behaviour. However, the most useful advice recognises that these are usually not separate risk issues. The impact of generous amounts of alcohol, with or without additional drugs, is to lower inhibitions, blur judgement and impair risk assessment. Young people put themselves at risk of different kinds of assault, including sexual. But they also increase their chances of physical damage through road accidents, often simply by wandering into the path of a vehicle. Serious dangers arise from a social life, and friendship network, that regards being completely drunk as an essential part of a good night out. Peer pressure in some groups – not only young people – normalises having no memory of the previous evening and uses drunkenness as an excuse for antisocial or sexually exhibitionist behaviour.

It is crucial not to forget that adolescence is a time traditionally for pushing out at least some boundaries. The most cooperative of young people may rebel if required to be too 'sensible'. Effective programmes in school or other services weave in ways to deal with peer pressure towards any high risk choices. Appropriate initiatives also recognise that adolescence is a time of life when even popular young people usually have doubts about their own attractiveness. Both sexes need sensitive help about boosting self-confidence without legal, or illegal, substances or agreeing to doubtful or indiscriminate sexual activity.

If you want to find out more

✤ Coleman, Lester and Cater, Suzanne (2005) *Underage 'risky' drinking: motivations and outcomes* York: Joseph Rowntree Foundation, summary and report on www.jrf.org.uk/knowledge/findings/socialpolicy/0045.asp

✤ *Drug Education Forum* – briefing papers www.drugeducationforum.com

✤ Lynch, Jeanie and Blake, Simon (2004) *Sex, alcohol and other drugs: exploring the links in young people's lives* London: National Children's Bureau

TROUBLED RELATIONSHIPS BETWEEN PEERS

Children and young people need the experience of adults who handle their behaviour in a positive way, without using threats, verbal humiliation or physical forms of intimidation or punishment. Your setting or service should have a clear policy on how you deal with behaviour and the ideas and approaches should be shared with parents. A positive approach is underpinned by values that view adults as having responsibilities towards children and young people, not just a set of rights over them. The accompanying supportive approach builds on the rights of children and young people to be heard and experience fair treatment, alongside their growing responsibility for the consequences of their own actions.

Dealing with bullying

Some children and young people are abused and neglected by adults. However, a proportion of the troubles for the younger generation arise from each other. A wide range of studies with vulnerable children and young people in residential care has established that they want effective help from adults against persistent verbal abuse, unwanted sexual attention and actual assault from their peers. Practitioners in any setting would normally use policy related to bullying for behaviour between children or young people that aims to hurt, either emotionally or physically. Bullying should always be taken seriously, although a wise adult response is proportionate to what has happened, when the facts are clear.

Bullying behaviour between children or young people includes:

▪ physical attack or intimidation through the threat of attack;

- taking another child or young person's possessions or ruining them;
- persistent verbal and emotional cruelty to peers, including direct offensiveness and spreading rumours through conversation, text messaging or other forms of cyberbullying.

Some elements in bullying between children and young people could raise further concerns. High levels of cruelty, whether emotional or physical, or sexual overtones to harassment raise questions about what has happened to this child or young person that their behaviour is so outside normal range.

WHAT DOES IT MEAN?

Bullying: persistent ill-treatment that is intended to hurt the person on the receiving end, physically or emotionally.

Cyberbullying: a campaign of ill-treatment using words or images through the technology of mobile phones, email or the internet.

Signs of possible bullying

You need to be attentive to changes in a child or young person, without, of course, assuming that any change is evidence of bullying. You will notice that many of the signs of ill treatment by bullying are similar to those that could indicate possible abuse or neglect by adults. The common factor is that a child or young person is being ill-treated and needs appropriate protection:

- Children and young people may tell a trusted adult directly that they are being bullied or answer a friendly question of, 'Is something the matter?'
- Alternatively, they may let you know in a more roundabout way, for instance by saying they do not like school or club any more. They may say they do not want to attend a leisure or sporting activity that they previously enjoyed.
- Children and young people may have injuries, for which they give odd or evasive explanations; their clothes may be torn, their possessions missing or broken, or they may inexplicably run out of their lunch or allowance money.
- A child or young person's behaviour may change, such as a loss of confidence or fear of particular children. Children may regress in development, for instance bedwetting, or experience sleeping difficulties or nightmares.

- Children or young people may show serious over-concern about their hygiene or weight, because they have been targeted as 'dirty', 'smelly' or 'fatty'.
- Children on the receiving end of bullying can show the effects in their physical and emotional health. They may appear depressed, express feelings of hopelessness and in extreme cases resort to self-harm, even suicide.

Why might children and young people bully?

The work of Kidscape has demonstrated that there are different reasons underlying bullying. Adults who genuinely want to help need to keep an open mind about what is happening and why. Reasons are not excuses and responsible adults can still be tough on bullying. But efforts need to be directed in an informed way, given a better understanding of what probably underlies the bullying pattern on this occasion.

- Some children and young people bully because they have no conception that they should limit their demands. Michele Elliot has pointed out that such a child can be a 'spoiled brat' who uses harassment to get what he or she wants.
- Children and young people who have not been indulged by their families may still have learned through life experience that intimidation of others makes them feel good and is a quick route to getting what they want.
- Some older children or young adolescents are essentially 'victims-turned-bullies'. They were bullied when they were younger, nobody helped them and now they are bigger it is 'payback time'.
- Some children or young people have very poor self-image and confidence, despite the appearance of being strong and forceful. They have learned to use bullying, physical or verbal, to boost themselves and feel powerful. However, it is an inaccurate cliché to claim that all bullies have low self-esteem.
- Some bullies are part of a group that intimidates others. The less enthusiastic children or young people feel reluctant to object. The activity is part of the group identity and they will have to find new friends if they refuse to be part of bullying. They may also fear, on the basis of reliable experience, that refusal will lead to their becoming the new targets.

Helpful adult responses

Children and young people who are being bullied need reassurance that adults in whom they confide will take them seriously and help them to resolve the situation. They want adults to understand the situation from

SCENARIO: BREAKSTONE SECONDARY SCHOOL

Consider the following scenario which has a marked choice point.

- **What are the likely consequences of the choice taken by the school?**
- **At the end of the scenario 'rewind' to the choice point. What could have been a wiser option at that point?**
- **What should the school team learn and what might be done now?**

You will find a commentary on page 227

This year Breakstone school introduced a revised behaviour policy with a more specific message that bullying would not be tolerated. Soon after the introduction of the policy, 13-year-old Kelly accused two of her classmates of a campaign of verbal bullying against her. The two girls, who were close friends, agreed they had had several loud arguments with Kelly, but denied all the other details in her accusation of harassment.

Choice point: Kelly's version was believed and everyone involved was told that the school had a zero-tolerance approach to bullying. Kelly's two classmates were given detailed, written warnings about their behaviour. Additionally, their timetable was changed so that they were no longer together in classes with Kelly.

A month later, Kelly accused a teacher of shoving her against the door. There were witnesses to the alleged assault; Kelly's version was disproved and she had to apologise to the teacher. In the discussion that followed, it became clear that Kelly's home circumstances were very disrupted and she seemed desperate for attention. Within the same conversation, she admitted fabricating the allegation against her peers. Kelly was offered support within the school pastoral system, but no further steps were taken about her false accusation of verbal bullying.

'Rewind' to the choice point.

their perspective, and they do not want thoughtless action that only makes matters worse.

- Listen carefully to what is said by the children or young people on the receiving end. Take what they say seriously; it has upset or frightened them, even if at first hearing the events seem minor to you.
- A child who has been bullied may not want you to tackle the children who have done the bullying. It is important to listen and

certainly not to take sudden action. But you may need to explain your responsibility to keep people safe, which means that you cannot simply ignore what has happened.

- If the bullying is happening within your setting or family home, then find an appropriate opportunity for a calm, yet firm, conversation with the accused child, young person or group.

- Avoid adult behaviour that is bullying in its turn. Check out what has happened and listen to what the accused children have to say.

- Challenge children or young people who claim, 'He said we could have his bag' or 'It's just a joke!' You need to communicate that real jokes are shared by everyone involved. These boys or girls did not stop when the child they were harassing was upset and frightened. So this was not a piece of fun at all.

- Reach an accurate view of what happened. Impose consequences where appropriate; these may include an apology (but there is no point in insisting on a 'sorry' that will be insincere) and the return of anything 'borrowed'.

You need to consider, with your colleagues in group settings, what further action needs to be taken beyond this incident.

- Children and young people who have been bullied need support, as appropriate. Affirm that they were right to tell and work to help boost their self-confidence or skills of assertiveness, if this focus might help.

- Consider what you could do to re-direct the children or young people who did the bullying. In some cases they may need continuing support, in order to meet their legitimate emotional needs in less harmful ways.

- Less keen participants within a bullying group may need help to establish other friendships. Adults can make headway, so long as the local culture has not become violent as the norm.

- In some cases, there may be a need for more general discussions to take place, in order to mobilise the power of bystanders, exploring how they felt unable or unwilling to tell or help.

- Does this incident raise more general issues for your setting? For example, have children let you know about times of the day, parts of the building, or outdoor space that need better or different adult supervision?

- Do you all need some new ground rules, discussed with the children and young people themselves? You may well say that hitting must not be children's first reaction here. But they need to be able to raise their voice to a peer who is harassing them, without being told off by an adult for 'shouting'.

In some neighbourhoods, adults need to understand the pressures on older children and young adolescents to join gangs. It is extremely difficult for boys, and to an extent now also girls, to step aside from aggression, including intimidation involving weapons. In some areas it is not an option for young male adolescents to say effectively, 'I don't want to join'.

In settings with a strong and positive approach to behaviour, it can be possible to work alongside the children and young people through the power of group discussion, meetings or an effective school council. Children cannot be expected to tackle and resolve bullying on their own; adults have serious responsibilities. However, supported group work creates an atmosphere in which it is clear to everyone that bullying is unacceptable behaviour from anyone: child, young person or adult.

Guided group discussion can highlight the feelings of the bullied child or young person in ways that the children who have bullied will find harder to ignore. Bullying works best alongside de-humanising victims: their feelings do not matter, they are not 'like us', they deserve what they get, and so on. Children or young people who have bullied should also have a chance to speak up and be heard, so that the group can understand what their thoughts are. Group meetings should be supportive of changes in the behaviour of a child or young person who previously bullied others; the main goal is to change behaviour. An over-emphasis on punishment, rather than consequences, deflects attention and emotions from that goal.

If you want to find out more

✤ Barter, Christine; Renold, Emma; Berridge, David and Cawson, Pat (2004) *Peer violence in children's residential care* www.nspcc.org.uk/Inform/informhub_wda49931.html and go through *Research* and *Research findings*

✤ Elliott, Michele (ed) (2002) *Bullying: a practical guide to coping for schools* Harlow: Pearson Education

✤ Gill, Tim (2007) *No fear: growing up in a risk averse society* London: Calouste Gulbenkian www.gulbenkian.org.uk – summary can be downloaded

✤ *Kidscape* materials about bullying www.kidscape.org.uk

✤ Save the Children (1999) *I've got them. You've got them. We've all got them* Booklet about rights – www.savethechildren.org.uk/en/ 54_90.htm

✤ Peter Smith (2005) *An investigation into cyberbullying* www.anti-bullyingalliance.org.uk

Young sexual abusers

Disclosures about bullying sometimes reveal that children or adolescents have a limited idea of how to relate appropriately to peers because of their own experience of sexual abuse.

Undoubtedly, practitioners, and parents, have to keep a perspective, drawing on their knowledge of development and judging the details of any situation. Every instance of curiosity about private parts is not evidence of abusive activity by children and each example of under-age sexual flirtatiousness is not exploitation by one of the adolescents involved. But neither must practitioners swiftly assume that activity is consensual, especially if that message arises from only one of the involved parties. It is not wise adult practice to decide easily that intimate contact between children or young adolescents is simple, ordinary experimentation. The behaviour of siblings and step-siblings, as well as unrelated children, sometimes goes far beyond a game that pushes into what children say is 'just a bit rude'.

Adult judgment over concerns needs to draw on issues of relative power between children and levels of discomfort of either child in the play.

- In the case of children, the problem is much better described as sexually inappropriate behaviour rather than labelling a child as a 'sexual abuser'.
- Older children and young adolescents have a broader grasp of what is unacceptable, although the whole point is that some boys and girls have had that understanding distorted through sexually abusive adult behaviour.
- In all families – stepfamilies as well as birth families – it is important that parents create clear ground rules about privacy and respect between siblings of either sex. Children and adolescents can bully within their own family and harassment may continue, if parents fail to take a firm line over doubtful behaviour, such as spying on an adolescent sibling in the bathroom.
- Some practitioners have to deal with vulnerable siblings, whose experiences have distorted their understanding of boundaries and led them into sexual activity with each other.

Certainly, practitioners must pay attention when children or young people confide or complain about physical contact imposed on them by a peer. The Cabin Hill Statutory Inquiry Report (2005, www.deni.gov.uk and search by title) investigated events over 1992–3 at the Cabin Hill preparatory school (Belfast, Northern Ireland) arising from claims of sexual abuse of boarding pupils by a 13-year-old in a position of authority over younger boys. The report concluded that more than one boy had been abused and that the activity could not be judged to fall within ordinary adolescent experimentation. The assessment was also that the school staff had failed to handle indications of a serious problem at the time and that it was reasonable to expect a more responsible approach in the 1990s.

NCH was one of the first national charities to address the experiences of young sexual abusers and was part of the Committee of Enquiry into Children and Young People who Sexually Abuse other Children in 1992. The work identified underlying patterns in this kind of abuse.

- An adult sexual abuser may coerce a child or young adolescent into inflicting abuse in their turn. This activity can be part of sexual satisfaction for the adult.
- Abused children can become very sexualised in their behaviour: meaning that they seek to make physical contact with peers in intimate ways that are outside the normal range of behaviour for this age group.
- Children may seek sexual encounters with peers because this is the only way they have learned to make close contact, to express commitment and affection.
- Children may act in a sexual way to a younger or weaker child, more as an exercise of power. The abused child has been made to feel powerless and may be trying to feel powerful in his or her turn.
- All young abusers have not been sexually abused through physical contact. Some have been exposed to pornographic material or exhibitionist adult sexual activity. The child's judgement of normal behaviour has been distorted.

Young abusers can experience a mix of emotions when they abuse others and they do not necessarily experience sexual satisfaction. They may feel:

- very angry at the time they sexually abuse others;
- excited by the sense of power and secrecy;
- temporarily relieved of their feelings of worthlessness through sexual contact with younger children;
- guilt and fear that they are becoming like the person who abused them.

The professional approach has to include support for the young abuser and guidance is usually clear that there should be two, separate child protection investigations. One investigation and assessment focuses on the child or young person on the receiving end of this abusive activity. But another investigation must focus on the young abuser; their actions must be curtailed but the approach to this child or young person must not all be punitive. Practice is sometimes confused by steps to control the abusive actions of an older child or adolescent. In some cases, individuals have had their name placed on the sex offenders register and received minimal support for their own trauma.

If you want to find out more

❖ Department of Health (1998) *Caring for children away from home: messages from research* Chichester: John Wiley

❖ Lovell, Elizabeth (2003) *Children and young people who display sexually harmful behaviour* www.nspcc.org.uk/Inform/informhub_wda49931.html and go through *Research* and *Child protection research briefings*

❖ NCH (1992) *The report of the committee of enquiry into children and young people who sexually abuse other children* London: NCH

❖ Parton, Nigel and Masson, Helen (2002) *The current state of child protection; tensions, contradictions and possibilities* www.hud.ac.uk/hhs/research/acs/hcm.htm

Sexual awareness and relationships in adolescence

Part of growing up is for children and young adolescents to gain an understanding of close relationships, including sexual relations. The unacceptable nature of sexual abuse is that such activity forces children and young adolescents into what should remain a matter of informed consent between people of adult years. The legal age at which it is judged that a young person can agree to sex (heterosexual or homosexual) is 16 years of age across the UK, with the exception of Northern Ireland where the age is 17 years.

Sex and relationships education

Across the UK, secondary schools – and sometimes primary as well – offer some level of sex and relationships education (SRE). However, children and young people usually want to be able to talk with their parents, as well as familiar practitioners. Families share with schools the responsibility to prepare their sons and daughters for the events of puberty and the facts of adult sexual life.

▪ Children and young people need to build age-appropriate knowledge in a context that enables self-respect and respect for the feelings and rights of other people in any relationship.

221

■ Part of safeguarding is to ensure that children are not exposed to inappropriate or distressing aspects of the adult world. However, they are not protected by being denied any level of knowledge until practitioners, or parents, have no choice.

■ Throughout childhood, it is wise for adults to respond to children's curiosity and answer their questions or comments. Any practitioner's response needs to be informed by knowledge of children's usual development: what are ordinary questions and interest and what raises concerns about this child or adolescent because their focus is out-of-the-ordinary.

■ Young people usually welcome the chance to talk, in a safe environment, about practical issues and to fill in the information gaps that exist, even for apparently knowledgeable adolescents.

LOOK, LISTEN, NOTE, LEARN

Some clothes and toys, aimed at girls in particular, have increasingly sexy overtones. The American Psychological Association became very concerned about the prevailing culture in the United States; see the *Report of the APA Task Force on the Sexualization of Girls* (2007) – summary, full report and other links on http://www.apa.org/pi/wpo/ sexualization.html. This problem of blurred boundaries between adult sexuality and the world of children has definitely reached the UK. (I share this concern and do not accept that objections are evidence of misplaced prudery.) Look around at:

■ Clothing stores and toy shops: what products are pitched at under 8s or 8–12s? Are there dubious items for children? If so, in what way?

■ High street newsagents and service petrol stations: what 'adult' magazines are displayed (without masking paper covers)? Would it be acceptable for literate children to read the front cover headlines out loud in the store?

■ What messages do these products give to children or adolescents of either sex?

Programmes may be offered within mainstream school or delivered through other means to young people, whose experiences mean their schooling has been intermittent. Disabled children and young people also need access to well-judged SRE. Their needs are sometimes overlooked, with the assumption that they will not be sexually active or are less likely to be at risk from people who will take advantage, neither of which are accurate assumptions.

The sensitive task for practitioners, whether through an SRE programme or within informal conversations, is to be a responsible grown-up, yet avoid breaching the privacy of adolescents and their personal relationships. Adults need to raise the key issue that it is possible to decline as well as agree to sexual activity. This focus for discussion is about recognising pressures on young people; it does not have to rest on a total abstinence option. Young males, as well as females, may feel under pressure to become sexually active, or to lie about what they have actually done so far. Both sexes can be harassed with insults around, 'What's the matter with you?' if they express reluctance in this arena.

Giving information and advice
Health professionals are bound by rules of confidentiality in their helping relationship with over-16 or 17s, who for most legal purposes count as adults. The usual assumption would be that adolescents were competent to ask about their own health issues, and make some decisions on the basis of information, supported ideally by their family. Doctors or school nurses are not obligated to inform parents that their daughter or son has asked about contraception or other sexual health matters. The right to confidentiality would, however, still be over-ridden by safeguarding concerns if a young person appeared to be sexually active as the result of coercion, or exploited in some way.

Practitioners in daily or residential services, who are a trusted adult to this adolescent but not a health professional, can find themselves in an uncertain situation, if young adolescents seek very specific advice. Conversations may move towards choices of action about sexual activity below the legal age of consent, or dealing with unwanted pregnancy. The advice from the Children's Legal Centre is for practitioners or teams to be very cautious about taking on a role that assumes a level of parental responsibility.

LOOK, LISTEN, NOTE, LEARN

Many young people are likely to seek information on the internet. It is therefore wise that practitioners are aware of reliable sites and consider using materials from those sources as a feed for discussion. Take a look at these websites: www.likeitis.org.uk, www.need2know.co.uk or www.ruthinking.co.uk. Notice that more general issues like dealing with peer pressure are connected with feelings and exercising genuine choice over sexual activity.

Responsibility to protect but not intrude

No younger generation wants the grown-ups, parents or otherwise, to be unduly curious about their adolescent flirtations and early sexual exploration. It would be right to be suspicious of any adult showing a zealous interest in exactly what young people were doing and with whom. However, responsible adults need to be alert to the well being of young people of both sexes, whatever their sexual orientation. Coercion and sexual bullying can happen across any boundary.

It is often not straightforward to reach a judgement about whether a close involvement between adolescents is unequal in ways that raise concerns. Considered judgement, and careful discussion with colleagues, has to weigh up the ages of the young people involved and what is within normal range for close physical contact or flirtatious activity for this age group. You would interpret the same behaviour differently for children of 7 or 8 years of age than for 13- or 14-year-olds and for 16- or 17-year-olds. It is not judged possible for an adolescent who is younger than 13 years of age to agree to any kind of sexual activity. So such behaviour immediately raises concerns about undue pressure and likely abusive patterns of behaviour. If another, equally young adolescent is involved, concerns would also arise about his or her experiences so far.

Responsible practitioners should be aware if clues of words or body language suggest that one young person, even of a similar age, is applying high levels of pressure, coercion or threat to the other young person, in even low-level sexual activity. This situation would remove the possibility of informed consent between peers and can arise from a very forceful young woman, as well as females being intimidated by their male peers.

- A key issue is about equality, or inequality, of power between the two people. Relevant factors include individuals' learning or physical disabilities, which could make them less able to understand or refuse approaches of their peers.
- Careful risk assessment by concerned adults also needs to allow for whether one young person appears to insist on a level of secrecy beyond the usual wish for privacy. A similar cause for concern would be if alcohol, or other substances, were used to ensure the agreement of a less keen partner.
- Whatever else is happening, adults would be right to feel concern if one of the young people involved had a track record of coercion or sexual maltreatment of peers, either acting alone or with accomplices.
- Even 14- or 15-year-olds, ably supported by friends, can exert real pressure over a peer. Sexual bullying may be more common when led

by young males. But groups of young females have made life miserable for a young male of similar age. Actions that would be called inappropriate touching, even sexual assault, when carried out by males, should not be overlooked just because the shouters and gropers are female.

An inequality of age between young people would not automatically be a source of concern. But an older partner might be a reason for adults to worry, if that person wielded considerable influence over the younger one and appeared keen to detach him or her – usually her – from family and friends. It is, however, a responsible first step to ensure that a male adolescent or young adult is aware of the real age of a girlfriend who looks older than her years.

Within the culture of some families living in the UK, it is utterly unacceptable for young women to be sexually active prior to their marriage. However, within cultural traditions tolerating more flexibility, young women who are sexually active outside a couple relationship are still more likely to be judged harshly than their male peers. Despite many changes in UK society, a double standard still operates between the sexes. It is socially unjust and inconvenient to a working definition of female empowerment that focuses on saying 'yes'. Nevertheless, there are serious negative consequences for the well being of young women who agree to sleep with many young men in their neighbourhood, often assuming that sex indicates some level of affectionate commitment. However, female adolescents can also put themselves at risk from males outside their immediate group, differing by age, ethnic group or cultural background, who cultivate young women for whom they have no respect whatsoever. Such patterns of deliberate exploitation and grooming have occurred now in several neighbourhoods.

LOOK, LISTEN, NOTE, LEARN

Download *Hands off,* the NSPCC magazine-style leaflet that explores what is meant by sexual abuse. Discuss the content with colleagues or fellow-students **www.nspcc.org.uk/documents/hands_off_pdf_ wdf36237.pdf**

■ Look at pages 1 or 7, which raise hard-to-judge issues with someone who is known, including peers, who pushes an adolescent beyond the comfort zone.

■ In your view, are these situations meaningful for young people?

If you want to find out more

✛ Find out more about sex and relationships education from the Sex Education Forum www.ncb.org.uk/sef and Learning and Teaching Scotland www.ltscotland.org.uk

✛ Hamilton, Carolyn (2006 6th edition) *Working with young people: legal responsibility and liability* Colchester: Children's Legal Centre

✛ London Child Protection Committee London *Procedure for Safeguarding sexually active children* (2007) www.londoncpc.gov.uk/ safeguardingsexuallyactivechildren2.htm

Commentary on the scenarios

Each commentary offers some possibilities. You and your colleagues may raise other ideas and perspectives.

Meadowbank Nursery (page 192)

Good practice with very young children is shown by attention to their personal care and giving time. There is no 'just' about care or personal care routines and young children's learning can only be supported in an emotionally warm atmosphere. The current situation needs to be resolved on a team basis and with proper leadership from the head of centre. Thorough discussion is needed within a room, and maybe also a staff meeting. But continued professional development will be necessary for the practitioners who devalue care. If they are sent on a training course, a senior practitioner must follow up with links into their practice.

Further problems arise if the more caring practitioners do not get support from the head of centre. A possibility is to talk in confidence with a local advisor: raising the concerns in a professional way and communicating that some active intervention in this setting would be appreciated.

Selena (page 204)

You are faced with a situation that needs proper attention and checking out for reliable information, including whether your colleague was as unhelpful as Selena describes. If Selena's account is accurate, her class teacher has shown poor practice. Such lack of respect for young people's concerns undermines any policy about bullying and the principle of telling. The teacher's behaviour needs to be addressed within the team.

The students, not only Selena, need to know that an adult is taking the situation seriously. Some of the alleged problems occur in school, so it is appropriate and necessary to explore the claims. There needs to be proper exploration of Ian's alleged behaviour so far. This discussion will need to address whether he has also sent the text messages. If you are confident the sender was not Ian, then that issue needs a separate approach. Some 15-year-olds lack social skills, but Ian's actions have gone beyond awkwardness: he seems not to understand 'Stop' and that he has distressed and scared Selena.

The next steps depend on the extent to which Ian responds to clear direction from the school about acceptable and unacceptable behaviour. It is likely that Ian's parent(s) should be informed, especially if there is any written agreement about his behaviour from now on. Ian and his family need to understand that, assuming Selena's allegations are true, then the young man's behaviour could become a police matter if he continues to harass any young woman in this way.

Kimberley (page 210)

You need to tell Kimberley how pleased you are that she has spoken and confirm that she should not be her friend's support. Kimberley needs to be encouraged to talk with her parents about the situation, with your help if she wants. Her family can then contact the family of the friend who is putting herself at risk.

Breakstone Secondary School (page 216)

The school team needs to understand much better how an effective behaviour and bullying policy should work in practice. At the choice point, the first incident with Kelly was poorly handled and it seems likely that a more thorough exploration would have at least queried Kelly's version.

After the second incident with the teacher, the two girls accused in the first incident will now feel even more badly treated. Young people have a strong sense of justice and these girls deserve a full apology not only from the staff, but also from Kelly. It is not acceptable for the adults to walk away from that responsibility.

The school team need to reflect on their written policy and their practice. All staff need to appreciate that mishandling will shape the attitudes of the students as a whole, not only the students who were unjustly punished. A policy to combat bullying will not work if adults fail to listen or take unthinking punitive action, so that they come across like 'bullies' in their turn.

7 Supporting children and families

There is no single pattern of how best to help children and young people or to offer support to their families. A common strand is for practitioners to connect general good practice of partnership with families, most often parents, with their approach to safeguarding. This chapter also covers practice issues that especially arise for working with families who are involved in the child protection process.

> **The main sections of this chapter are**
>
> ✳ **Working with parents to support children**
>
> ✳ **Child protection and the courts**
>
> ✳ **Families and children under stress**

WORKING WITH PARENTS TO SUPPORT CHILDREN

Good contacts between your service and the local child protection team should include practical discussions about the contribution of your setting and your own skills as an individual practitioner. You might be asked to be especially attentive to a child's regular attendance, their well being, play and conversation, without distorting their experiences with you. Children and young people need a place and familiar people, with whom everything is as 'normal' as possible.

Supporting children in need or at risk

It will be helpful to know whether other specialist input is being offered to the child, young person or family. You are not asking for confidential details of counselling or therapy. However, some shared information will help you know the identity of 'Lisa', for example, who apparently talks with this child every week. Counselling for children and young people, including play therapy, is a specialised task and practitioners should not attempt to undertake this kind of work unless they have been trained. But not all children or young people who have been abused want or need special therapy. They can be well supported by what you offer within the ordinary day or session. You will share this understanding and knowledge in your partnership with some families.

Talking and listening

The key guideline for practitioners is to treat children and young people as normally as possible, without pretending that nothing has happened. An abusive experience can make children and young adolescents seriously doubt themselves and the trustworthiness of adults. You can help in the following ways, all of which are applicable to the support of adolescents, although you would not use the same language when speaking to a 14-year-old as would be appropriate for a 5-year-old.

- If children say critical things about themselves, you need to offer positive emotional support. Avoid saying simply to the child that 'It's not true' and do not deny the child's feelings with, 'You don't think that, really'.

- Acknowledge that the child has expressed a strong feeling with a phrase such as, 'It must be difficult for you to feel that way'. You do not bluntly disagree with the child's negative remark, but reply warmly 'I'm glad you come here to the club' or 'I don't think you're a waste of space' (an adolescent's own words).

- Take the time to encourage a distrustful child and do not feel that your skills are in question. Some children take a long time to open up and you have to be pleased with small successes. Adolescents can have experienced years of rejection or unpredictability from adults and they then often persist in rejecting any help in their turn. Such a relationship is emotionally very wearing for the practitioner, which is another reason why support for adults is so necessary.

- Children need your support and sympathy, but pity is rarely a helpful emotion to express to a child or young person in distress. Avoid talking about children in hushed tones or expressing the message of 'Poor little Wesley', whether you communicate through spoken words or your body language.

- It is important to relate to abused children in play as you would to any child: enjoying their satisfaction and looking for opportunities for them to learn. It will not be helpful to seek deep meanings in every drawing they do, or find greater significance in rough physical play than you would for another child.

Children do not forget about distressing events just because adults avoid talking about the topic. It is more likely that children decide that adults are cross with them or believe that the young person did something very wrong. The ways in which you offer time and attention will vary according to your work. Ideally, you would respond when a child starts to talk. However, there may also be times when you have to say carefully to a child or young person, 'I really want to hear what you want to tell me, but there is no way for us to have privacy until (give a time). Can we please talk together then?'

A positive approach to behaviour

Children need your understanding of the likely impact of distressing experiences and you may have to adjust the expectations you usually bring to a child or adolescent of this age.

SCENARIO: ANGIE

Angie (9 years old) has seen many angry rows between her parents. This afternoon she has started a conversation with Jane, her key person at the after-school club.

Angie: Do you shout at Mark (Jane's partner)?
Jane: No, I don't. We try to talk about things when we disagree.
Angie: Do you yell at Bella (Jane's child)?
Jane: No, you know me, Angie. I try hard not to raise my voice unless there is a really good reason.
Angie: My mummy shouts at daddy all the time.
Jane: Yes, I realise that. But not all mummies and daddies shout at each other.
Angie: Mummy yells at me and I haven't done anything.
Jane: Yes, I know. You hear a lot of shouting, don't you, Angie?
Angie: Mummy says I'm a 'useless little cow'.
Jane: I'm sorry your Mummy says that to you, Angie. I don't agree with her at all. You're a real help here and I like you very much.

Questions

■ **What is probably on this child's mind?**

■ **What issues are raised for you by the conversation and how might it continue?**

You will find a commentary on page 261.

■ But children and young people will not benefit from a tolerance that is without limits. Practitioners may be concerned that keeping to ground rules will add to the burden of an already distressed child. On the contrary, it can reassure a child or young person that these grown-ups take responsibility and act in a predictable manner. They may complain, but this behaviour is in the usual 'job description' for being a child or adolescent.

■ You need to be prepared for individual reactions from children. When children have witnessed bouts of domestic violence, they may become aggressive in their turn and need to be guided towards non-disruptive ways to deal with ordinary conflicts. However, some children become distressed by even mild altercations, or expect fierce words from you for minor problems. They need a great deal of reassurance, such as, 'It's alright, Barry, everyone makes mistakes. We'll mop it up together'.

■ When one child brings her problems into a group, the other children need to feel reassured that you are aware of what is happening.

Children who have been abused should not be allowed to release their misery or anger on their peers through unacceptable behaviour. It is unfair to the other children and will not help the distressed child in the long run, not least because their actions will undermine their peers' inclination to offer support.

- Even younger children can be caring towards each other and react well to simple explanations that do not break confidences. Perhaps you might explain, 'It's okay, Melissa, I know you didn't say anything mean. Paresh gets upset if people shout at him (including Paresh in your glance at this point – so he does not feel excluded). Just say things in your indoors voice.'

If a child's abusive experience is emerging through behaviour in the group, you may have to give an explanation to other parents, which does not breach confidences about the other family. Explanations should never become excuses and parents should not be expected to tolerate their own children's pinch marks, or emotional distress, because another child is experiencing family problems. Explain simply to concerned parents those steps you are taking in your provision to deal with the situation that their child has faced. In a small community, some parents may be fully aware of the stresses in a particular family. You take a professional stance by listening to any concerns expressed by other parents, or information about a household. However, you do not allow such exchanges to slip into a regular conversation.

Supporting parents involved in child protection

In most cases children and young people will stay in the setting they are already attending or with their childminder. The exception would be if safeguarding issues have arisen about the setting or childminder. Otherwise, relationships with the parent may not be easy, but partnership can still be possible. Parents do not necessarily turn against their child's setting or childminder, even if it was you who first raised the concerns. Parents may feel that, despite mixed emotions, their child's key person or class teacher is basically on the side of the child and family. It is also possible that a parent is looking for support and trusts the practitioner to provide it. Some parents ask for help when they recognise that they are close to ill-treating their child.

Families who feel convinced that a practitioner or entire team has behaved badly may choose to move their child to another school or cancel a childcare arrangement. If worries about the child have been fully resolved, the change has to be accepted as the family's choice. However, if any concerns still remain, it is crucial to inform social care services that the family is no longer in regular contact with your setting or service.

Your partnership with parents, or other key family carers like a grandparent, may take several forms as you:

- continue a working relationship with parents who are alleged to have abused or who have admitted ill-treating their child;
- support a non-abusing parent who is distressed and confused that their partner has abused the child(ren);
- work with parents whose child has been abused by somebody else, either within the family, a trusted person allowed contact with the child, or less usually a stranger.

Even when children are taken into care, it is good practice for every effort to be made for a young child to continue at a familiar nursery, or for an older child or adolescent not to have to change school. In this situation, practitioners in nursery, school or club establish a partnership with the child's foster carer, or an adolescent's key person from the residential home. You need to work closely with these fellow-professionals and deal with practical details (alongside the child or young person) about how you will refer to someone who is in a parental role, but is not a carer from the birth family.

Only practitioners in more specialist settings, and those with additional training, would undertake counselling or other therapeutic work with fellow-adults. But a very great deal of support can be offered through daily communication with parents and other carers. A friendly face and a continued welcome to your setting may be exactly what some parents need. Their life has been turned upside down and their child's nursery, school or out-of-school club is the only element that is constant. Non-abusing parents may really appreciate a place where they and their child are well known from before the current crisis. You are available to talk about difficulties if they wish, but you still show the collage their daughter completed, or tell how their son had such good ideas about the garden make-over.

Sharing the support for an abused child

The confidence of non-abusing parents in their own skills can be severely shaken. They may try to make everything up to the child with treats or by abandoning normal family rules. Or perhaps a parent feels that the child needs the security of positive family boundaries, but is overruled by someone else in the family. You can listen to this parent's dilemma and explain how you are dealing with similar choices and concerns during your time with the child or young person.

Parents may need to be encouraged to respond to their child's overtures in conversation. Non-abusing parents and other carers are still sometimes told that it is better not to talk about a distressing experience with their child or adolescent on the 'least said soonest mended' principle. You may be able to reassure them that, although children should not be pressed to talk, parents should show that they are responsive and will listen.

A child who has been sexually abused may make inappropriate physical approaches to other children or to adults. Parents may not realise that such consequences could follow from their child's experience. You can offer support by acknowledging the seriousness of this kind of behaviour, but explain that it is not unusual for sexually abused children. Explain to the parents how you deal with this situation through the twin messages of 'I like you and I am happy to have you close to me' and 'The way you want to touch me is not the right way between a child and an adult'.

Talking and listening

Some parents may wish to talk with you about what has happened and is yet to come. These supportive conversations should be private. Parents may have deep and confused feelings; they may become distressed or angry (not necessarily with you) and they may talk about their child(ren) in the hearing of other children or parents. If what seemed to be a quick question about information is turning into what ought to be a longer and private conversation, then you should attempt to halt the parent at this point. Explain by saying, for example, 'I want to give you some proper time, but it's impossible now. Can you can come back at . . . ?'.

There is no single blueprint for how parents will feel. They may express any of the following emotions, and feelings often change over time. They may feel:

- Shocked and unable to take in what has happened. A non-abusing parent may still find it hard to believe what has occurred. An abusing parent may feel stunned that matters got this much out of hand.
- Angry that someone else has abused their child. Or an abusing parent may feel aggrieved that justifiable discipline has been called abuse, or that a child's word is believed over an adult's counter-claim. Parents feel anger towards the person(s) who first raised the concerns, even if they also feel a sense of relief.
- Guilty about not realising earlier or not facing nagging worries about a child's physical or emotional state. A non-abusing parent may fret over why the child did not tell. An abusing parent may feel very guilty about what has been done and may be willing to accept help, or not, of course.
- Relieved that the abuse has been discovered and is being challenged. A neglectful parent may feel many other emotions but still feel that it is better to get help than to struggle.

- A conflict of loyalties between commitment to the child and to the alleged abuser, when this person is a previously trusted partner or friend. Sometimes rejection is directed, at least initially, towards doubting or blaming the child or young person who has disclosed abuse.

- Shame and embarrassment about what has happened and that family life has become public. Once a child-abuse investigation starts, professionals have the right and obligation to ask many questions that intrude into what otherwise are private family matters.

- Distress and pressure from other family members, or local people, who are not being supportive. Non-abusing parents may have to deal with relatives and neighbours who want to disbelieve the child, who blame the parent, or who feel that the whole matter should have been handled within the family, immediate community or faith group.

Parents can doubt their ability to protect their own children. Non-abusing parents whose child has been ill-treated by a relative or close friend feel a serious loss of confidence about their own judgement. In cases of sexual abuse, for instance, children may have been abused for some time and have said nothing; or what they did say earlier was not recognised as a serious cry for help. When the facts emerge, the non-abusing parent(s) are faced with a time of weeks, months, or even years, when their perception of events was completely wrong. This kind of discovery of abuse has been likened to bereavement or loss.

You will support parents if you acknowledge their feelings and recognise the mixed and changing emotions. You are not saying that they are right to feel that way – for instance, in almost blaming a child for keeping the abuse a secret – but you show that you have heard what they said. You may be able to present an alternative perspective, for example, explaining why children can have such difficulty in telling. It is also important to recognise that once an abuser has been removed from a family or denied any more access to a child, the situation does not suddenly revert back to what was normal before the crisis. Children have distress to work through and so, too, will the non-abusing adults of the family.

Safety and risk assessment

If parents are angry with you or with your team as a whole, you need to acknowledge that anger, rather than try to argue or get cross in return. There is no sure way to deal with anger and defuse the power of that emotion, but the following guidelines will help:

- Stay calm and do not answer the parent's anger with your own angry or hurt replies, or counter-claims that the parent is being unfair.

When emotions run high, there is little point in trying for rational discussion at that point.

■ Show that you recognise the feelings. You are not saying a parent is right to be angry, nor agreeing, perhaps, that all social workers are interfering busybodies.

■ Explore if a parent is ready to listen. You might try, 'I appreciate that you're really fed up with what has happened. You feel the social worker won't answer your questions. Do you want me to explain what happens next?'

You still have a responsibility for children in the setting, who can become distressed by adults who lose control. A furious adult or one who is using offensive language needs to be told firmly, 'This isn't the time and place to be this angry. You're frightening the children.' All practitioners have a right to their own safety and any setting should have clear procedures on how staff come to a colleague's aid when an altercation risks getting out of hand.

When your setting or service is involved in child protection, it is appropriate to make a risk assessment about the behaviour of adults who are alleged to have abused or neglected their children, or who may already have admitted to their actions. Adults cannot neglect children unless they are responsible for them, so this pattern of maltreatment would not usually have a direct impact on other children in your setting. Physical, emotional or sexual abuse could be a potential risk issue while a parent was present legitimately, for instance to pick up their child. But this risk could only become a serious issue if a parent were left alone with a group, which should not happen in any case.

It is appropriate to remain alert to the actions or words of an alleged or identified abuser, without over-reacting. Practitioners have to deal immediately with unacceptable behaviour from any adult that occurs within the boundaries of the setting, regardless of whether words or actions are directed at a parent's own child or another. Perhaps an accused parent or other family member is involved directly in your setting, for instance as a volunteer. Then it is necessary to take appropriate action that is proportionate, and does not assume guilt when none is certain – see page 165 about allegations.

Information about the child protection process

If there is an investigation ongoing, then parents should definitely be kept informed of what is happening. The assigned social worker should be ready to explain to parents, but they may prefer to talk with you. Practitioners should understand the child protection process, so they can explain what will happen next and that some events (for instance, taking children into care) are definitely not inevitable. You can ensure that parents know about case conferences and their right to attend. Explain your role in such events and that, although the parent may appreciate a familiar face, you have to give your setting's impartial report as a contribution to the meeting.

Normal practice is now that parents are invited to case conferences on their child or adolescent, unless there is good reason to exclude them. Parents can see the process for themselves and, at least sometimes, will feel reassured that people are not simply condemning them. Parents should also see that different professionals work together and want to understand how far family members are motivated to take an active part in the plan for this child or young person.

The focus within the case conference must be on the child or young person. The professionals present have to be ready to express the more difficult issues about the family situation. As the practitioner who will give a report, you should not make comments that will surprise a parent. You should have had any difficult discussions with the parent prior to the case conference. Nevertheless, it can be hard for any professionals to listen to parents' distress or fear about what is happening. You may be discomforted by an articulate defence by parents of their actions, or a verbal attack about professional assumptions or attitudes.

CHILD PROTECTION AND THE COURTS

All the professionals involved in a child protection case work to achieve a plan to protect children without court proceedings, unless there is no option, in order to keep a child or young person safe from harm. Practitioners are therefore unlikely to have to go to court, especially if you do not work in specialised services for vulnerable children and young people. However, you could be involved as a witness yourself, or in supporting children who have to go into the witness box.

The two broad types of courts are civil and criminal, and there are significant differences in how they operate.

Civil proceedings

Civil courts are less formal than the criminal courts and the standard of proof is different. In civil proceedings for child protection, there has to be evidence that suggests on the balance of probabilities that a child has been abused and that a named person (or persons) is the likely abuser. (In criminal proceedings, the evidence has to be on the basis of beyond reasonable doubt, which is a tougher test of any evidence.) Child protection legislation across the UK allows for some strong legal steps to be taken to protect children and young people, that do not require a criminal court case and prosecution of the alleged abuser.

Civil proceedings in court can lead to rulings that the named alleged abuser stays away from the child, or can only have supervised contact. A social worker might be involved in such contact, or some arrangement might be made with a daily setting that supported vulnerable children and their families. Alternatively, a ruling might be made that children should be removed from the family home as the only way to ensure their safety. Foster parents or the staff of a residential children's home might then be supervising the agreed contact. Civil proceedings allow for a range of serious steps to protect the child(ren) but do not involve any prosecution against the alleged abuser(s).

Civil proceedings are not only less formal, but tend to be less confrontational than the legal process in a criminal court. Yet there can still be disagreements and arguments. If an acceptable solution had been found between social workers and the family, the case would have been resolved outside the courtroom. Civil proceedings are more likely to occur when:

- The local authority social workers cannot reach an agreement with the family about what has happened, or is continuing to happen, to the child and the family's response to the situation.
- The child protection team judges that children need to be removed from the family and no voluntary arrangement has successfully been made with the parents or other relatives.
- Custody and access issues in a matrimonial dispute hinge on an allegation of abuse by a parent of the children.

Children do not have to appear in civil proceedings (whereas they may be a witness for the prosecution in a criminal case). Children in civil proceedings have an independent legal representative, different from the solicitor for the local authority and another solicitor representing the parent(s). The court also appoints a Guardian *ad litem* (GAL), who is a person who will continue to represent the child's best interests and wishes. GALs are advocates on behalf of the child. In Scotland, the independent representative for the child is known as a safeguarder. Scottish law is especially strong on providing ways for children's views to be heard.

It is possible that early years, school and out-of-school practitioners might be called to civil proceedings to give evidence about a child. You might have knowledge and records of a child's physical health, development or behaviour that had a bearing on the child's need for protection. You may have observed important incidents between a parent and child, or the child may have chosen to disclose an experience of abuse to you. The procedure in civil courts is not as adversarial as criminal proceedings, but many of the key issues about being a reliable and credible witness are equally important.

Criminal proceedings

Only a minority of child abuse cases reach the courts as part of a criminal case. A prosecution will only be undertaken when the abuse, if proven, falls into the category of a crime and there is sufficient evidence to support the case. So, most practitioners will not experience court process as part of their work. However, it is not appropriate that any practitioner should be a witness without prior support. Practitioners who work with vulnerable families, and certainly those in services for looked-after children and young people, should have training about the court experience sufficiently well in advance of their need to enter the witness box.

Preparation to be a witness

The local authority lawyer should find time to meet you before your appearance, in order to explain what will happen and go through any practical issues about your evidence. The lawyer can alert you to the kind of questions that they will ask you as the case is developed. Other people in court will not necessarily be experienced with children, so you will need to explain any specialist terms or preferably use ordinary language. The local authority lawyer should help you prepare in this way.

If you are uncertain about anything or have new information, speak up at this point. Lawyers' nightmares are court scenes in which their witness suddenly reveals new facts or voices doubts. You should raise, if the lawyer does not, any potential problems of inconsistency in your account, gaps in your written record, or likely disagreement over interpretation between you and other witnesses in the case. The lawyer may also have made some good guesses about the questions likely to be put to you by the defence lawyer. If there seems to be a delay in your being contacted, then phone the local authority lawyer yourself, especially if you are facing your first time as a witness. You might also welcome a prior visit to the courtroom. Unless you have been on jury service, you may have very little idea of what to expect.

The experience of being a witness

Smart clothes are appropriate dress for attendance at court; on the day of the hearing avoid wearing very casual clothing, even if this style is usual for your work. If you are going to use your notes in the witness box, ensure everything is in your bag. You should arrive at the court with time to spare, so that you do not feel rushed. Do not let yourself be drawn into discussions or disagreements with other parties outside the court, for instance parents or other relatives who dispute the events.

Once you are in the witness box there are practical guidelines to bear in mind.

- You will be asked to take an oath on a holy book, that is relevant to your faith, or make an affirmation that you will speak the truth. Then you are guided through your evidence by questions from the prosecution lawyer.

- Speak steadily and clearly. Look up and not down at the floor. Although the lawyer asks you the questions, you should direct your reply to the magistrate or judge sitting at the bench.

- You probably need to talk slightly slower than a normal conversational pace. The clerk of the court takes notes and magistrates or judges usually make their own notes as well.

- If you could not hear all or part of a question, ask for it to be repeated. If you do not understand the question, then say so.

- Witnesses are not expected to remember everything when they are going to be asked for many details, as you could be. It is acceptable for you to take notes into the witness box and to consult them to ensure the accuracy of your answers, for instance about dates or what a child said.

- However, as soon as you use notes you can legitimately be asked when you made this written record; this is another reason why you should be prompt in your record keeping. Your notes can also be copied as evidence and made available to the defence lawyer in criminal proceedings.

- Your evidence should be limited to what you personally observed, what you can honestly say 'I saw' or 'I heard'. Quote a parent's or child's actual words only if you are certain that those were the exact words used. Otherwise give the gist of the communication.

- Answer the question and do not move onto other topics unless what you have to say is a relevant explanation. You would normally reply more than 'Yes' or 'No' to a question, although this simple answer is sometimes appropriate.

- In some cases, your evidence may include positive points about a parent or other adult. Express these as honestly as you would any negative evidence.

- Part of your legitimate evidence may be second-hand, in that you were told something by another person. Express this accurately with, 'Mrs Jones asked to speak with me on the 25th May. She told me she had seen Lena's mother hit the child and Lena had fallen against the concrete post.' You know what you were told but you did not directly observe that Lena was hit by her mother.

■ You may be asked to express an opinion based on your knowledge of the child or of children in general. Support your opinion with 'because . . .' or 'my experience has been . . .'. Do not go beyond issues on which you can reasonably express an opinion.

■ If you do not know the answer to a question, then it is better to say, 'I don't know' or perhaps 'I wasn't able to hear what Teddy's father said to him. I could see that Teddy was crying and pulling away from his father.'

In criminal proceedings, witnesses are first questioned by the prosecution lawyer. There should be no surprises in this part of your evidence, since your answers are part of the local authority and police case. You will then be cross-examined by the defence lawyer. In civil proceedings the parents' lawyer may ask you questions. The job of defence lawyers is to defend their client, so their responsibility is to challenge the reliability of any evidence. Lawyers use a number of adversarial tactics in order to achieve this aim. The end result for witnesses can be anything from slightly to highly uncomfortable.

Defence lawyers are not being personally vindictive, although some tactics are very unpleasant. Their job is to express public doubt about your observations or professional experience; your role is to remain focused and calm.

■ Avoid getting either annoyed or distressed. Do not relax, even if the approach is initially friendly. You are not having a conversation together; the defence lawyer is cross-questioning you on behalf of the accused.

■ Take no notice of theatrical tactics used by some lawyers, such as looking contemptuously at bits of paper and throwing them onto the table. Ignore doubtful expressions, shrugs or other dismissive body language and concentrate on the questions.

■ Answer only the question that is asked and reply with what you can contribute from your direct observations and professional experience. If you are asked questions to which you cannot honestly give an answer or opinion, then do not guess. For instance, you might be asked, 'What did Steven's uncle think about the child's claims?' and you may have to reply, 'I don't know. Mr O'Hare didn't say anything to me.'

■ If you are asked the same or very similar questions again, do not feel provoked into giving an extended or different answer, as though you were wrong the first time. If a lawyer uses this tactic, you could say courteously, 'I have already answered that question'. The magistrate, judge or the prosecution lawyer should also step in to prevent your being harassed.

- Take each question on its own and do not be afraid to think for a moment before replying. You may experience the defence tactic of asking you a series of quick questions to which you can honestly reply 'Yes', followed by a question to which your answer should be 'No', but the lawyer hopes to establish a pattern of your agreement.

- If you have inadvertently said something that is inaccurate or not what you meant, then correct yourself straightaway.

If you are called as a witness, it is unlikely that all the practical issues about evidence outlined in this section will arise. But some of them will be part of your court experience. Be prepared and remember that your time in court is a particular kind of exchange. Concentrate on the task in hand and do not relax until you have left the witness box. This section assumes you will be called as a witness for the prosecution. It is possible the defence team may call you. Most of the practical points are still relevant; certainly do not be tempted to go beyond what you know, however much you like a parent.

LOOK, LISTEN, NOTE, LEARN

After you emerge from court, it is important to give yourself a short time to re-adjust and, later to reflect on your experience in the witness box.

Avoid reworking the details and certainly do not spend ages on regrets. Take the opportunity to talk with someone in your team, if the experience has actually caused you distress.

Otherwise, what have you learned – for yourself and to share with colleagues?

- In what ways was your experience more or less what you expected and in what ways different?

- In what ways did your preparation, which may have included a training workshop or support from the local authority lawyer, help you to be ready?

- What would you add in terms of advice to other practitioners?

- What might you do differently next time? But realise that each experience as a witness will vary in the details.

Children and young people in court

Children and young people can be directly involved in court proceedings because they are called as a witness, or because they themselves are accused of a crime. The age of criminal responsibility is 10 years of age in England, Wales and Northern Ireland and 8 years of age in Scotland. Practitioners who work with vulnerable children and young people may support them because they are involved with the police owing to the child's own behaviour. The resources on page 244 are also helpful for this situation. But the main focus here is for the support of children or young people who give evidence against their abuser.

Young witnesses

If a child protection case involves a criminal prosecution, then children or young people could be called as a witness. If the alleged abuser pleads 'guilty', then children do not have to go to court. But if the plea is 'not guilty', then children's evidence has to be heard in court and they have to undergo cross-examination. Adult witnesses can find the experience daunting and need to be prepared. The situation can be even more distressing for children, especially since in these legal cases, they are the person who has been ill-treated.

Children are in a particularly vulnerable position when there have been no adult witnesses to the abuse and there is no clearcut physical evidence of maltreatment. This situation often applies over allegations of sexual abuse, since abusers put immense effort into ensuring secrecy and are not necessarily violent. The evidence of a young witness, or more than one, may be the only strand of the prosecution's case. The evidence of children has become more acceptable in court, partly as a general recognition in child protection that children can understand the difference between truth and lies. However, prosecutions are rarely taken forward when children are younger than 6 or 7 years of age.

Apart from considerations of the weight of the evidence, police and social workers are also concerned about a child's well being. They have to make a balanced decision about the likely distress for a child of being a witness, against the public interest that an abuser is prosecuted and punished in law. This decision should be taken in partnership with the family, unless they are involved in the abuse. Older children and adolescents should be enabled to understand what is involved and give their informed consent or refusal.

The court process in a prosecution is confrontational and can be distressing for any witness. The defendant must be presumed innocent until proven guilty and it is the job of the defence lawyer to question and undermine the evidence against their client. The judge should control inappropriate tactics, especially when children and adolescents are involved. However, it is still difficult to decide whether individual children and young people will be able to cope with cross-examination and having their word doubted in public. Young witnesses state from experience (see the NSPCC report *In their own words*) that you have to be ready for accusations of lying. They also recount that the prosecution lawyer will make it difficult for you to tell your story: by interrupting and talking over your replies and using complicated words that you do not understand.

There are strict guidelines that govern how children and young adolescents give evidence in any court case, not only one about child protection. If guidance is followed, then it should be possible to reduce potential distress for children, as well as to ensure a good quality of evidence.

- Children can be interviewed for their evidence before the court hearing. The child is interviewed in a special police suite that looks like a living room and the whole interview is video recorded.
- Children must not be prepared for the interview and there must be no leading questions from the adult. In other words, there must be reassurance that children's evidence has not been shaped by anyone, including the police.
- A video link between the courtroom and a separate room can be used so that children do not have to be in court, and they do not have to face their alleged abuser. Alternatively, some courtrooms have a screen that shields the child or young person from the majority of the court. However, some courts do not offer this facility.
- Each court should have a child witness officer who supports the familiarisation process for a child or young person and ensures that, on the day, they are able to access the court and a waiting area without risk of contact with the alleged abuser, their family or other supporters.
- Young people older than 14 years will usually be asked to take an oath or make an affirmation: the same commitment to speak the whole truth that is required of adult witnesses.
- Children will still be cross-examined by the defence lawyer, whether in open court or via the video link, and have to answer questions about their evidence, including details of the abusive experiences. In sexual abuse cases, in particular, young witnesses find this experience embarrassing and intimidating.
- The main thrust of the defence is likely to be that the young witness is lying or, at the very least, confused and mistaken. Some lawyers have insinuated that children have been complicit in their own sexual abuse.

It is important to know about local support facilities for young witnesses. Apart from the child witness officer of the court, Victim Support often have someone who can support in a similar way. Additionally, the NSPCC has several witness support projects around the country. If there is a programme in your area, they may be able to provide a trained supporter for a young witness.

A practitioner who is closely involved with the family can have an important role in supporting a child, young person and non-abusing members of their family. Everyone needs to have realistic expectations of what may happen. The more you understand court process, the better you can prepare the child or young person, as well as offering support after an unpleasant court experience. You may need to work hard to reassure the child or young person that you believe them and rebuild their confidence.

Children and young people who are deeply distressed by their abuse may need the support of specialised therapy or other forms of counselling. Such support used to be postponed until the criminal trial was complete. This process could take months and it has now been accepted that it cannot be in the child or young person's interest to have their necessary help delayed.

If you want to find out more

✤ *Criminal Justice System* – the Witness Virtual Walkthrough interactive facility www.cjsonline.gov.uk (click on *Witness*, then a search for 'Child Witness' brings up a list of resources)

✤ Plotnikoff, Joyce and Woolfson, Richard (2004) *In their own words: the experiences of 59 young witnesses in criminal proceedings* London: NSPCC – summary on www.nspcc.org.uk/Inform/informhub_wda49931.html and go through *Research* and *Research findings*

FAMILIES AND CHILDREN UNDER STRESS

All the key laws about child protection across the UK include the option to use family support services in order to ensure the welfare of children judged to be in need, as well as sometimes the best way to protect individual children. Some of the low-key support will be offered by practitioners who are already involved with families through their child or adolescent. Families under serious stress or those who have put their children at significant risk will need more specialised services. Practitioners in early years, school and out-of-school services still need to know about those possibilities.

Support in child care and parenting skills

Parents whose neglect or abuse has largely arisen through ignorance of their child's basic needs may accept help within your setting. The different types of community-based centres for children and families aim to offer informal support, as well as easy links with local family support services. Specialist family centres, known by many different names, will be organised in a more formal way; for instance, a firm agreement (maybe called a contract) will be made with parents for their attendance, as well as that of their child. Any setting has to be clear about the boundaries to the service they offer and what can realistically be done, without reducing the quality of work with children and young people.

Some parents may genuinely have very little idea about children's physical and emotional needs. The problem may have arisen because the parents are very young themselves. Some adults might have had a disrupted childhood from which they have no useful memories of how to treat children well. In other families, serious stress may have overwhelmed the parents and blotted out concerns for their children. Depending on the other calls on your time and energy, practitioners who are the key person for this kind of family may be able to offer advice on basic child care, usual patterns of development and ordinary 'problems'. You need to be familiar about the other local services, which parents may be willing to approach.

Family support services are offered in different forms and their extent and availability varies considerably between different areas of the UK:

■ Home visiting schemes can be a great support to families under stress and those who would welcome some advice about play and dealing with their children's behaviour. Home visitors, from schemes such as 'Home Start', are part of a broad-based family support service. They do not only visit families about whom there are child protection concerns.

■ Some early years and school settings are able to offer supportive parents' groups that can cover a range of issues and again are not only for families about whom there are worries. Some groups and sessions follow one of the parenting programmes that are widely available.

■ Some schools have organised the funding for home-school link workers, whose role is to help families who are struggling. If schools are successful in creating a welcoming atmosphere, many families may regard them as the best first contact point for seeking help.

SCENARIOS

Imagine if you were the practitioner facing each of these situations. Consider the following questions:

- ■ **What do you feel are the main issues here?**
- ■ **What would be your next steps?**

You will find a commentary for each scenario on pages 261–2.

Winston

15-month-old Winston often seems to be grumpy in the morning but today he was very out of sorts and wandered around in a daze until lunchtime. When his mother picks him up you ask whether Winston has been unwell. She replies, 'I think we overdid the sleeping medicine.' You look puzzled and she continues, 'Winston is an awful sleeper. My mum said to give him a tot of sherry. She said that was what she used to do and it didn't do us any harm. I was having a terrible time and one night I started to shake him. So I thought the sherry would be safer.'

Janice

Janice is 3 years old and has attended the pre-school for several months. She started when her mother, Ruth, had not long given birth to a baby boy, Sachin. Janice's brother is very unwell. He has been in hospital several times, but as yet with no definite diagnosis of what is wrong and his illness has caused Ruth to become distraught; she has told you that she is getting very little sleep because of Sachin's screaming and Janice wanting to get into bed with her and her husband.

When she started pre-school, Janice was a relatively quiet child but made friends and joined in the play activities. But over the last few weeks you have noticed a significant change in Janice and she spends a lot of time rocking and hugging herself. She has complained to you of stomach aches and one day says that her bottom is 'so sore'. You tried to speak with Ruth, but she rushed off the premises, taking Janice with her to a hospital appointment for Sachin. The next morning Janice comes to pre-school with a long scratch mark over one cheek. Her mother asks to speak with you in private and as soon as you are alone together, she bursts into tears.

Janice's mother admits that she hit her daughter the previous afternoon. She had found Janice trying to put Sachin in the dustbin. Janice said, 'I just snapped. I hit out at her and my ring scratched her cheek. It's terrible. I said I would never, ever hit one of my children. My father used to hit us; I can't believe I did it.' You take the opportunity to ask about Janice's remark of having a sore bottom. Ruth replies straightaway, 'It's the constipation. Janice won't go to the loo for days, then of course she's in pain when she finally does go. And then she has stomach aches as well.

> We've taken her to the doctor and he just says Janice is obviously jealous of all the attention for Sachin and she'll get over it. I'm at my wits' end!'

Clement

You work in a local authority children's centre. Clement, who is 2 years old, has started in your group this week. Clement seems happy and he talks with single words and a few 2-word phrases. But he has very little idea about what to do with the play materials that you would usually give to his age group and is keener to handle the baby toys. He cannot walk but stands steadily holding onto a firm surface and cruises along by hand holds.

The health visitor has told you that Clement was found a place in the centre because she realised that the boy's mother and grandmother did not let him out of his cot. They both expressed great worries about the potential dangers to Clement if they let him roam around their flat, or if they took him out into the local neighbourhood. Both women seem caring towards Clement but the settling-in time at the centre has been hard, as his grandmother has been especially concerned about Clement's safety in the playroom and the centre garden.

- Specialist family support workers may be assigned as a response to child protection concerns. In that case, the family can be well aware that noticeable improvement in the well being of their children is essential, or else more serious intervention will be the next option.

A consistent theme is encouraging, and enabling parents to put their child's needs to the forefront. It is not only families in poor or deprived neighbourhoods who put their children or young people at risk. Some two-parent families with substantial incomes place such a high priority on their adult careers that children struggle with a patchwork of different carers or inadequate supervision. Different issues arise when older children and young adolescents are at potential risk. In this case, family support may be more about setting boundaries for an older child, who is allowed dangerous levels of freedom, or who is expected to take significant domestic responsibility to enable adults to continue with their life.

If you want to find out more

✤ Allard, Amanda (2003) *'The end of my tether' The unmet support needs of families with teenagers – a scandalous gap in provision* (a report and advice leaflet) www.nch.org.uk/uploads/documents/EOMT.pdf

✤ Barrett, Helen (2003) *Parenting programmes for families at risk: a source book* London: National Family and Parenting Institute

✤ NCH Children and Families Project (2001) *Creating a safe place: helping children and families recover from child sexual abuse* London: Jessica Kingsley

✤ NCH (2007) both these reports also discuss family support and parenting programmes – *Literature review: the emotional harm and well-being of children* www.nch.org.uk/uploads/documents/Emotional_ harm_lit_review2.pdf and *Literature review: resilience in children and young people* http://www.nch.org.uk/uploads/documents/Resilience_ Literature.pdf

✤ Utting, David (ed) (2007) *Parenting and the different ways it can affect children's lives: research evidence* www.jrf.org.uk/bookshop/eBooks/2132- parenting-literature-reviews.pdf

Domestic violence

Domestic violence, or domestic abuse, is not only linked with poverty or stressful living conditions; the situation can arise in any social class or ethnic group. Some writers use the term only to mean male violence towards their female partners or ex-partners. Statistics indicate that men are most often the perpetrators of violence in the home. But it has to be recognised that in a small minority of cases, it is the woman who is violent towards her partner or their children.

WHAT DOES IT MEAN?

Domestic violence: use of aggression towards fellow-adults, often partners, within the family home.

Children and young people are adversely affected by living in a home in which there are regular violent disputes. Their emotional well being and psychological development are poorly affected, even if they do not suffer any physical abuse themselves. The problems of domestic violence have been brought into a more central position within safeguarding, with the recognition that the situation always affects children and young people; the only question is by how much. The likely risks are that:

▪ Children are distressed by continuing arguments in their home and by the threat of possible violence. They may be torn by conflicting loyalties between their parents and can also be pulled into the damaging secret that nobody outside the family must know how bad matters have become. It has been accepted that significant harm can be experienced by children when they frequently see and hear the ill treatment of someone else.

- Children may fail to be protected in a home full of violence. Conflicts between the adults may erupt into physical attack and the children are caught in the middle. The adults may not intend that the children are injured and they do not directly attack them, but adult violence injures children as bystanders.
- Parents who are prone to violence sometimes also attack their children, or step-children, or threaten to do so in order to control their partner. Domestic violence directed at adults is sometimes part of a more general abusive pattern in which children are directly abused, physically or sexually, and family pets are also cruelly treated.
- Parents under extreme stress are not in a position to offer their children the kind of support that is necessary for healthy development. Additionally, some mothers or fathers divert their frustration and anger onto the children. Children in their turn may become aggressive to other children, or turn in on themselves to become distressed and withdrawn.

In order to help parents, you have to have some understanding of the complex situation that they face. People who have very little experience of the problem often say, 'But surely, she could just leave'. Yet women, or the smaller number of men, who are on the receiving end of domestic violence often have very few options of where to go; and the extended family is not always supportive. Despite the violence, abused adults may still be attached to their partner and continue to hope the violent person will eventually change or hold to their promise to do so. They may excuse violent actions as explained by drink or stress, or feel that they somehow provoke outbursts. Parents in violent homes may be afraid their children will be taken into care, unless the violence remains a family secret into which the children are inevitably drawn.

You may not be the person to help directly but you could be invaluable in alerting a parent to other sources of help and support.

- You may be able to reassure parents that they do have resources for the children, when failure to protect them from a violent partner has seriously undermined this confidence. Parents sometimes also have mixed feelings, seeing the violent partner in the actions of one or more of the children.
- It is a practitioner's responsibility to alert parents to the fact that children are affected by violence in the home. Sons and daughters

can suffer serious emotional distress, even when they are not physically harmed. Parents may feel that they are protecting children, perhaps by tolerating the violence and that the children are not really aware of what is happening. You may also support a parent who needs to be honest with children about what is happening or the steps their non-violent parent has taken to protect them.

▪ Another issue, relevant to the whole staff of any setting, is that children whose fathers are violent need models of caring, non-aggressive men. A positive image may be offered if you have male practitioners or volunteers.

Substance abuse in the family

A significant number of children and adolescents live in families where life is seriously disrupted because of their parents' alcohol consumption or use of illegal drugs. A noticeable proportion – some sources estimate this to be up to about 25 per cent – of children on child protection registers have reached that position because their parents' use of drugs or alcohol has put their children at significant risk.

Local services often need to be more effective in working together. For instance, professionals involved with addicted adults should always be alert to whether individuals, who can scarcely take care of themselves, are responsible for the well being of children or young adolescents. The same principle of practice applies to adult mental health services. It is important not to stigmatise adults who seek help for alcohol or drug dependency, but all professionals involved must pay attention to children in the family. Drug users and alcoholics are not necessarily bad parents, at least not deliberately, but it is irresponsible of any service team to ignore the fact that the capacity to be a safe parent is seriously compromised.

Some adults who are addicted to alcohol or drugs make significant efforts to take care of their children and get help for themselves. However, any kind of addictive behaviour absorbs an adult's attention and will often affect parents to the extent that they cannot possibly ensure the well being or direct safety of their children. Carelessness about bottles of alcohol, drugs and the paraphernalia that accompanies drug addiction inevitably places young children at risk. Parents who are regularly drunk, or otherwise unaware of their surroundings, are also opting out of keeping their children, or young adolescents, safe from dubious behaviour of the adult's friends or acquaintances.

In some families, one parent may work hard to protect children from the impact of the other parent's addictive behaviour. However, in some households both parents are involved and children are unsafe in what operates as an open house. An unknown number of grandparents have taken on primary responsibility for their grandchildren because the parents are unable to cope as the result of their addiction. Sometimes addictions remain a family secret, or older children step in as young carers to mask the problems. Older children or young adolescents coping with this situation often want help but are blocked by not knowing who to ask and because they fear that telling a teacher, for example, will result in the break up of their family by social care services.

Much like other young carers, older children and young people who have stepped into an adult role because of addiction in the family often still care deeply about their parent(s). They want help for themselves and effective support to get their parent back on a safe track. Like many other young carers, these young people have become knowledgeable about their parent's problem and want professionals to respect that knowledge.

Children and young adolescents should be seen as 'in need' whenever drug use affects family life. They are also affected when older siblings have a drug problem and parents are struggling to deal with that situation. Family life is disrupted by the continuing anxiety and the actions of young addicts, such as stealing from family members. The presence of drugs increases the risk that siblings may try them and some addicted young people have deliberately introduced their siblings to drugs.

If you want to find out more

✣ Advisory Council on the Misuse of Drugs (2003) *Hidden harm: responding to the needs of children of problem drug users* www.homeoffice.gov.uk

✣ Barnard, Marina (2005) *Drugs in the family: the impact on parents and siblings* York: Joseph Rowntree Foundation, summary and report on www.jrf.org.uk/knowledge/findings/socialpolicy/0215.asp

✣ Gorin, Sarah (2004) *Understanding what children say about living with domestic violence, parental substance abuse or parental health problems* London: National Children's Bureau summary on www.jrf.org.uk/ Knowledge/findings/socialpolicy/514.asp

Children who run away

Many children and young people who go missing have not been abducted by strangers, or taken without permission by family members such as their non-custodial parent. Safety and safeguarding issues arise because some children or young people run away from their family home or other place where they are supposed to be living. Young people under 16 years of age

> **LOOK, LISTEN, NOTE, LEARN**
>
> Unless you work in a specialist centre, it will not be appropriate to attempt direct work with parents on complex problems, such as severe depression or alcoholism. Your support will be through knowing about local facilities and sharing this information. It is not your role to push parents into using helplines or support groups; such decisions remain their choice.
>
> Develop a file or folder, updated at regular intervals, containing details on local services and special units. You can add national organisations that offer advice on reliable websites, telephone helplines or practical leaflets. If you already have such a resource, then check it covers these safeguarding issues.

cannot legally live on an independent basis in the UK. But the circumstances of a missing 16- or 17-year-old could still trigger serious concern.

Different patterns

There is no typical reason why children and young people run away. The one consistent theme is that children and young people run away because they face some kind of problem that they cannot see how to resolve in any other way. Running away should always be noticed and not treated as an ordinary event of every childhood or adolescence; many families never have the experience of sons or daughters running away from home.

- Most individuals who run are within the years of adolescence but some children as young as 9 or 10 years of age go missing as runaways.
- Runaways are not the same as homeless young people. Some runaways become homeless and some homeless young people started as runaways. Children or young people on the streets, or in unsafe places to stay, can become involved in what are called survival crimes in order to live; such crimes include stealing, begging and prostitution.
- Some children and young people go missing for short periods of time. Generally speaking, children who are absent within a single day would not then be described as runaways. However, their actions might still be a matter of concern, depending on where they went and with whom.
- Running often seems to be largely unplanned: a spur of the moment choice. However, some runaways have thought ahead about this

SCENARIO: JEROME

You are the class teacher for Jerome, who is 13 years old and the eldest of a family of four. His mother has a history of alcoholism and has been physically violent in the past. The view of the current social worker is that Jerome's mother has 'turned the corner' on her alcohol problem and is better at dealing with her anger. A new partner in the household is regarded as a stabilising influence.

Jerome's mother came into school today to tell you that her son had gone missing for most of the weekend. The police were called and Jerome was found safe at a friend's house, but his mother is concerned he may run away from school. You were ready to talk with Jerome this week because the standard of his work has fallen in the subject for which you take him. Your colleagues have also found that Jerome misses most homework deadlines.

Initially, Jerome appears surly and launches into, 'Not you too! My mother's been on at me non-stop. I just went to my mate's for some peace and quiet.' You have had a good relationship with Jerome, so you look thoughtful and ask, 'Do you want to talk about what's going on for you?'

Bit by bit, it emerges that family life is far from stabilised. Jerome appears to take most of the responsibility for his siblings and his mother wants to talk at length to him about her own abuse as a child, which he finds distressing and embarrassing. Jerome resents the new partner for trying to take over as if he is their father, and says that this man and his mother have started heavy drinking sessions. The family social worker rarely talks with Jerome, and only does so when his mother or new partner is present. You are concerned about the burden of responsibility placed on Jerome, but realise he is afraid that he will be split up from his siblings if social care services decide that his mother cannot cope.

Questions

■ **What main issues should concern you about this situation?**

■ **What should probably be your first step now?**

■ **You will find a commentary on page 262.**

option, although they have not necessarily found a safe place to stay. Sometimes, a residential home has to deal with organised runs which seem to be motivated by a desire for drama and excitement.

■ It appears that most runaways do not go far and many return to their own family, foster or residential home of their own accord. There is no neat pattern about the level of risk and how far runaways travel. Some individuals want to reach a place or people with whom they were once happy and they may be safe at some distance from where they are now supposed to live. Some young people go no further than just across town, possibly to the home of an abusive individual.

- Some runaways have left because of a single incident that may seem minor to the adults. However, some children and young people run away to escape from persistent and serious distress, sometimes direct abuse or neglect from their carers, or a campaign of bullying from their peers, for which no adult is offering help.

- Some adolescents have not run out of choice but have effectively been thrown out by their family. Parents, other relatives or a step-parent have made their life impossible or have sometimes literally pushed them out of the door.

Some adolescents run off only once, others continue in this pattern. Not surprisingly, what matters is whether they have been helped effectively with what led them to run away in the first instance. A common factor is a lack of communication or mis-communication, including a serious row with parents or other carers, or children anticipate trouble because of something they have done. Older children or young people feel, with justification sometimes, that nobody will listen to their problem and adults will blame them.

WHAT DOES IT MEAN?

Runaways: young people under 16 years of age who have left home or substitute care without agreement and stayed away for a significant time, given their age or disability.

Survival crimes: actions taken by children or young people, that may be anti-social or criminal, in order to cope when they have run from home.

Missing from school or college

Absences from school or colleges of further education should also be taken seriously; they should be neither dismissed, nor treated only by punitive means.

- Children and young people who truant are often becoming enmeshed in a social network that divides them ever more from their peers in school and raises the possibilities of further risks.

- Additionally, some children or young people who have patchy attendance at school are absent because they are young carers (see page 257). They do not deserve to be punished for choosing to take care of a mentally or physically sick parent, when no service has offered effective help.

■ Some young females who go missing may have been forced into marriage (see page 135), taken abroad for the illegal procedure of female genital cutting or are very ill as a result (see page 133).

MAKE THE CONNECTION WITH . . . REGULAR ATTENDANCE

Unexplained absence of a child or young person should always be followed up in nursery, club, school or your home as a childminder. Practitioners in any setting have a responsibility to check, when this child or young person should have arrived today, or when they should have been seen by now, even on an irregular pattern of attendance.

It is good practice that parents, and, as appropriate, young people themselves, realise that you are concerned to know they are alright. Most times, such follow-up will prompt an apology that you were not told about a planned absence or unexpected illness. However, there have been cases where a nursery or other setting has sounded the alarm and young or vulnerable children have been found with a desperately sick parent, or children have been abandoned in their home.

Possible reasons for running away

It would be important for any family to consider why their child or young person felt compelled to run away. Residential settings, such as boarding schools, as well as homes for looked-after children and young people, need to take a serious look at patterns of running. Studies of children and young people who run away have found that looked-after children are significantly over-represented in the group. Of those, the great majority had run from residential units rather than foster care. The problems that led them to run might well pre-date their becoming looked-after, but some residential settings were noticeably more successful in reducing the risk. Certainly it is important that running should not be regarded as 'just an occupational hazard' in services for vulnerable children or adolescents.

Several projects have noted that similar residential units in the same authority can have significantly different rates of 'running away', sometimes called absconding. The atmosphere of a unit, as well as the reaction to the event of running, seems to be important. Several broad issues emerge for practice and much of the advice also applies to children who run from their family home.

■ A positive approach to handling behaviour in a unit creates a better atmosphere in which troubles do not escalate and children do not have to run in order to get attention, for example either personal or effective help against fellow-residents who are bullying them.

- Running away should be treated as a potential child protection issue and not exclusively as 'bad' behaviour from children; it may also reveal problems about life in this group setting. In the past, scandals around abuse in residential settings were highlighted, and in some cases ignored, when significant numbers of the children tried to run away from the home: the location of their abuse.

- Good relations with other agencies, including the police, should build a response that acknowledges the seriousness of the situation, without punitive labelling of runaways as deviant. The police should immediately be involved if a missing child or young person is on the child protection register. (Not all looked-after children have been judged at risk in this way.)

- Children or young people should be collected or welcomed back if they return of their own accord. Some discussion needs to follow: a delicate balance between addressing the serious issues and avoidance of nagging or a row.

- Conversational sessions can communicate that the child or young person was missed and workers should try to explore reasons for an extended and worrying absence beyond the agreed return time, as well as absconding.

- Some basic strategies can help, such as encouraging young people to phone in, so that they are not 'absent without leave'. Such a process helps to show adolescents that practitioners genuinely worry about their well being.

- The concerns and distress of some runaways has highlighted the need to involve children and young people more effectively in choices about their placement, as well as negotiating time with their family and friends.

If you want to find out more

✤ Biehal, Nina and Wade, Jim (2002) *Children who go missing: research, policy and practice* www.dfes.gov.uk/qualityprotects/pdfs/missing-children.pdf

✤ Morgan, Roger (2006) *Running away: a children's views report* www.rights4me.org.uk (Reports are under 'Be Heard' on the website)

✤ Rees, Gwyther and Siakeu, Jean (2004) *Thrown away: the experiences of children forced to leave home* www.childrenssociety.org.uk/NR/rdonlyres/ 2BE2E581-5A56-4378-9ABB-CCA06AE0D08C/0/ ThrownAwayFullReport1.pdf

❖ The Children's Society – reports and the Safe and Sound campaign on www.childrenssociety.org.uk/what+we+do/Our+work/Children+at+risk+on+the+streets/

Young carers

A considerable number of daughters and sons are responsible for much of their own family life: taking care of their parent(s) and sometimes also younger siblings. Their situation is still often overlooked, despite more public awareness of the extent of the problem since the 1990s. These young carers are in a different situation from children and young adolescents who are effectively raising themselves with no adult help (see page 259). Many young carers have loving parents who do not in any way ill-treat them. These adults are unable to be a full mother or father because of chronic physical or mental ill-health, or the impact of disability of different kinds. However, some young carers have to step into adult shoes because their parents are incapacitated by drug or alcohol abuse.

WHAT DOES IT MEAN?

Young carer: children or young people who take on a parental role within their family, looking after themselves, one or both parents and younger siblings.

From available statistics it seems that most young carers are adolescents, but some older children carry similar levels of family responsibility. The problem has been long-standing and often hidden. Young carers, together with their parents and young siblings, can be very anxious about the family situation becoming public, out of fear that a blunt social care response will be to take children into care. Such a response is unlikely, unless there was significant risk, and family support services should be the chosen option. However, young carers frequently say that help is delayed, sporadic and sometimes a poor fit, given the family's needs.

Young carers share all the stresses that are experienced by adults who care for an incapacitated family member: the normal household duties, worrying about money, dealing with a range of health and other professionals, responsibility sometimes for medication, disrupted sleep and trying to take care of younger family members. It is hardly surprising that young carers, whether an only child, the eldest or most responsible of a sibling group, often struggle to take good care of themselves, feel tired and worried much of the time. Older children and young people can also be troubled by health problems like back troubles, arising from lifting or helping to support the full weight of an adult.

The plight of a young carer often comes to light because the school takes action about unauthorised absence or frequent late arrival. Sometimes a sympathetic teacher finds out about the young person's domestic burden when following up the lack of homework. However, many of the signs that should concern practitioners could indicate other problems, including neglect by an able parent. It is another reminder about recognising a serious concern, but keeping an open mind about the origin of the problem.

- Young carers may be frequently late because they have to get their parents up and dressed and walk siblings to another school before they arrive at their own. They may have many unauthorised absences: staying home to deal with a crisis or simply being exhausted. The last item on their daily list may be to do their homework, so teachers challenge the quality or absence of set tasks.
- Adult concerns may arise about personal hygiene and presentation, including clothes or proper school uniform, of the young person or younger siblings.
- They may appear very tired (and not from adolescent partying), anxious or depressed. Other patterns of behaviour present as playground problems, but are actually an indication that this child or young person has no emotional reserves to deal with the ordinary ups and downs of life with peers.
- Some young carers have to deal with verbal bullying about their parent's mental health or substance abuse. They may also have difficulty in ordinary socialising with peers (or not, of course). Young carers appear mature but have often missed out on ordinary childhood experiences. They may feel they have little in common with their peers and are wary about confiding in them.

Apart from well-judged family support services, including respite care, young carers most value support services for themselves and with peers who are in the same position. Organisations like the Princess Royal Trust for Carers (which also supports adult carers) provide drop-in sessions, dedicated support workers and an online support service. Young carers can be very cautious about talking in general with peers about their situation, fearing gossip and taunting. Some have additionally been disappointed in school practitioners, whom they trusted with their confidence, but who revealed their situation in a public way, sometimes with the misplaced aim of getting peers to be sympathetic.

Practitioners can support young carers by keeping confidences appropriately, but clearly not joining in a secret that blocks appropriate help. Young carer support services will often work with schools, to extend knowledge and find ways for young carers to cope with the long list of responsibilities in their daily life. Like any other aspect of support, it is important that you find out more in general, as well as aim to locate services in your area.

If you want to find out more

✤ Bibby, Andrew and Becker, Saul (2000) *Young carers in their own words* London: Calouste Gulbenkian Foundation

✤ Shah, Robina and Hatton, Chris (1999) *Caring alone: young carers in South Asian communities* Barkingside: Barnardo's

✤ Young carers – useful information from these websites: Help the Hospices has www.timetocare.org.uk with a young carers section, the Princess Royal Trust has www.youngcarers.net, also www.childrenssociety.org.uk/youngcarers

Children who raise themselves

Some children and young people are especially vulnerable because they have little or no security from their family. Their parents may be unpredictable, often absent or unreliable because of alcohol or drugs. Some of these children have experienced direct abuse and neglect, yet have not been supported by social care services. Some young adolescents have failed to come to helpful adult attention and now are firmly classified as behaviour problems posing an anti-social threat: labelled as 'feral' or 'yobs'. Their patterns of behaviour can be completely unacceptable, but exclusively punitive responses worsen the situation.

The aim, often in the media as well as political responses, is to demonise individuals who are still young. Such responses also push to one side how many of these children have been damaged by experiences and the real level of physical danger that exists in neighbourhoods where some of them live. Punitive reactions are also ineffective against children or adolescents whose young lives are already full of adult aggression and ill-treatment.

Working with emotionally damaged children and young people is exhausting, whether practitioners are in residential and foster care services or therapeutic youth work. Practitioners who do not work in these services benefit from understanding the basics of what can be involved.

- Children can be highly confrontational. But what is usually ignored, except by involved practitioners or therapists, is that many of these young people are themselves very scared: of peers who can out-shout or out-fight them and of the pain of their own emotions.
- At least some of these children harm themselves as well as other people. They can still be a genuine threat to peers or adults, because

they have such a limited sense of self-preservation. They do not think they are worthy of care.

- Emotionally damaged children and young people can be hyper-vigilant. They have been comprehensively let down by their family and sometimes also by social care services. By middle childhood, and certainly by adolescence, they have limited ability to empathise with peers, become angry very quickly and have great difficulty in calming down, even with help.

- These children and young people need firm boundaries, sometimes placed with safe physical containment and restraint. But the efforts of practitioners to provide a much delayed experience of safe adults – some kind of parenting – have to work alongside the aftermath of what children have done to cope.

- Camila Batmanghelidjh explains how children and young people feel shamed by survival crimes like theft or prostitution, actions that seemed unavoidable in order to obtain food and clothing, for themselves and also younger siblings. Feelings can be buried under a cold facade and rejection of help from the adult world that failed to protect them.

Some services deal with children who are still living with their family, although adults are far removed from acting as parents. Some children will have been taken into foster or residential care to ensure their own safety. Sometimes looked-after children are very distressed to be separated from their parents, even those who have treated them with disdain and continued abuse. Boys and girls struggle with accepting the affection and care offered by a committed practitioner, wanting desperately that this support is offered by their own parent. They will often test that commitment by repeatedly rejecting the foster carer or key person in a residential home. The carer needs emotional stamina, and good support systems, to outstay the continual rejection.

If you want to find out more

- ✣ Bailey, Shaun (2005) *No man's land: how Britain's inner city youth are being failed* London: Centre for Young Policy Studies
www.cps.org.uk

- ✣ Batmanghelidjh, Camila (2006) *Shattered lives: children who live with courage and dignity* London: Jessica Kingsley

Commentary on the scenarios

Here are some ideas. You and your colleagues or fellow-students may have brought other perspectives.

Angie (page 230)

Jane accepts Angie's questions about her own family life and answers honestly, because Angie is asking and not prying. But on other occasions, when asked inappropriately curious questions, Jane could decline to answer with a comment such as, 'That's private to me'. It seems very likely that Angie will have found this conversation helpful and it is her right to know that not all families have 'shouting matches' and rows on a regular basis. If the club team is already aware of Angie's family situation and has taken any steps that are appropriate, this conversation may not raise any other issues around protection.

Conversations with older children and young adolescents will range over broad topics and they are often genuinely interested in your personal and family life. In daily and residential settings, as well as when working as an individual practitioner, it is appropriate that you share some personal information. You are working with children and young people in a professional capacity. But when children have a friendly relationship with you, they regard you as a person, who should relate to them as individuals.

Winston (page 246)

Some parents have resorted in desperation to alcohol to deal with night waking children. It is not a safe option, since young children can easily be made ill by alcohol. It is additionally against the law, since they are younger than the legal drinking age (5 years of age under the Children and Young Persons Act 1933).

Winston's mother needs advice for coping with the sleep disruption and empathy for this very tiring period. The nursery may be able to give suggestions within friendly conversation. Additionally, the local clinic or health visitor team should offer constructive support on this common problem. The next step would be to check with Winston's mother if she has asked for help and let her know about local facilities. You would not speak with these professionals without asking her.

His key person should monitor Winston's behaviour each day. As long as it seems very likely that Winston's mother has stopped dosing him with alcohol, then the incident need go no further than support and advice.

Janice (page 246)

The pre-school team are right to be concerned about the changes in Janice's behaviour, since she sounds like a very unhappy child. The family seems to be under heavy stress and Janice's mother (Ruth) is scarcely coping with all the problems. Her explanation about the constipation is feasible and she is open, and distressed, about having hit Janice.

If this pattern of behaviour is consistent, the pre-school team could feel confident to monitor and support Janice. They need, through a relationship with Ruth, to communicate their awareness that the situation is very stressful and that it is not acceptable for Janice to be hit. The situation needs to be written up in the notes and monitored with care. It is one of those occasions when it would be very helpful for Janice's key person or the CPO to talk with someone in confidence for a second opinion. However, if the explanation from Janice's mother seems feasible, then the next step would be to support her in contacting a local source of family support. If Ruth is willing to accept this option, then it reduces the immediate level of concern for the pre-school team.

Clement (page 247)

Young children who have had a caring but restricted early experience can develop quite quickly when their horizons are stretched, but this change cannot be assumed. It is important to monitor Clement and ensure that his development progresses well.

Clement's mother and grandmother sound caring yet seriously anxious. Family support could be a great help to guide them in more positive child care and play for Clement. It would be worth exploring whether the family would accept, even maybe welcome, someone from a local home-visiting service. Supportive conversations may also help to determine whether there are genuine dangers within the family home or the local neighbourhood, and what needs to be done.

Staff need to welcome Clement's grandmother but cannot agree to inappropriate restrictions on his movement, either indoors or out in the garden. A positive approach on partnership means that the staff are careful to explain and show how they keep young children safe.

Jerome (page 253)

The conversation with Jerome raises serious concerns about him and his siblings. They seem to have been lost in the social work focus on his mother. You can empathise with Jerome's fears but cannot keep quiet for this reason. It is important that the general family situation does not get lost in understandably anxious reactions to Jerome having gone missing overnight.

You should speak with the CPO who, perhaps with yourself, needs to have a meeting with Jerome's mother. Ideally, you want her agreement for you or the CPO to talk with the family social worker. Given the long-term concern about the family (this is only the current social worker), social care services should have been working closely with the school. If Jerome's mother refuses to agree, this is most likely a situation in which it makes sense to explain that contact will have to be made without her permission.

It is not inevitable that the family will be split up, but some level of family support is really needed and it would seem that the social worker needs to take a whole family view. It will help Jerome if the school can be flexible on his homework deadlines and offer as much support as possible.

FURTHER RESOURCES

Most suggested follow-up references are placed within the relevant section in each chapter. This list covers useful, general resources and many of the websites have information that can be downloaded.

★ *Barnardo's* www.barnardos.org.uk Tanners Lane, Barkingside, Ilford, Essex 1G6 1QG Tel: 020 8550 8822. National children's charity responsible for a wide range of projects.

★ *ChildLine* www.childline.org.uk Free 24 hour helpline UK-wide, 0800 1111 for children and young people. The website has information sheets.

★ *Children and Young People Now* www.cypnow.co.uk A weekly update of events and developments across services for children and families. Free if you are a member of the National Children's Bureau or by subscription subscriptions@haymarket.com

★ *Children in Wales (Plant yng Nghymru)* www.childreninwales.org.uk 25 Windsor Place, Cardiff CF1 3BZ. Tel: 02920 342434. Works with services involved with children and their families in Wales.

★ *Children in Scotland (Clann An Alba)* www.childreninscotland.org.uk Princes House, 5 Shandwick Place, Edinburgh, EH2 4RG. Tel: 0131 228 8484. Brings together professionals working with children and families in Scotland.

★ *Children's Law Centre* www.childrenslawcentre.org 3rd Floor, Philip House, 123–137 York Street, Belfast BT15 1AB. Tel: 028 90 245704. Information about the law in Northern Ireland.

★ *Children's Legal Centre* www.childrenslegalcentre.com University of Essex, Wivenhoe Park, Colchester, Essex CO4 3SQ. Tel: 01206 873820. Advice and information about the law in England and Wales.

★ *Children's Play Council* www.ncb.org.uk/cpc Wakley Street, London EC1V 7QE. Tel: 020 7843 6094. An alliance of organisations to promote children's play.

★ *Council for Disabled Children* www.ncb.org.uk/cdc Wakley Street, London EC1V 7QE. Tel: 020 7843 6082. National forum for policy and practice relating to disabled children, young people and their families.

★ *Joseph Rowntree Foundation* www.jrf.org.uk The Homestead, 14 Water End, York, North Yorkshire YO30 6WP. Tel: 01904 629241. Involved in social policy research, useful Findings series on www.jrf.org.uk/knowledge/findings.

★ *Kidscape* www.kidscape.org.uk 2 Grosvenor Gardens, London SW1W 0DH. Tel: 020 7730 3300, helpline 08451 205 204 for parents and other concerned adults. Information and advice on child protection, personal safety and bullying.

★ *Learning and Teaching Scotland* www.ltscotland.org.uk The Optima, 58 Robertson Street, Glasgow G2 8DU. Tel: 08700 100 297. Information about education in Scotland and general resources for professionals.

★ *National Centre for Excellence in Residential Child Care* www.ncb.org.uk/ncercc 8 Wakley Street, London EC1V 7QE. Tel: 020 7843 1168. Collaborative initiative to improve practice for children and young people in residential care.

★ *National Children's Bureau* www.ncb.org.uk 8 Wakley Street, London EC1V 7QE. Tel: 020 7843 6000. Works with services for children, especially within England and Northern Ireland. The NCB hosts a wide range of projects and groups and publishes summary Highlights.

★ *NCH* www.nch.org.uk 85 Highbury Road, London N5 1UD. Tel: 08457 626579. National children's charity responsible for a wide range of projects.

★ *NSPCC* www.nspcc.org.uk 42 Curtain Road, London EC2A 3NH. Tel: general 020 7825 2500, helpline 08 08 800 5000. Wide range of information, much of which is best accessed through this home page www.nspcc.org.uk/Inform/informhub_wda49931.html

★ *Parentline Plus* www.parentlineplus.org.uk See website for contact details of local offices. Tel: helpline 0808 800 2222 for advice on any aspect of parenting. National charity working for parents and other family carers.

★ *Office of Public Sector Information* www.opsi.gov.uk Website information about legislation across the UK and bills in progress.

★ *Save the Children* www.savethechildren.org.uk 1 St John's Lane, London EC1N 4AR Tel: 020 7012 6400. Supports a wide range of research projects and other units, such as on supporting children's rights.

★ *Scottish Child Law Centre* www.sclc.org.uk 54 East Crosscauseway, Edinburgh EH8 9HD. Tel: 0131 667 6333, freephone for under 18s 0800 328 8970. Advice and information about the law in Scotland.

★ *Teachernet* www.teachernet.gov.uk. Information and guidance for practice in schools (England) but relevant more generally.

★ *Young Minds* www.youngminds.org.uk 48–50 St John Street, London EC1M 4DG. Tel: 0800 018 2138. Focus on improving the mental health of children and young people, helpline for anyone concerned about a child or young person.

INDEX

abduction 56, 117, 136, 200, 201, 205

abuse of trust 57, 64

access to records 183

accident book 175

accidental injury 47, 66, 70, 81, 84, 90, 111, 139, 144, 180–1, 197, 200, 212

addictions 11, 51, 55, 250–1

age of consent 4, 14, 57, 223

allegations 9, 10, 90, 107, 116–7, 145, 160, 165–174, 192, 227, 242

assessment framework 16–18, 23, 35, 184–5

behaviour policy 130, 199, 216

benign skin markings 87, 191

Bichard report 12, 14, 17, 154, 158

body outline 86, 88, 179

bullying 41, 44, 83, 87, 90, 102, 120, 151, 213–9, 224, 226–7, 254, 256, 258, 264

Butler-Sloss report 4, 48

CCTV 161–3

Carlile report 10

civil law 6

child protection
   conference 21, 26, 28, 34, 36
   officer (CPO) 66, 67, 71–4, 77, 79–80, 82, 106, 108–10, 113–4, 126, 128, 141–2, 145, 148, 150–1, 166–7, 170, 184–8, 262
   plan 16, 26, 30–6, 69, 83
   register 2, 16, 18, 21, 26, 30–2, 36–7, 69, 250, 256

Children's Hearings 20

Climbié, Victoria 13–15, 125–6, 129, 139

Clywch report 10

Clyde report 7

confidentiality 7, 11, 13, 58, 73, 88, 103, 128, 148, 163, 170, 175, 182, 186, 223, 228

ContactPoint 16–17

criminal law 6

cruelty to animals 1, 90

cultural background 2, 117, 121–39, 141, 225

cyberbullying 41, 209, 214, 218

cybersexual behaviour 209

disabled children 5, 16, 36, 47, 51, 81, 85, 94, 118–21, 140, 145, 179, 190, 196, 222, 264

disciplinary procedures 112, 168, 170–1

disclosure of abuse by
   adult 79, 107–8, 152, 182
   child 20, 41, 64, 73, 98–107, 109, 182, 219

domestic violence 33, 41, 45, 130, 132, 136–7, 230, 248–51

emergency court orders 33

emotional abuse 5, 26, 31, 39–44, 54, 83, 136, 178, 194

equality practice 116–142, 144

extended family care 125

fabricated illness syndrome 4, 148–9

faith 2, 19, 62, 90, 117, 121–9, 134, 136–9, 141

false allegations 107, 162, 168–70, 192

faltering growth 50, 92

family group conferences 29–30

family support 4, 5, 9, 28, 31–4, 41, 54, 113, 128, 184, 244–8, 257–8, 262

female genital mutilation 4, 48, 133–5, 255

forced marriage 135–7

grooming 61–2, 225

Guardian *Ad Litem* 237

hitting children 129–33
home alone 51
home visiting 245, 262

illness induction 4, 48–9
images of abuse 62–3
induction of staff 146, 154–6
information sharing 11, 14, 16, 73, 182–3
informed consent 56, 163–4, 182–3, 221, 224, 242
Integrated Children's System 16, 30
internet 63–4, 98, 145, 207–11
intuitions 178

kinship care 29

Laming report 13–14, 18, 125–6

male practitioners 116–8, 250
malnutrition 50, 54
masturbation 57, 94, 113
medical examination 27, 35, 97
Megan's law 160
missing children 7, 60, 136, 139, 200, 251–7, 262

neglect 2, 5, 9, 10, 12, 26, 31, 44, 49–53, 66, 91–3, 125, 170, 197, 235, 245, 258
non-abusing parent 41, 232–4
non-accidental injury 45, 88–9, 119, 191

obesity 34, 91, 93
observations 11, 71–2, 75, 82–3, 94, 176, 178, 180–1, 187, 202, 240

paedophiles 61–3, 160, 206–8, 211
partnership with parents 42, 66, 80, 93, 109, 115, 117, 128, 141, 144, 157, 187, 209, 228, 231–2, 242, 262
practitioners who were abused 150–2

personal safety
    children 46, 104, 145, 200–11
    practitioners 9, 234–5
photographs 163–5, 179
physical
    abuse 2, 4, 5, 41, 44–9, 63, 85, 90, 98, 102, 116, 134, 191, 197, 248
    care 35, 118, 155, 190–202
    contact – see touch
    intervention 198–9
play (concerns about) 76, 85, 92, 94, 100, 112–4, 121, 133, 146, 169, 180, 185, 187, 228, 229, 247
play therapy 228
police role 6, 14, 19, 21–2, 24–6, 28, 29, 46, 59, 63, 78, 105, 136, 153–4, 159, 171, 205, 227, 240–3, 253, 256
policy 4, 9, 41, 52, 71, 90, 108, 130, 138, 141, 143–50, 191–9, 213, 216, 226–7
pornography 57, 60, 62–3, 138, 153, 207
private fostering 123, 125
procedures 4, 9–10, 13, 18, 27, 31, 71, 78, 118, 120, 143–50, 165–8, 171–2, 235
professional
    dangerousness 8–9
    notes 182–3
prostitution, abuse through 59–62, 252, 260
public inquiries 6–8, 11–13, 17, 35

recruitment 3, 144, 153–6, 193
referral 20–3, 28, 32, 67, 73, 78–83, 110–1, 141–2, 148, 166, 186
religion – see faith
risky behaviour 97, 208–9, 212
risk assessment 147, 159, 181, 212, 224, 234–5
running away 252–6

INDEX

secrets 68, 106, 202
security 152–61
self harm 84, 95, 97, 208
sex and relationships education 221–3
sex offenders 158–60
sexual
    abuse 2, 4, 5, 7, 10–1, 26, 31, 41, 44, 55–65, 94–8, 101–2, 116–8, 120, 207, 219–21, 225, 234–5, 242–3
    exhibitionism 57, 211
    exploitation 55–6, 58–60, 62, 97–8, 219, 225
sexualised behaviour 120, 211, 220
sexually transmitted diseases 97
siblings
    abuse by 66, 78, 84, 157, 178, 219, 251
    care by 52, 77, 91, 93–4, 102, 141, 253, 257–8, 260, 262
sign and image systems 104
social worker (role) 19–35, 50, 69, 74, 79, 82, 104, 111–2, 115, 166, 184, 235, 237, 242
Soham 14
spirit possession 138–9
sport and leisure 19, 44, 96, 102, 149, 151–2, 172, 214
stranger danger 56, 118, 200–11, 232, 251
students (in training) 42, 66, 151, 156–7, 167, 192
substance abuse 17, 33, 55, 250–1, 258

suicide 208, 215
survival crimes 252–4, 260
supervision (staff) 9, 112, 151–2, 156, 171–2

taking children into care 33–4, 41, 232, 236, 249, 257
therapy 61, 228, 244
trafficking 60
toileting 42, 197–8
touch 64, 94–5, 112, 170, 186, 191–7, 219, 220, 224

United Nations Convention on the Rights of the Child 5, 132
Utting report 7–8

vetting and barring 14, 152–8, 210
visitors 157, 162
volunteers 144, 146–8, 155–8, 167, 172, 250

Waterhouse report 9–10
webcams 162–3, 187, 211
whistle blowing 167–8
witness in court
    children 236, 242–4
    expert 48
    practitioners 236, 238–41
written records 79, 145, 175–85

young
    carers 51, 251, 254, 257–9
    parents 46, 54
young sexual abusers 56, 219–21